D0778536

LIBBY HOLMAN
Body and Soul

LIBBY HOLMAN
Body and Soul

Hamilton Darby Perry

Little, Brown and Company — Boston – Toronto

FIRST EDITION

Library of Congress Cataloging in Publication Data

Perry, Hamilton Darby.
  Libby Holman: body and soul.

  1. Murder—North Carolina—Winston-Salem.   2. Holman,
Libby.   3. Reynolds, Zachary Smith, d. 1932.
4. Criminal justice, Administration of—North Carolina.
I. Title.
HV6534.W65P47   1983   364.1′523′0975667   83-13545
ISBN 0-316-70014-2

For permission to reprint material from previously copyrighted sources, the author gratefully acknowledges the following individuals and companies:

Newsweek, Inc. for excerpts from two articles: "Watch Out for Trial Lawyers," by F. Lee Bailey, *Newsweek,* January 2, 1978, page 7. Copyright © 1978 by Newsweek, Inc.; "Fortress Law," by Peter Prescott, *Newsweek,* February 16, 1976. Copyright © 1976 by Newsweek, Inc. All rights reserved. Reprinted by permission.

The New York Times Company for excerpts from a review by Brooks Atkinson of "Blues, Ballads, and Sin Songs," a concert by Libby Holman, *The New York Times,* October 5, 1954. Copyright © 1954 by The New York Times Company. Reprinted by permission.

The Raleigh Times for excerpts from a July 11–12, 1932 editorial on Libby Holman. Reprinted by permission.

Warner Brothers Music for excerpts from three songs: "Body and Soul," Lyric by Edward Heyman, Robert Sour, and Frank Eyton, Music by John Green. Copyright © 1930 (Renewed) Warner Bros. Inc.; "I Guess I'll Have to Change My Plan," Lyric by Howard Dietz, Music by Arthur Schwartz. Copyright © 1929 (Renewed) Warner Bros. Inc.; "Something to Remember You By," Lyric by Howard Dietz, Music by Arthur Schwartz. Copyright © 1930 (Renewed) Warner Bros. Inc. All rights reserved. Used by permission.

The Winston–Salem Journal for quotations from two editorials, one from July 15–16, 1932, and one from November 16, 1932, on Libby Holman. Reprinted by permission.

VB

*Published simultaneously in Canada
by Little, Brown & Company (Canada) Limited*

PRINTED IN THE UNITED STATES OF AMERICA

For
Hamilton Darby,
who showed me where the good music was,
and
Katherine Wilson Addinsell,
who came to take on Broadway and won

Acknowledgments

I was only eight years old in 1932 when most of the events that are described here took place. So the impact on me of nostalgia from all this is questionable. And I have no firsthand recollections of this story being in our local papers, although the headlines of the Lindbergh kidnapping and the pictures of the Bonus Army marching on Washington — other 1932 events — are still vivid in my mind.

But while I was growing up in the South, as the years went by certain references to the story — mostly references to the mystique of Libby Holman — kept floating through the conversation of adults and, when I began paying more attention, coming up in news stories and columns. And there were usually big question marks at the end of the references: "Oh! Libby Holman? Wasn't she the one who was accused of killing her husband? What do you suppose really happened?"

When I read a *New York Times* story in 1971 that Elizabeth Holman Reynolds Holmes Schanker had been brought dead to a Stamford, Connecticut, emergency room, the static bits of recollection and conversation began to buzz more clearly again.

I regret that I never saw Libby Holman in person. Everyone I knew who had seen her said she was always memorable — and generally memorable to different people for different reasons. I think I would have particularly liked what Brooks Atkinson called "the dark purple menace of Libby Holman in the blues." But I have heard most of her records and have been interested to see some singers today following her style, with Carly Simon ending her current hit record singing Libby's theme, "Body and Soul," in a wonderful Holman-like delivery; one reviewer of the 1920s called this tone "Libby's throat-tearing contralto." And there were scores of anecdotes of her rather high-binding life: Libby, topless in a Tiffany's employees' coffee room, trying on a necklace that she couldn't get the look of when she tried it on over a turtleneck sweater . . . Libby and Montgomery Clift leaving a series of New York restaurants in disarray after another one of their "therapeutic" dinnertime quarrels that seemed to leave them refreshed and smiling, but everyone else in collapse. . . . And many of the anecdotes ended up with ". . . and what do you suppose *really* happened down there in North Carolina?"

Several years spent as a sometime police reporter on a Florida daily stirred my interest in the procedures of murder investigations. And I became intrigued with another mysterious, never-solved shooting — the death (followed by a haphazard and cavalier investigation) of New York financier Grenville Baker shortly after World War II at his West Florida plantation. That story strengthened my suspicion that "this sort of thing" just happened from time to time to wealthy people and did not, after all, require too much close investigation. The death of Smith Reynolds in North Carolina seemed to be all in the same vein.

So this book began as a simple narrative of another one of those glittering things: rich people's tragedy — as opposed to the preponderance of American homicides, which generally seem to happen with the family carving knife in a kitchen full of dirty dishes. But as I got into the sequence of events, it became clear that it was no wonder nobody was sure what really happened down there in North Carolina. The only sure thing seemed to be that the logical procedure of the North Carolina judicial system had been tampered with rather highhandedly. And so my story comes in this final form.

As always, a reporter needs a lot of help along the way. Whatever truth comes through in a story usually is the result of listening carefully to little bits of information, rather than a blinding flash of investigative reporting. There was a general reluctance in "Reynolds country," the territory around Winston-Salem, to talk much about the Reynolds shooting, even this many years later. Some of that was probably because the people most likely to know something firsthand had gotten tired of being asked the same thing by various burning-eyed writers. But some of their reluctance came about because Winston-Salem is still a town the Reynoldses own, and the feeling of their power — as well as their benevolence — is not hard to detect there. However, little by little the bits of information began to come.

Perry Knowlton of Curtis Brown, Ltd., who had seen me through two earlier books, gave initial encouragement and good background leads: he had been Libby Holman's houseguest as a young college student on a couple of occasions and he was as fascinated as I was. It became clear that much of the story would have to be followed in North Carolina, and having been born in the South and having lived there for about half my life, I knew what a "closed corporation" the country could be without some introductions. The start of these was supplied by former New York City Police Commissioner Michael J. Murphy at the suggestion of William Bostelman. Commissioner Murphy's letters introduced me to Manley Lancaster, an enthusiastic University of North Carolina graduate who was sheriff of Forsyth County, embracing Winston-Salem. Lancaster gave me valuable information about how a Southern city works and how the 1932 Forsyth sheriff's department might have operated at the time of the Reynolds shooting. And he turned up the only surviving deputy from that investigation, Guy Scott, brother of the 1932 sheriff, Transou Scott. Lancaster also provided introduction to the man who had followed Scott into office, E. G. Shore, the former Boston Red Sox baseball star. Shore saw the case from unique dual vantage points, having sat on one of the investigating grand juries before becoming sheriff and trying to reopen the case himself against what turned out to be formidable opposition. The Forsyth county clerk, A. E. Blackburn, tried to be helpful with records, but could only be apologetic that the files that would normally contain essential data in such instances had been carefully looted of material long before his time in office.

Fine background on Libby and the Broadway musical stage in the twenties and thirties came from a number of individuals and theatrical collections, and notably from Howard Dietz's excellent book *Dancing in the Dark*. Personal recollection of Libby on Broadway, and off the stage with the theatre crowd, came from Katherine Wilson Addinsell, my godmother, who was another young actress tackling the New York stage at that point and often saw Libby for one reason or another. Pamela Perry, daughter of Jennings Perry, a superb Southern newspaperman, editor, and foreign correspondent and a longtime friend of Libby's, provided sparkling description of the weekends at "Treetops" when Libby hosted a wonderful array of celebrities and unknown strays at that gracious Connecticut estate. Linda Gutiérrez, Lee Perry, Frances Weaver, and Margaret Happel were careful researchers into what for them must have seemed like a lot of ancient history. Dr. Philip Bond provided an important clue in the Leo Frank lynching case that helped explain to me why Carlisle Higgins, the intended prosecutor, made some of the unusual decisions he did.

When investigating the complexities of trial law, trial procedure, the selection of jurors, and the approach and ethics of both prosecutor and defense attorney in a criminal trial, I valued the observations of Angelo T. Cometa, a former New York prosecutor and a distinguished Manhattan trial lawyer. In trying to understand how people react under trauma and the pressure of such events, I was helped by Dr. Frederick Flach, an authority on mental depression in its various phases — from conventional January "blahs" to total disablement.

Patient and sensible advice at various points in the writing came from Ken McCormick, in my opinion the dean of American editors working today, and from Jacques de Spoelberch and Ray Roberts. And Audre Proctor and Mary Bruce kept asking questions, when working with the manuscript, that I hope enabled me to show you what I think "really happened down there in North Carolina." It shouldn't happen again.

H. D. P.

New York
February 1983

The Seats of Power

Immediately after Jimmy Carter was elected President of the United States, he announced he needed a rest from the grinding months of the campaign. He took that rest at Saint Simon Island, Georgia, on the estate of Smith Bagley.

Bagley's name was relatively unknown in the national press at the time, though he has since been the center of an unpleasant corporate scandal. But his heritage was readily identifiable. He was a beneficiary in the vast R. J. Reynolds tobacco fortune. And in newspapers, radio, and television the Bagley name was invariably followed by the Reynoldses'.

Carter's avowed role as the simple farmer from Plains, Georgia, was in sharp contrast to the powerful family background of the host. The Reynolds family has been an awesome force in the business and political life of North Carolina for almost one hundred years. Hospitality to a President is a matter-of-course thing to such people. But for the last fifty years, spurred quite by accident, the Reynolds name has also become a force in education, social reform, public health, civil rights, and other good causes. The accident that began the Reynolds altruism was a murder — and an attempt to keep the details of that murder from becoming a scandal in the press and the subject of a trial. You will have to judge how successful that attempt was. And if it was justified.

On the surface, the story that follows is the story of that murder. It was never officially established at the time just why the murder took place or who the murderer was. Because that was the way the Reynolds family wanted it.

A major part of the investigation of the murder was hushed up, with the examination of certain of the witnesses, and of those later indicted for the crime, mostly conducted in hearings closed to the press or difficult for them to cover. Then and later, evidence was altered, misplaced, destroyed. Normal steps in the orderly investigation of a murder were delayed until they could no longer be performed accurately enough to result in evidence.

Certain portions of this book are based on the original and single stenographic transcript taken during some of those closed hearings — a transcript made exclusively for Carlisle Higgins, the man who was selected to prosecute the case. He went on to a distinguished career that included a major role in prosecuting the Japanese war-crimes prisoners at the end of World War II. And finally he occupied a seat on the North Carolina Supreme Court. He made this transcript available for the preparation of this book.

Higgins was on the scene for virtually all the events in this book that followed the shooting and was a major participant in them. Because he was so immediately involved and because he was one of the few principals who would talk about the case, even so many years later, his transcripts and his recollections were vital if anything perceptive was to be written. His decisions had to be made, as you will see, under great pressure from various quarters.

Strangely enough, the other most important "witness" whose observations are critical here is a man who was only a boy living some 3,000 miles away in Wales when the shooting occurred. Bernard Knight, who has spent most of his life in the study of forensic pathology — the branch of medicine used in the detection of crime — is today Home Office Pathologist for Her Majesty's Government and has earned a worldwide reputation in his specialty. He speculates in this book on the forensic aspects of the case, the critical area that was first ignored and then pursued only reluctantly and sloppily, and confusedly interpreted when the pressure became too much to ignore. His opinions are part of the summary that you will read in making your own decisions.

The reader, by examining the testimony reported here and by reading the recollections of those who participated in the case, is able to sit as a juror on a celebrated murder trial — the announcement of which attracted international curiosity.

In the events that are related in this book, Reynolds family power apparently influenced the orderly legal procedure of the State of North Carolina, in an effort to quash a first-degree murder indictment and prevent a trial. Then, having succeeded in this, the family closed ranks to keep its wealth from going to "an outsider," who earlier was supposed to have been welcomed as a member of that family.

The means of protecting the wealth was the establishment of a family philanthropic foundation. So, as a result of the murder, there has been some notable assistance to the public good.

Did it matter that justice may have been manipulated along the way?

You are free to judge. The power of a wealthy family can be awesome. It was awesome in Winston-Salem, North Carolina, in the summer and fall of 1932. It was awesome at Chappaquiddick. It can be awesome today.

But why revive a fifty-year-old crime in which perhaps no one except the victim suffered and from which almost everyone else got rich?

First of all, the number of people peripherally connected with the incident who suggested that the book was "not such a good idea" persuaded that it might very well be. The initial idea for this book had been simply the story of a somewhat mysterious accident that struck a talented young couple who seemed to have the best of everything. Then the more I found out about the accident, the less it seemed that — and the more it was clearly a murder, resulting from the tangled antagonisms of jealousy, pride, fear, sexual avarice, and anti-Semitic anger. But perhaps what finally appeared to me as most sinister and chilling of all was the way in which a rich and powerful family manipulated the law to suit its own needs.

If this concept of being somewhat above the law was rare fifty years ago, today it is a belief that has shown itself to be a most misguided policy on too many occasions in vast corporations, in the White House, in the FBI, in the CIA. . . . If that is an accepted code of behavior of the rich, of the powerful, perhaps it bears examination at any time.

True, the murder made everyone rich. And it has been responsible for passing out some $125 million to causes that have made a lot of unfortunate lives more fortunate.

But that was not anyone's aim at the time.

And is that chance result any justification for setting yourself above the law?

This is the reader's decision to make. There is no statute of limitations on murder. The reader can still act as juror here. Over the seats of power.

Contents

LIBBY HOLMAN
Body and Soul

1

"Don't Talk! Don't Say Anything!"

TUESDAY NIGHT AT Baptist Hospital, on the western edge of Winston-Salem, North Carolina's "Country Club" district, was not a peak period; Friday night was more nearly a peak — but still a dress rehearsal; Saturday, payday, was opening night, when all the excitement took place. Saturday meant the cuttings, shootings, multiple car accidents after drinking parties. But Tuesday was usually a more casual time, when the emergency room personnel might be expected to get only a sampling of what would face them on the weekend. In the middle of the week in the summer, there was likely to be milder fare. A firecracker burn, a fishhook in a fleshy palm. Sunstroke. A routine car smashup. Such was Tuesday night, July 5, 1932.

Then, shortly after midnight, out of the soft Carolina night came an expensive sedan. Fast. Screeching up the curved hospital drive from the street. Braking to a halt with a smearing of rubber on asphalt. The pulsing of the powerful engine — even at idle — was like some exhausted animal panting after a hard run. The car had slid into the main entrance of the building, where autos of hospital visitors normally pulled up. And from it stumbled three people, who then reached in to struggle with something still inside. The three stumbling out were two women and a man. One woman was dark and handsome, but barefoot and clad only in a negligee that kept gaping open. She was tugging hard at what turned out to be a body. The second woman, a striking blonde, reached in to try to help but was pushed aside. The dark woman tugged again. Then, losing her grip, fell back against the side of the car."Oh, my God! Oh, Jesus!" She slumped to the ground.

The man who came around from the driver's side was wearing only a bathing suit, a black knit pair of trunks with a white top that carried an American Red Cross lifesaving badge. He was unsteady. Cursed at the limp form. The rear door was too narrow and the limp body offered no handholds. He cursed again and leaned against the side of the car to catch his breath.

Because they had come up to the main visitors' entrance of the hospital, it took a few moments for the nurse on duty there to get the emergency room people on the scene. But when they arrived, the young man in the bathing suit cursed them too, and shoved them back.

Determination occupies a vacuum. The professionals drew back at first. The amateurs, urged on with little cries by the stocky blonde, continued to heave at what might have been an ungainly sack of Checkerboard flour. Finally, somebody from the hospital moved forward to take charge. The man and dark woman were being *given* orders now. Their resistance collapsed. They gave up command as readily as they had taken it. The body was slid from the car with the sureness of the professionals and carried out across the lobby into an elevator. It was a young man with a sharp, almost Indian face.

But the swarthy countenance which should have gone with the Indian features was now pale. A neat, clean wound — not rich red like a Hollywood Technicolor injury, but dark maroon like a loganberry — was evident high in the man's right temple. From somewhere below and behind the left ear, blood oozed — slowly, like syrup that had been too long in the icebox. It did not pulsate. There seemed to be no life in the form.

The young man in the bathing suit, who had driven the car, and the dark woman followed. Slowly. With some hesitation. Before, they had been the focus of the drama. Now they were pushed aside. The limp, deadweight body was center-stage. The medical people were calm but fast, examining the injured man, whispering terse instructions.

It was ten more minutes before the importance of the bleeding man — and the importance of the three who had brought him — came again into dramatic focus. Ten more minutes in which all three could have gotten back into that sedan and fled — somewhere, anywhere. In the days ahead, two of the three probably wished they had.

The victim was young enough to be a college boy, hurt while out partying. But the problem was no country-club brawl. Or roadster smashup. Or riding accident. Or drunken fall. The problem was a gunshot wound. And whoever it was, that was going to take a little explaining.

When the victim was wheeled into the operating room of the Baptist Hospital, and the frosted swinging doors closed behind him, the three who had brought him were led to rooms upstairs to wait. They were docile now. The blonde woman took each companion by an arm and had to hang on tight when they wavered and stumbled on the stairs. A staff nurse led the way, another followed. The only sounds were occasional sobs from the dark woman.

The identity of the patient and his companions and the circumstances surrounding the shooting came in fragments to the personnel of the operating room and to the first doctors called to assist. The patient was not someone whose face the emergency room staff immediately recognized. But the big expensive car that brought him spelled money. The dark woman was in turn hysterical and morose. And clearly quite drunk. The man in the bathing suit was sullen, obviously also trying to fight off the liquor, and wasn't saying anything that was making much sense. The blonde was trying to be very methodical and calming with both, as if it were not clearly a crisis.

The doctors started to work without waiting for any identification. The condition of the injured man did not look promising. But to most of the medical staff who had lived through the violence of many a Winston-Salem Saturday night, the wound did not look immediately fatal. With a lucky break in the trajectory of the bullet, some useful part of his brain might be uninjured. Who knew what would happen if they could buy a little time?

They worked rapidly and efficiently. With the operating room procedure under way, some of the clerical staff sought out the distraught dark woman and the man in the bathing suit where they were waiting, pacing, on another floor. From the dark woman came only a shaken head and sobs. From the man in the bathing suit came incoherent and slurred speech. The blonde woman finally produced the information for the forms.

When the injured man's name became clear to the admitting nurse, she knew right away what she had on hand. If interest in the rescue effort speeded up considerably, the tempo probably did not; the medical people were already doing all they possibly could. Now the operating room crew was rapidly adding other doctors and nurses. Staffers from the late night watch found reason to come down to the operating room balcony to study the complex surgical effort. That was how you learned. Third and fourth transfusions were going in. The movements of the surgeon were more hurried now. Clamps and tubes were hastily pulled aside so something new could be tried.

The specialists, arriving separately in the operating room, insisted later that there was little they could have done that had not been done by the first attending resident doctors. The young man would probably not recover consciousness before dying. There was little to do except wait. It was the staff nurses outside who were having the problems.

The dark young woman was most of it. The night supervisor at the hospital found the dark woman roaming, disheveled and barefoot, around the fifth floor, her negligee open, trying to find the operating room where the injured man had been taken. The nurse had finally taken her in hand, led her to an alcove near the elevator where there was a small cot, and washed the blood off her neck, chest, arms, hands, and feet. Then she changed her, for modesty's sake, into a black kimono supplied by the blonde woman, and fastened it securely with some big hospital safety pins. When the dark woman settled down a bit, they led her down to a spartan private room on the third floor. She had stayed there quietly for a while. The supervisor and the blonde woman left her sobbing softly but exhausted.

A short while later, the dark woman suddenly erupted from the room with a shriek, running toward the stairs that led to the operating room level. In the postmidnight stillness of the hospital corridor, the slapping of her sandaled feet and her wail seemed louder than they actually were."Oh, my God! How did it happen?" It took two nurses and a male ward attendant to get her back to the third-floor room. The two nurses were pummeled with her fists, which had no force — and with her tongue, which did. "You dumb bitches! I've got to see him before he dies!"

It took a long time to calm her down. A sedative was out of the question; she had clearly drunk so much that sedation might take her past total relaxation — straight through to a heart stoppage.

Sometime around two o'clock, the night floor nurse was annoyed to see the flushed young man, still in his bathing suit, enter the dark woman's room.

He had angered the nurse earlier, making frequent and agitated calls on the phone at her desk, and had generally been bossy and commanding. When she followed him into the room and asked him to leave, he had rudely ordered *her* out. Surprised, she started to obey, somewhat uncertainly, when she heard him say to the dark woman in an equally angry voice: "Don't talk. Don't say anything. To anybody! Goddamn it, do you understand?"

The nurse was concerned at the threatening tone. "Can't you talk to her with me in here? I don't like to leave this patient alone in her condition."

"No!" The young man looked violent now. "Get out!" The nurse decided she had better get help. She started out — then turned back to warn him to ring the nurse's buzzer if the young woman became hysterical again, when he pushed her out with a blast of abuse. The young woman started to sob: "Oh, my baby! My baby!"

"What do you mean by that?" the young man's voice sounded more startled than angry now. Then he turned and yelled at the nurse, who had halted just outside the door, "Will you get the hell out of here!"

She retreated, but not before she heard the woman wail, "Don't you know that I am going to have a baby?" The high crying began again.

The nurse hesitated. Should she go for help — or face another blast from the drunken young man in the bathing suit? The dark woman seemed to be building toward hysteria. All the while she had been sloppily waving a cigarette, ashes falling all over the place. She was perfectly capable of setting herself and the room afire. A loud crash from the room resolved the situation for the nurse.

Her first thought when she entered the room was that the sobbing woman had been attacked by the young man. Her second thought was that she had intruded on a private, but violent, love scene.

The couple was on the floor, the dark woman sprawled on top of the drunken and muttering young man.

2

"Good Night! Look at the Blood on the Bed!"

WHILE THE STAFF AT Baptist Hospital was hurrying the form of the dark young man into the operating room, out in the rolling country northwest of Winston-Salem on the well-tended grounds of the large and handsome estate called "Reynolda," a crusty countryman, W. E. Fulcher — sometime farmer, sometime quail-hunting guide, sometime deputy sheriff — was coming in from another of his hourly rounds as Reynolda's night watchman. There had been a barbecue on the grounds earlier in the evening, down by the lake of the estate, with a large fire to cook it, and he was responsible for seeing that all the coals were doused. They had been through a long, hot, dry period, and fire was a problem around Winston. It was all part of his job as being responsible for general security of the estate at night. And there was a lot of territory to cover. A break-in at the main house was always something of a concern. Heavy family silver was easily melted down and was the first target of that generation of amateur burglars spawned by the Depression. A great deal more valuable than the silver, he had been told — but who the hell would want it? — was Reynolda's superb collection of antique china, porcelain, and nineteenth-century American paintings. To watchman Fulcher the china and porcelain just looked like a lot of fixy stuff you wouldn't dare drink coffee out of or serve a mess of greens in. But they had told him over and over again how dear it was. More to his concern, because the loot was so tempting and easy to get at, were the prizewinning rose bushes in Reynolda's large and scattered gardens. What he called "shrub rustlers" often tried to sneak into the gardens to dig up and steal the bushes, probably for sale to landscape gardeners in nearby Greensboro and High Point. Hell, the roses likely ended up with the Reynoldses' friends. That evening, with the cars of all those kids going in and out of the long winding drive, he hated to think how easy it might have been for some of those shrub rustlers to slip onto the grounds. He couldn't check everybody.

Reynolda was several cuts above any of the other estates nearby. It was more like a rather isolated and self-reliant English country manor — which was exactly how it had been planned — than simply a large estate less than fifteen minutes' drive from the nearest Piggly Wiggly "groceteria."

As you moved closer to town, the gently rolling land leveled off and the prevailing breezes off the Blue Ridge Mountains had less zest to keep down the smells of roasting tobacco from the factories of East Winston-Salem. The graciousness of the real estate rapidly moderated, until clustered around the tobacco factories themselves were the wood-framed, tin-roofed bungalows of the factory workers. Dullingly alike in both design and drabness, the little houses sat perched above their crawl spaces on rickety red brick supports. They hugged the high-crowned tar and gravel streets that the hard-pressed city government was trying to weave out through the poorer parts of town to replace the red clay roads. The Piedmont clay gave off a fine, irritating, into-every-thing dust in summer and fall — then turned to slippery rust-colored gumbo with the rains of winter and spring. To the south of the down-town area were the shabby remains of the old Moravian village of "Salem," yet to receive the restoration fervor of the mid-twentieth century. The paint flaked and the screen doors flapped. But "out north-west" around Reynolda and the other big homes and estates, even in that darkest-before-dawn Great Depression year of 1932, there seemed to be plenty of money for fresh siding, bright paint, taut copper screens, grass seed and sprinklers and gay porch furniture.

At Reynolda, watchman Fulcher had been glad to see the last guest drive out. Now there was welcome quiet after the hurrah of another of the Reynoldses' children's parties. At about 12:45 there had been one interruption. He had been having a sandwich and some lemonade by the basement door under the kitchen when he heard what could have been a gunshot. His watchdog sat up sharply. Fulcher went out toward the far end of the house where the noise seemed to come from, leaving his dog behind.

He had stood some distance from the house, listening for any other noise from there . . . or for any sound coming from down at the lake where the kids had been having the barbecue. There were still plenty of lights on in the big house — but he couldn't see anyone moving around or hear any voices. There was silence too from the direction of the lake. After standing there out off the east wing for a while, he shone his light on his pocket watch, saw that it was coming up on one o'clock, time for his next round, and so he headed down for the lake to make sure no coals had burned through, leaving his dog tied up back at the basement door.

It may have taken him ten, fifteen minutes to circle the end of the lake — he sure as hell wasn't going to rush in that heat — check the barbecue site again, and circle back around through the trees, before he came out of the woods up on the formal grounds out front of the house. He'd better see if any cars from the party had come back. Those kids didn't know when to go home. As he came up out of the dark of the woods with his light playing on the path ahead of him, he was surprised to hear a car engine start and race quickly. Headlights flashed on back at the house. There was the quick screech of tires on the asphalt of the loading area under the entrance porch as the car got away fast, then a rattle of gravel being kicked out by the wheels as the car careened down the far drive. By the time the car got abreast of him — and he was only about a hundred yards from the house — he figured it was going about forty or fifty miles an hour and still accelerating. It looked like young Smith Reynolds's big buggy — but it was going too fast for him to see much of anything. Damnfool kids!

Fulcher trudged back toward the big house, looking briefly up to the sky to see if there was any sign of clouds with rain that could help with the heat and the dry spell. There were just stars . . . and the mosquitoes were starting to come again. Way off toward town somewhere he could hear the wail of a siren.

By the time he reached the house the siren was louder and coming his way, probably out on Reynolda Road. Smashup somewhere, most likely. The way ol' Smith was driving, that boy would probably be next.

As Fulcher headed across the sedately laid out "English rose garden" in front of the house to close the big french doors that led from the living room onto the porch, the siren screamed through the Reynolda gateway. Fulcher turned to see headlights heading up the driveway. Now what the hell! He hoped it wasn't a sheriff's car with some problem about someone who had been at the party smashing up full of liquor. That would be trouble for Reynolda. And for him.

When the lights got even with him and the glare was out of his eyes, he could see that it was not a sheriff's car, but an ambulance. It braked sharply at the main entrance of the house, and the two attendants got out as Fulcher dogtrotted over. The siren was just winding down: God, *that* wail could wake up the drunks, Fulcher thought. Be some hell-raising from the house directly now. He threw a glance at the upstairs rooms, waiting to see the lights start to flash on. Then he greeted the ambulance crew.

"What's the trouble, boys?"

"Hell, you tell us," one of the attendants answered. "We got a call to get the hell out here. Bad accident."

A mistake somewhere, Fulcher thought. Better get these boys packing — quiet, with no siren — before everybody from the house came down on him. He knew the madam had a temper and he didn't want it dead at him.

"Nothing here. This here is Reynolda House."

"We know that. They said Reynolda House."

"Must be a mistake. Maybe they meant something on the road *near* Reynolda House. There was a party here tonight. But it's all over now. Folks all cleared out. Mister Reynolds just lit out for town. But he'll be back soon, so you better clear out."

"That's a damn pretty way to do. Call us out here and it ain't nothin'." One attendant was doing all the complaining. The other fellow was already headed back toward the wagon.

"Well, take a look inside, if you want to," Fulcher said. "Won't hurt none. Then you fellows are in the clear. Must be a mistake, though. Must be something out on Reynolda Road. We had some whistler drivers here tonight, that's a fact."

The three men walked through the front door into the great living room that went the depth of the house. It was sure mussed up like a party. Off to the right they could see into the library, brightly lit also. Fulcher noticed whiskey bottles and glasses on the big table in the center of the library. He hoped the ambulance attendants did not.

"That's it, boys. They is all gone to bed. Except for ol' Smith." He threw an arm around the shoulder of each, steering them back toward the entrance, walked them down to the ambulance, and thanked them for coming out anyway. "And how about *not* hitting that siren on the way out? OK?"

The ambulance headed sedately back down the drive. He watched until the lights swung out through the entrance and turned left, onto Reynolda Road, heading back toward town. Better wait around front now till Smith got back.

He remembered the french doors then, still standing open to the front porch. Now that wasn't like Smith. He was usually sort of careful about the place, careful about closing up and turning off the lights at the end of an evening — even when he had been drinking pretty hard: Better make one more check. Wonder if somebody got sick? Or hurt? Smith had took off in one hell of a hurry.

When he got back into the house he was just plain disgusted. They had had themselves a party, all right. Plenty of glasses. Half a dozen whiskey and gin bottles, most of them pretty well worked on, some empty. Ashtrays sloppy full and a whole pack of cigarettes spilled out on the floor by one of the sofas. Three or four cold ribs in a greasy paper napkin sitting on top of one of those little rugs they put on top of their tables. A piece of cake on another napkin in the seat of a chair. Somebody had tried to play the old moviehouse organ in the corner of the room and had left it turned on and humming, with music sheets spilled out all over the floor. Bunch of damn spoiled rich kids! Well, hell, *he* didn't have to clean it up. Just lock her up, turn out the lights — except leave a couple on for Smith — and go back outside. Outside was Fulcher's territory.

Still . . . something seemed funny. The ambulance men had been positive about the call coming from Reynolda House. Bad accident, they had said.

There was a phone booth off the entrance hall, put there mostly for outside calls. The house phones were hooked up on a private system that went to all the buildings on the Reynolda grounds: stable, garage, shop, greenhouse, pool house. Fulcher went to the booth and gave the telephone number for his boss, Stewart Warnken, the manager of Reynolda. Fulcher popped open his watch again as he placed the call. It was almost 1:30 A.M.; Warnken was going to be mad at getting called out in the middle of the night. But then those were Fulcher's instructions. Warnken had said Smith was just a kid and it was part of Warnken's job to see that the kid — as well as the house and grounds — got a little adult supervision as far as the smooth running of things went. Fulcher had better call.

Warnken sounded annoyed at the other end of the phone — but resigned. Fulcher just better lock up good. And be sure to give Smith a once-over when he came back. And if anything looked wrong, Fulcher should call again and Warnken would come if necessary.

Fulcher went back into the living room, relieved. He had done all he was supposed to do. He picked the cake up out of the chair and took the congealed spareribs off the table, wadded them up in paper napkins, and tossed them into a wastebasket. To hell with the rest of the mess. He turned off the organ and most of the lights. He pulled closed the several sets of french doors to the porch and latched them from the inside, then went around through the entrance pulling the doors closed behind him, but leaving the lock off; he didn't want ol' Smith standing there in a fog, battering the damn doors down trying to get back in. Then he went out to the garden between the drives and sat down on one of the big stone benches to wait for Smith to come back.

It was almost an hour later before the next car came up the drive. And it was not Smith's, but Mr. Warnken's. Fulcher had already learned not to be surprised by anything that occurred around Reynolda. He figured Warnken had gotten curious and decided he would come over anyway and take a look for himself. Hell, that was what they was all paid for, to mother Smith a little bit. Fulcher walked over to the drive to meet him.

"What's been going on around here tonight?" Warnken asked casually as they strolled back toward the house. Fulcher told him about the party, that there had been a good bit of drinking and kids wandering around in the bushes, the usual stuff. Then Fulcher took him around by the east wing of the house so he could show Warnken just where he stood when he came out after hearing what he thought was a shot. Then they went around to the kitchen entrance and sat for a while on the runningboard of Fulcher's car, both smoking, Warnken looking up at the house from time to time and asking some other casual questions about the evening, before saying equally matter-of-factly; "Smith's been shot, you know."

"Well, I'll be damned! I thought he left here in a hurry. What happened?"

"That's what I came down here to find out," Warnken answered. "I guess we better go through the house and see who's up there." He sure was in no damn rush, Fulcher thought.

They went in through the back, turning off the kitchen and pantry lights as they passed through. Those rooms were relatively neat, since the staff had cleaned up that area before they left. Fulcher reported how he had come into the house earlier with the ambulance men. When they reached the living room, Warnken switched on all the overhead lights. "What a mess!" He walked toward the rear of the room to the matching staircases that went to the second floor, stopping along the way at a big sofa, picking up a white jacket and a pair of grass-stained white slacks that lay there, shaking his head. Under the slacks was a light tan wallet. He opened it."Smith's. Funny."

They started up the stairs, Warnken first. The two formal curving staircases that descended into either side of the rear of the living room came together at the top. Several of the bedroom doors in the east wing were closed, but there was a light burning on the sleeping porch at the end of the wing. Walking toward the sleeping porch, Warnken stopped and listened for a moment at each of the closed doors along the way. At the open doors of the sleeping porch, Warnken started in — then lurched back, as if he had been roughly shoved! He turned, grabbed Fulcher, pushed him ahead into the room. The dim light came from one of the wall sconces above a double bed, but it was enough to show Fulcher what had jolted his boss.

"Good night! Look at the blood on the bed! Better come in here."

Warnken's shaky voice came from the hall."You look. You look. . . . I don't want to see it."

Fulcher went carefully through the room, flashing his light along the floor, the walls, along both sides of the bed. It was a mess! The place was pretty well marked up with dark red blood splotches, across the bed, on the rugs. He shined his light in the bed looking for a gun. There had been that shot. Warnken had said Smith was shot. He nudged the pillows aside with the head of the light until he was sure no weapon was underneath them, swept the beam along the rugs on both sides of the bed and under the edges of the bed. More blood patches. But no gun.

When he came out, Warnken had already retreated down the hall to the top of the stairs, where he stood, white-faced, waiting for Fulcher.

"I better call Barnes," Warnken said, descending the stairs somewhat unsteadily to go to the first floor telephone closet.

It took a little time to find J. T. Barnes, Warnken's boss, in the confusion of Baptist Hospital that night; he had been called to the hospital when the identity of the gunshot victim was discovered. The young man was Zachary Smith Reynolds, one of four heirs to the R. J. Reynolds tobacco fortune. And Barnes, as well as Warnken, worked for the Reynolds family. Barnes had arrived at the hospital to find that he had not only a dying man to look after, but also Smith Reynolds's three distraught bearers. And the nurses quickly let him know what a problem the two drunken ones had been. Barnes found that they were Smith's wife of a few months, Libby, and a childhood friend, Albert Walker. The third person in the car that had brought Smith to the hospital was identified to him as Blanche Yurka, a New York actress and a houseguest at Reynolda. Over the phone Barnes heard Warnken's report about the bloody bedroom and about the mess left from the drinking party. There was nothing he could do at the hospital to influence the events in the operating room; he told Warnken he would be right out. Fulcher and Warnken sat in the big living room, all lights on now, waiting for him. There were a lot of thoughts going through both their minds. But Fulcher was reluctant to volunteer his to his superior without being asked.

It did not take Barnes long to get there. The three men went up immediately to the sleeping porch. Barnes and Fulcher went through the room thoroughly, with Fulcher again playing his light on the bed, floor, rugs, walls. Fulcher cautioned them all not to touch anything; hell, he was a deputy sheriff; he knew that was what you were supposed to do. Warnken hung back outside, not even looking through the door at the bloody mess. Barnes was shaken, too.

"Boy! There's enough blood for a machine gun." To Fulcher: "And you only heard *one* shot?"

"That's right, sir. Just the one. And it wasn't too loud."

"You didn't find any gun?"

"Nope. Looked. Must of took it with them."

When they returned downstairs, Barnes called Clint Wharton, the Reynolds corporation executive who dispensed all the money it took to run Reynolda, then said he would head back to the hospital, promising to be back at Reynolda by the time Wharton could dress and get there. It was sometime after 3 A.M. when he hung up on Wharton. Wharton thought he might be there about 3:45. Off to the west some big thunder rolled around, but no rain came, and the cool of the late evening had not yet seeped through the house. All were sweating. Heat. Nerves.

"You fellows better get all this whiskey and stuff out of sight before the sheriff gets here," Barnes had told them as he hurried out. Prohibition enforcement in North Carolina in 1932 was mostly aimed at bootleggers. But it would not help to have illegal whiskey as one more thing to have to sweep under the rug. "We got enough trouble without getting the moonshine squad down on us. Goddamn!" He headed down the drive almost as fast as Smith's car had.

Warnken did most of the cleaning up of the bottles, capping and carefully marking each one with a line on the label to show the amount still in it, then storing them downstairs in a locked closet off the big game room. Then he rinsed the glasses Fulcher had carted to the kitchen, so that there was no liquor smell in them. They dumped the ashtrays and Warnken made an attempt to straighten up pillows, magazines, the spilled music sheets, the piles of records strewn around the table next to the big upright phonograph cabinet. They were barely finished sometime before 4 A.M. when they heard Barnes's car come back, followed by another. Barnes came through the front door, guiding Albert Walker by the arm. Clint Wharton followed them.

Walker was still in his bathing suit. Dull, brownish red spots streaked much of the white top around the American Red Cross insignia. His hair was disheveled, he had a bandage on one cheek, and he wore a pair of sneakers which were a couple of sizes too big for him. His eyes were glazed and Barnes had to steer him into the room.

"You better get cleaned up, young man, and dressed, and then we'll need you back down here." Wharton headed him toward the stairway, and they all watched silently as Walker made the climb as if he were starting up a mountain, and then disappeared down the east hall to his room.

Barnes had talked a little to Walker on their way back from the hospital. Walker said Smith had shot himself, but he didn't know why. When asked why they had taken the gun with them, Walker said they hadn't taken any gun. Now Wharton wanted to find the gun. Soon they were going to have to call the sheriff. And when the sheriff got to Reynolda, Wharton wanted to make sure that everything was in good order. The publicity was going to be bad enough as it was. But it sure as hell was important not to have any funny-looking loose ends, and that included finding the gun Smith had shot himself with.

Barnes reminded him there had now been two searches with no results. "But Walker told me that the gun has got to be up there on the sleeping porch."

Wharton was puzzled. "Let's take another look."

He motioned to Barnes and Warnken to come with him. In the four-o'clock-in-the-morning quiet of the upstairs hall there was only the low sound of the shower running in the bathroom off Walker's room. With the one dim wall light on and because of what they knew had gone on inside, the sleeping porch had taken on a weird murk for all of them. Barnes had Fulcher's flashlight, and he went in first, Wharton behind him. Warnken again hung back outside. "I've seen it enough." He shook his head.

The two men made a thorough search of the room, even lifting up the dust ruffles that fell around the legs of the bed and playing the light back and forth underneath it. There was nothing to be seen except some dust feathers among the blood drip where it had seeped through.

"A goddamn mystery," Wharton complained. "Did anybody look in the car? Maybe they took it with them in the car with all the excitement." But the car was still at the hospital. On his hands and knees, Wharton searched the second floor hall. But there was nothing, fortunately no bloodstains either. "I've got to make some calls." He herded them downstairs again. As he passed Fulcher in the living room, he had a second thought.

"Mrs. Reynolds and the actress lady — Burke, or whatever her name is — are down at the hospital. Any of the servants asleep in the house?"

"Don't think so, sir. The servants' area is locked."

"Somebody else up there now? A lady?"

"There's a teacher fellow lives all the way down in the west wing. Works with Smith. The other doors up there are closed. Don't know. Maybe some of the party people stayed over. Don't know exactly about any lady."

Wharton cussed. "Walker said something about a lady being up there when he left — but he either didn't want to wake her . . . or couldn't wake her." He swung around to Barnes.

"If there is any lady up there, wake her up and get her the hell out of here. Take her home yourself, or to a hotel or whatever you have to do. Better leave the teacher where he is."

Barnes grimaced and started toward the stairs.

"And don't tell her a goddamn thing," Wharton called after him, then disappeared into the telephone closet.

Barnes had his job cut out for him. A search of the second-floor rooms did produce a lady. And she was in no shape to get up, first a rag doll — and then fighting mad. But she was asleep in her clothes, so the problem of getting her dressed, which he had been apprehensive about, disappeared. In a few minutes he was back down again with an awkward armlock on a cussing young woman. He collected the light coat she pointed out on one of the divans and, as she mounted one last protest, led her to his car.

Barnes was back by the time dawn was up.

The others were still sitting there. There was sporadic talk in low voices. Nothing to do until they heard from the hospital. Wharton had decided that if the sheriff didn't arrive, as a result of having heard of the shooting some other way, they should hold off calling him until they heard about Smith's condition.

About 5 A.M., Dr. Fred M. Hanes had called to say that Smith was close to dying. Shortly after 6, Hanes called again; Smith was dead. The doctor said he would gather up Mrs. Reynolds and Miss Yurka and bring them out to the house. At least it would get them away from a reporter who was already snooping around at the hospital. When Dr. Hanes arrived, he had Mrs. Barnes with him; she had stayed at the hospital to help the two women and now she saw them to bed at Reynolda, placing the groggy Mrs. Reynolds in a room next to Blanche Yurka's at the extreme end of the west wing, as far from the shooting scene as possible.

Downstairs, Wharton and Barnes questioned the doctor about Smith. He told them as well as he could in layman's terms what they had done to try to save Smith, and why at first they had thought they might be able to. When Dr. Hanes mentioned the relative smallness of the entry and exit wounds, Wharton interrupted: "Sounds like it might have been a twenty-two. But damn if we can find a gun, doctor. The only thing is, a twenty-two doesn't fit with the amount of blood splashed around that room."

"I suppose I should look at the room," Dr. Hanes said after thinking for a moment. "I guess I might be questioned about that."

Dr. Hanes, Barnes, Wharton, Warnken, and R. E. Lasater, another Reynolds executive, who had driven to the house about 4 A.M., all trooped up again to the second floor sleeping porch. The others stood at the door as if deferring to Dr. Hanes's professional eye.

An overcast day was dawning. The light was still a bit dim, but they didn't need a flashlight anymore. On the north side of the bed, Dr. Hanes noted a large pool of clotted blood on the floor beside the bed. The mattress sides were streaked with blood and there was blood on the bed and one pillow. Indeed it was an amazing amount of blood, thought Hanes, for the small wound he had been working on; Smith must have lain there for a while.

When he had first circled the bed to examine the bloodstains, Dr. Hanes had probably very nearly stepped on the pistol. But it wasn't until he came back around the bed that he noticed it. It was lying in the clear on the rug about three feet from the south side of the bed, toward the headboard end. Dr. Hanes picked up the gun and placed it on one of the night tables at the head of the bed. Warnken, seeing what had been found, moved quickly into the room he had been so fearful of before and picked it up from the table. "I can take the clip out of it, the cartridges."

"Maybe you'd better. For safety," someone said.

Warnken struggled with it for a few moments, turning it around several times to look for a catch and get a hold — but couldn't remove the clip. He laid the gun back on the table, muttering at it. It was a small automatic, and none of them was familiar with the type.

It had taken four searches to find the missing gun — now suddenly there it was in clear view on the bedroom rug. Or, perhaps more properly, it had taken three searches to establish that no gun was there. And the fourth search had ended with two people handling the gun and ruining any chance of finding a useful set of fingerprints on the weapon.

When old man Fulcher, waiting downstairs, heard about it, he was just plain disgusted.

3

"That's Something I'll Take to My Grave!"

THE OFFICE OF sheriff Transou Scott did not get its first indication of any trouble at Reynolda until sometime before 7 A.M. The call came from one of the estate men at Reynolda and was taken by deputy Guy Scott, sheriff Scott's brother, who was manning the phones and was in charge of the watch that was going off duty at 8 A.M. The estate man did not identify himself. And Guy Scott knew from the imperious tone of the voice on the other end that it was not the time to press for details. The Reynolda man simply said there had been "some trouble" at the estate. And sheriff Scott should get out there.

A short time later there was also a guarded call from W. E. Fulcher, who was on his way home from his night shift. He and Guy were old friends. Had they gotten a call from Reynolda? Yes. Well, said Fulcher — and his relief at not having to be the first bearer of the bad news was apparent — they sure *better* get *out* there. What was the trouble? Guy wanted to know. Fulcher said there had been a shooting, but damned if he really knew the details. Somebody sure better get out there. Was Transou "OK"? Was he in shape to go? Fulcher wasn't much on the diplomatic phrasing. Guy said he was okay, and hoped to hell he wasn't all hung over. Fulcher rang off. "I guess I'll be seeing you later."

Transou Scott was probably better qualified to hold down the often powerful office of a North Carolina county sheriff than perhaps 50 percent of the other men who wore sheriffs' badges in the state that sum-

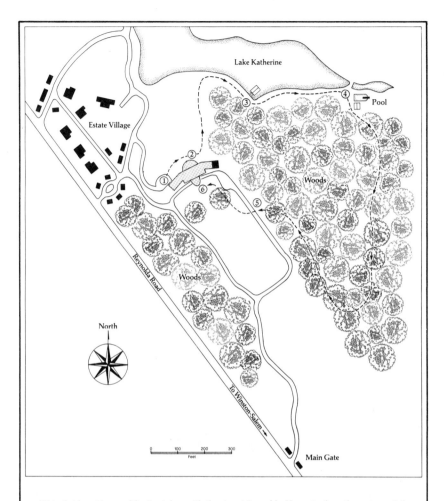

Lake Katherine

Estate Village

③

④ Pool

② ① ⑥ ⑤

Woods

Reynolda Road

Woods

North

To Winston-Salem

0   100   200   300
Feet

Main Gate

This sketch, with some liberties taken with the size of Reynolda House to show the contour of it, indicates the general plan of that part of the estate involved in the shooting incident. The watchman, Fulcher, was standing near the kitchen ① when he heard what he thought was a shot about 12:45 A.M. He walked out to a point behind the house ② and stood about 150 feet from the sleeping porch (the solid black point on the east wing), listening for any further noise or someone needing help. Hearing nothing after five minutes or so, he started out on his rounds, checking the canoe house down at the lake ③ and then the pool and barbecue site ④, to make sure all the cooking coals were out. Coming back along a sometimes-used "lovers' lane" in the east woods, he emerged at a point along the drive at about 1:05 ⑤ to see Reynolds's car headed toward the gate at high speed. After inspecting the party-battered living room of the house, he closed up and waited out front ⑥, expecting Reynolds to return. Instead, the next arrival — about 1:10 A.M. — was the ambulance from Baptist Hospital. It hadn't been called until 1 o'clock. Why hadn't anyone called for help or raised some alarm after the fatal shot at 12:45?

mer of 1932. Which spoke not so much for Scott's qualifications as it spoke for the traditional system of selecting sheriffs in North Carolina — and in many other states around the country.

North Carolina generally followed a tradition adopted from parent England, whereby certain law officials — often quite elevated ones — were chosen by ballot with no hard eye to their experience for the job. In colonial times there had been a certain logic and rightness to the procedure; most every North Carolina male had a good knowledge of firearms, some skill at the hunt, some dedication to simple principles of justice and the sanctity of following and enforcing "what was right." The maintenance of the peace was the concern of every responsible man. After all, soon the law even provided for "citizen's arrests" in instances that were not far removed from a sheriff's province. So it seemed logical that any conscientious citizen might then put himself forward for sheriff, to be elected by a vote of his fellows.

In this historical tradition, Transou Scott, with no special training to be a lawman, was by vote of his peers elected to the office of Forsyth County sheriff. His performance to date had been adequate. And though he knew little about the more sophisticated anticrime investigation and detection techniques that were being developed in the 1930s, there were relatively few occasions when that was a disadvantage. Moonshiners, car accidents, Saturday night cuttings, and domestic disputes were the routine. And he sure as hell knew how to handle *those*. He was a no-nonsense law-and-order man, was reasonably dedicated, went to church regularly — and drank a lot. But then so did many of his constituents. A number of things would surprise and disillusion him about the incident at Reynolda. But the big drinking party was not one of them.

After Guy Scott placed the call to his brother, Transou, he wrote up the brief log entry on the Reynolda calls. Transou had sounded OK, certainly sober, only slightly annoyed. He said he would check in at Reynolda first, then come down to the sheriff's office on the first floor of the Forsyth County courthouse in the heart of Winston-Salem. Guy headed across the street to a little café north of the courthouse where a lot of the night-shift people had their breakfasts. Then when he got home he could honestly say he was well fed and could crawl right into bed and wouldn't have to sit up and talk. He had the midnight-to-eight coming up again that night, and he wondered if he would be able to get much sleep that day. It looked as if it was going to be a screamer for heat.

Transou Scott got himself together in no particular hurry. Grits and eggs, which was the main thing going on in his kitchen, did not seem appealing. But some black coffee and buttered corn bread settled all right. He hunted up a black snap-on bow tie for his khaki shirt, much as he didn't like to wear ties, then shucked the shirt he had put on from the day before and selected a heavy twill one like the state highway boys wore. He pinned on his badge with only one false stab into his finger, strapped on his .38, settled the broad-brimmed tan Stetson on the back of his head — man, it was going to be hot! — and clomped out to argue with the reluctant Reo sedan that was the heritage of the sheriff's office. (Goddamn Reo salesman must have had something on someone down at the county to unload that thing on them!)

When he finally drove off, he wondered briefly whether he should try to pick up Guy or another deputy. Those Reynoldses liked to have lots of side laid on for them. But hell, Guy was probably home in bed by now. As for the rest of the staff, they were already spread too thin. Three men in three cars handling the midnight-to-eight shift; two men in the cars from 8 A.M. to 4 P.M. with only a two-man office staff in reserve; three men riding from four to midnight. Scott himself was always on call and rotated his time among the three shifts. Then there were perhaps two dozen deputized men whom he could call on in emergencies. (Damn good thing the emergencies didn't come too often.)

Scott's route to Reynolda would take him in a wide U from northeast to northwest, swinging south through the downtown area, past his courthouse headquarters, and then out through the affluent northwest suburbs, past the schools and hospitals and into the estate section that bordered Reynolda.

When Sheriff Scott turned into the Reynolda gate he was stopped briefly by a black man who had stretched a heavy chain between the two stout brick pillars on either side of the entrance road. It was the first time Scott had seen the gate closed off, and he was surprised. "Might have to keep some folks out today, cap'n," the man had explained.

Scott drove slowly down the curving drive to the main house. He had only been there two or three times before. It was an impressive spread. He hoped their problem was minor; anything that involved these kinds of people could be difficult — and could backfire on you if it didn't go just right. At least now he would see the inside.

The first thing that surprised him when he got to the parking circle at the end of the drive was the number of big cars parked there: a large gray Franklin sedan (they were expensive); a big black Buick with spare tires mounted into the runningboard on either side ahead of the front doors; a maroon LaSalle touring car with some of those funny-looking vacuum-cleaner pipes coming out of the hood; a sporty Dodge roadster that had its rumble seat open.

Scott parked his dingy Reo over to one side where it would not block the departure of any of the other cars, unbuckled his .38 and stuck it under the front seat (didn't want to look like some goddamn beat pounder), and walked up to the broad covered entranceway. The doors were opened back and it looked cool and inviting inside. Through the screen, he could hear men's voices off there somewhere, in low conversation. He rapped hard at the doorpost. The voices stopped — and then there were steps coming toward him. He recognized the man who appeared at the door as Mr. Warnken, the same man who had arranged to have the estate's watchman deputized under Scott's jurisdiction.

"Come in, sheriff."

Scott took off his Stetson, moved through the screen door into the coolness, and found himself in the biggest living room he had ever seen. It was bigger than his whole damn house.

There were four men waiting in the room when he entered behind Warnken. Scott was introduced all around and there were mumbled acknowledgments. He missed a couple of the names but he recognized Mr. Lasater, who he knew was something big down at the Reynolds headquarters and some sort of relative of the family. And also Dr. Hanes; his picture was always in the papers as chairman of some committee or head of the Christmas Ball or something like that.

One of the Reynolds men whose name Scott had missed took over right away. The others seemed to defer to him naturally. In short sentences he told Scott briskly what had happened. No starting forward and then backing up; it was almost as if it had been rehearsed. Or like it was being read, like a news broadcast on the radio. Several times Scott made to ask a question, but the man waved off the interruption; the Reynolds fellow made it clear he didn't want to stop for any questions. Shortly, he finished: "... and Mr. Reynolds died, we understand, shortly after sunup. You can look at the room uptairs if you want to. We found Mr. Reynolds's gun there. It's pretty clearly a case of suicide."

Jesus! In spite of the slow delivery, it had all come too damn fast at Scott. The five men were all looking hard at him. No one had sat down. The heat was pressing in and he was beginning to sweat. Why the hell hadn't Guy given him some warning? Why hadn't his boys been told anything earlier? By the hospital, at least! Needed a goddamn better system!

"I think I better talk to the madam," Scott began, to buy a little time to get his thoughts organized. He fumbled at the flap button of his shirt pocket. Damn it! He hadn't even brought in his report book. He looked past the men into another large room. He wondered if Mrs. Reynolds was waiting there. He would need his book.

The leader of the group gave one quick shake of his head. "Sorry, but that's not possible just now. Mrs. Reynolds has been put to bed under her doctor's orders."

Scott looked to Dr. Hanes to un-order. The doctor gave a shrug. "Her doctor is Dr. Johnson. And he's not on the grounds right now. Sorry. She's not under my care."

Scott felt a need to have that notebook with him to fuss with for a moment or two to give him time to think of the next question.

"That boy? He's here?"

"Walker?"

Scott didn't know the name. "The fella who went with her to the hospital. He's here? I guess I better talk to him."

The authoritative man turned to the others. Warnken spoke. "Mr. Walker just went home to get some clean clothes. He will be back directly."

"I better see him," Scott said. But now he wondered if they were going to give him a chance. Bastards were all making it hard for him.

"You'll see him," Warnken said. "As soon as he comes back, I promise you'll see him."

"I better get my report book." Scott was sweating in the formality of the room. And without waiting for any acknowledgment from any of the five, he marched out to the Reo.

Rummaging around in the debris in the front seat, he cussed bad. This goddamn thing was going to be real trouble; he couldn't focus on just what. He wished he hadn't had so much to drink last night. Still, the goddamn problems he had at home were enough to make a man take a drink or two.

The notebook turned up underneath a welter of old summons pads, *Wanted* bulletins, and Treasury Department circulars, all held together with thick rubber bands. He grabbed the book and felt better. Then he headed back to the ornate living room.

The men were all sitting now — but otherwise were just as he had left them — as if he had never left. He flipped his book open thoughtfully, past the daily burdens of his office: "Boy throwing stones at SR underpass 2½ mi. northwest." "NC #84 past Devers Gulf, first red brick on right. Man threatens kids. See JR." Now a blank page.

"Okay. I'll want to see Mr. Walker when he comes in. The actress lady from New York City. Is she here?"

Dr. Hanes spoke up again. "Yes . . . well, sheriff, she's here . . . but she has also been put to bed under doctor's care. As you can imagine, it was a severe experience for those women. . . ." The others nodded sagely.

Scott would acknowledge that. Ain't so damn easy for me either. But damn it, he had to start getting something out of these people. "Okay. Where's the watchman? Fulcher."

"He's turned in, sheriff." Then hopefully, "But we can get him back — though it may take a while. He lives off the place."

Scott felt hog-tied! A rich young man had gotten himself drunk and shot himself dead, and these dudes had everybody hidden away where nobody could find out where they had been, what they had done, what they had seen! Scott's voice showed his annoyance: "Then I guess I just better sit right here and wait for this Walker."

Warnken picked up the iciness. He rose and came toward Scott solicitously. "Let's wait out front for him, sheriff. Just so he doesn't stray off somewhere else first. We'll see him when he drives in."

They walked out to the gravel of the parking area. "Terrible business," Warnken said. "Terrible business for Reynolda. Such a peaceful place. And terrible for all this fine family."

Scott answered with all the show of concern he could muster. The fine family had one problem. *He* had another. They stood together stonily. "You don't have to wait out here with me, Mr. Warnken. I'll bring him in when he comes." Warnken shrugged, shook hands rather solemnly, as if they might never see each other again, turned and went back into the house. Scott wiped his brow, replaced his hat, and settled down against the fender of the Reo to wait for Walker.

The boy was not too long in coming. Good thing, too. There was some pretty fair shade around the parking area, but it was getting hotter and hotter, and the house was a sight cooler. Finally a shiny maroon DeSoto sedan came up the drive at deliberate speed. A man about Scott's age was at the wheel; a lady in a floppy white tennis hat sat beside him in the front seat. A young man was huddled in the back. That would be Walker, he figured.

Scott straightened up and nodded a greeting as the DeSoto rounded into the parking circle, and then he walked slowly to the front door of the car. Scott touched the brim of his Stetson in half-salute to the older man. Then held the door open for the young man climbing out of the back.

"Mr. Walker?"

"Yes."

"Sheriff Scott." He extended his hand. Walker's handshake was limp, perspiry, cold. "We need to talk a little bit."

"Right now?" Walker seemed surprised.

"Might as well. I know you been through a hard night. But things will be clearer now than later. And we got a real problem here."

Walker stepped around to the driver's side of the DeSoto and said a few words to his father. The older man nodded, pulled the car into an empty space in the parking area, switched off the engine, but made no move to get out. Scott took young Walker by the arm. "Maybe we better have you tell me everything from the beginning. As I say, we got a problem."

Scott guided Walker into the house. Walker took some guiding. He walked in a dumb, automaton fashion. The Reynolds men were seated in one corner of the living room, huddled together as before, talking in their low voices. They looked up sharply.

"I'll need to see the upstairs now, Mr. Warnken," Scott announced, walking through the living room toward the big curving stairs in the back. Scott decided he would give some orders. Warnken detached himself with a word to the others and led Scott and Walker up the stairs.

"Please be as quiet as you can," Warnken cautioned Scott. "The ladies are asleep at the other end. They need it."

Walker seemed to hang back. Scott took him again by the arm. Warnken followed. At one corner of the balcony that looked down into the living room, Warnken stopped and pointed. "That's the room, there at the end. The double doors. They're waiting for me downstairs." Warnken left. Scott started down the hall, guiding Walker ahead of him. Then he entered the sleeping porch.

Jesus! What a mess!

From what they had told him downstairs about the way Smith had been rushed to the hospital, he had expected a churned-up bedroom and some bloodstains. But the bed looked like somebody had butchered a goddamn pig in it!

He was taking it in slowly when Walker tugged his arm away. The boy was white. "Sheriff, can't we . . . let's talk about this somewhere else."

Poor kid. Scott looked around, trying to note quickly where everything was. Looked like someone had already tried to clean up. He would come back later. Then he steered Walker out.

"Where's an empty room? Unless you don't mind talking in front of those fellas downstairs?"

Walker shook his head — then walked a short way down the hall. "This is my room." He slumped on the bed.

Scott eased himself into an easy chair opposite and took out the notebook again. "OK, I'll hear it ten times, but you might as well tell me what you think happened."

Walker didn't answer for a minute. Then he took a deep breath. "Well, we had this barbecue out here last night — and it didn't go very well. . . ." The story that followed was disjointed. But because of what

Scott had been told downstairs, he was able to follow Walker's skipping around. He didn't try to interrupt, just let the boy keep talking, prompting him occasionally with a question when he seemed to start back over the same ground or stray too far.

Walker seemed vague about the events immediately before the shooting, the time when he said he had been locking up downstairs. Scott didn't know whether to put this down to the fact that Walker might have been pretty drunk at the end of the party — or whether he was holding back. Then Walker jumped to the part about riding back from the hospital in the early morning and coming upstairs, still in his bathing suit, to get on some clothes. He said he was suddenly afraid to come down the hall toward the sleeping porch and into his own room. He was silent. Then: "This used to be Smith's room, you know. It's kind of spooky now." He looked around him.

It was at that point that Scott spotted the pair of women's slippers under the bed. Scott pointed to them, chuckled.

"Those aren't Smith's, are they?"

It took Walker a moment to follow Scott's line of sight. Then Walker leaned over unsteadily and looked under the bed, reached, and came up with the slippers. Bewilderment.

"Damn . . . they must be Lib's."

"Who?"

"Ah . . . Mrs. Reynolds's."

"Okay. But what are they doing under your bed, son?"

Walker flustered and stared at the slippers. Then said slowly, "Well . . . I guess . . . before they went to their room — Smith and Lib — Mrs. Reynolds — must have come in here. I'm sure they came in here."

When Walker had leaned over to pick up the slippers, the smell of whiskey had floated strong across the space from Walker. Scott hoped *he* didn't smell like that.

"I understand, Mr. Walker, that there was a good bit of drinking at your party. Just how much drinking was Mrs. Reynolds doing?"

Walker seemed almost relieved to change the subject. "I wouldn't let *my* wife act like that." And slowly, a different tone crept into his voice as he told about Mrs. Reynolds's jollying the male guests. According to Walker, she kept moving around the group, putting her arm around one man's shoulder, a kiss on another man's ear, a soft laugh at a joke shared between them. "The truth of the matter is, Sheriff . . . the trouble is, Smith just thought too much of that woman!"

"I don't know what you mean by that, Mr. Walker."

Walker thought a bit, and then said that Smith seemed to be crazy about her, but she seemed to like to play up to just about everybody *but* Smith.

Like you? Scott wondered. But when the sheriff asked him to get more specific about Mrs. Reynolds's playing up to everyone at the party, Walker could only answer vaguely: ". . . you know, she just played up to everyone. And she kept coming back to me and joking around with me. Smith saw it. And he got mad, I guess. So when the party was over and everybody was gone, I tried to square it with him."

Scott tried to size up Walker. Kid didn't look like much. Still getting over his pimples. Hard to imagine him being a barn-burner with the ladies. And yet he had sure been Mr. Party the night before.

"Was there something to square?"

"Nothing, really. But Smith thought there was. Because of the way Lib . . . Mrs. Reynolds . . . was following me around." Walker told Scott that after the party he had found Smith in the pantry downstairs, and they talked for a while with Walker trying to explain. And then Walker said they got shouting at each other a little because Smith was really mad. Then it all calmed down, and Smith had told Walker he wasn't at fault.

"Where was Mrs. Reynolds when you fellows were talking?"

"Upstairs, I guess." A pause. "Maybe in here, in my room. They were in here together at one point when I was still downstairs . . . that must have been when she left the slippers."

"When Mr. Reynolds left you downstairs, Mr. Walker, did he look like a man who was going off to shoot himself?"

"No . . . at least I didn't think so. He just hadn't had a good time, and he thought his wife had been making a fuss over everybody but him. I guess I don't blame him for getting mad. But then he had had a lot to drink — otherwise I don't think he would have picked on me like that. We kind of settled down after that. He just went on upstairs, and I started locking up."

"And then?"

"Well, I worked around down here in the living room for a while — it was a mess — and . . ."

"How long would you say you worked around?"

"Ten, fifteen minutes maybe. And then I heard what I thought was a shot. And directly Miss Yurka came from down her end of the hall and she said she heard crying. So I came up here and met Mrs. Reynolds running down the hall, crying. And I went in *there* and found Smith."

Scott was going to ask Walker to describe the room as best he could. The sheriff needed to know how much things had been moved around in all those sightseeing tours the Reynolds company people had apparently made during the early morning hours. Then he decided to try something he had read about in the *Southern Peace Officer*. Surprise a witness. And sometime you might get something he hadn't intended to tell you.

"Why do you think she did it?"

Walker looked up startled. Scott stared hard at him. Then Walker dropped his face into his hands, and his shoulders shook with sobbing: "Damn it, that's something I'll take to my grave! Damn it to hell!"

Scott was not sure just what he had gotten onto. But maybe it wasn't just a case of simple suicide like those Reynolds men downstairs kept assuring him. Young Reynolds was deader than hell. And somebody better find out just what happened. Who did these people think they were, anyway, not letting him talk to anybody?

4

"Camel" Reynolds of the Smokers' Club

THE LATE Zachary Smith Reynolds, just shy of twenty-two years old at the time of his death, stood for some pretty heady society-page images in central North Carolina. His father, the late R. J. Reynolds, founder of the R. J. Reynolds Tobacco Company, was one of the most powerful men in North Carolina at the time of his death — in both the business and the political worlds. Smith was in line to inherit several million dollars on his twenty-eighth birthday. But on his own, he had already made a national reputation as an accomplished aviator.

Aviation was perhaps what Smith loved most of all. It might not be a challenge to someday become the president, chief executive officer, or some other influential policy-maker in the R. J. Reynolds Tobacco Company. For the rest of his life everyone would say, "Oh, well, he's R. J.'s boy." It was a challenge to get up there in the sky where only God knew he was R. J.'s boy.

Smith had attended Woodberry Forest School near Orange, Virginia, for three undistinguished years. He had left in June of 1928 at the end of his sophomore year — having hardly registered a lasting impression on the school.

Woodberry Forest was not a hard place for a young boy of no discernible young-boy talent to fail to register an impression. The school is an old one by Southern standards and is quartered in a handsome and dignified group of buildings atop a commanding hill in rich Virginia countryside. Over the years it has provided a sound preparatory school education for the sons of powerful Southern families. Along the way, many of them also learned how to hold their liquor, a Southern classical knowledge not unappreciated by daddies paying the bill.

At Woodberry, Smith had labored indifferently at "junior football" in years when Woodberry Forest was a Southern prep school power-house. He tried the track and boxing squads with no better results. Along with the rest of the North Carolina boys, he dutifully joined the country-of-origin Carolina Club and the "Smokers' Club," an organiza-tion where he was known as "Camel" Reynolds and where he pledged to uphold the motto "Smoke now for tomorrow you may burn." Per-haps his greatest distinction was as an assistant editor of *The Fir Tree*, the Woodberry Forest yearbook. In the winter of 1928, when Libby Holman was already testing her wings on Broadway, sophomore Reyn-olds was nervously squiring a cousin from Winston-Salem to the mid-winter dance — about which the *Fir Tree* reporter wrote, "Beautiful girls in shimmering silks and satins brightened the cold Virginia week-end" — for the typical frustrating prep school dance. At the end of it, *The Fir Tree* reported, "tender smiles and soft pats were the only things that serve to stimulate the dejected males." By June 1928, Smith had had enough of junior football, the "Smokers," and Woodberry.

He could probably have gotten himself tutored into college. But what the hell. Whatever effect Wake Forest or Chapel Hill or Virginia or William and Mary or Washington and Lee could have on his character was obviously not going to be the difference between success and fail-ure in his life. So there was no college. Nor was there any great family pressure to make him go. Even as a prep school dropout, he already had had a more polished education than his father possessed at the end of college. R. J.'s drive had been to sell tobacco and to concoct new ways of making tobacco palatable to the American public. Smith had a simi-lar drive — to be a fine flyer.

Smith knew he faced problems as an aviator. Whatever he accom-plished, however difficult the goal he staked out for himself in the air, somebody was bound to say that in flying it was also too easy because he was a Reynolds. Maybe it was. While other young aviators were building their own machines or eking out flying lessons by washing planes and working at the airport diner, Smith Reynolds was making ends meet by 1930 on a $50,000-a-year allowance.

At the same time, Reynolds would have been crazy not to use his money to the fullest in pursuing his flying. Aviation and airplanes cost money. Either you had the money or you had to earn it. Or you went in debt for it. Or you went to a group of backers who had it. Or you scrimped and saved and patched your airplane together with cannibalized parts, and then you took a hell of a chance with your own life and everybody else's. Or you gave up flying. Smith Reynolds was smart enough not to adopt any pretense or false poverty when it came to aviation.

Smith had taken his flying instructions early and he had learned well. He held a "license" at sixteen, signed by Orville Wright and attested to by the *Fédérale Aéronautique Internationale.* At the time, there was no regular examination for American pilots. The pilots of the world were a loose, high-spirited international club. If you could get the damned thing off the ground, no earthly authority would challenge your right to fly it. When the French F.A.I. came to the United States to give its credentials to American pilots, Smith naturally wanted to have that accreditation, even though no licensing or accreditation was necessary. By the time the United States started officially licensing pilots, Smith Reynolds already had had so much experience that he was issued a transport pilot's papers immediately. Everyone in Winston-Salem who could read knew Smith Reynolds was one of the state's most notable aviators . . . and perhaps one of the most accomplished. His exploits got more than the average amount of attention.

But in the thirties more than the average amount of attention was the lifeblood of aviation. The United States, in trying to emerge from the depths of the Depression, needed bright lights to hitch its wagon to.

And then came the stars of aviation. They were mostly loners. And if the aviators did nothing immediate for the public *good,* they at least were not roughing up others. Aviation deaths were fast, violent, and sad. To those left behind they were viewed sometimes as *romantic* deaths. You went down in flames. You crashed in a rainstorm. You disappeared out over the Atlantic. You piled into the Rockies. But you didn't starve to death on some sharecropper farm in Arkansas. You weren't hounded by the tax collector or the mortgage man at the bank. You weren't sitting in the World War I veterans' hospital while TB and phosgene gas poisoning crept through your lungs. Although most aviators on points of character, morality, and aim were hardly in the classic mold of the pioneers, at least they *looked* that way. The pilots were like movie stars. And America loved them.

The pages of the *Winston-Salem Journal* — and almost every other paper at the time — were full of aviation exploits. The names of many of the pilots who were famous then are hard to recall today, even for the dedicated aviation buffs. Yet each area of the country had its own local heroes. Then there was a handful of national heroes whose wild, charming, courageous, often pointless flights attracted an avid following.

Smith Reynolds was a local hero and something more. If he had been a polo player or a football star or a bandleader, he would have been just one more spoiled little rich boy. With an unusual accomplishment, perhaps, but one that a starving, Depression-filled America really couldn't admire too much. But as an aviator, Smith was somehow totally different. The local airport from which he flew was an inviting Sunday afternoon focal point for Winston-Salem. And if Smith were flying, or tinkering with his plane, or talking with the other pilots, he was suddenly removed from the "Big House" out northwest. Now he wasn't a poor little rich boy. He was an aviator, just like Gary Cooper in *Lilac Time.*

A Sunday afternoon visit to the Winston-Salem airport might enable you to see — actually *see* and *touch* — the same sorts of machines that were accomplishing the wonders. You could pop all the kids in the car, drive out the dusty road a few miles northeast of Winston-Salem to the field. It was small. Grass runways. A neat, tiny administration building. An airport diner. Some corrugated tin hangars. Some cattle-wire fencing around the edges. It was mirrored in a dozen cities. With a dollar or two for ice cream and cotton candy, you could keep everybody happy until sunset. The planes were there, all shiny with doped fabric and bright colors and brave mottoes lettered under the cockpits or on the cowlings. And if the mechanics weren't looking, or if the pilots were friendly, you could run your hands over the slick, fragile wings, move the ailerons, kick the magnificent fat, smooth black tires, and even try to turn the very propellers that were going to take those glamorous aviators on their wonderful adventures. You could peek into the cockpit and study the wires and gauges and petcocks that the heroes had to contend with. Amazing! And if the outsides of the aircraft looked smooth and sleek and brave, the insides looked amazingly frail, improvised, wired together with ingenuity — and hope. But by God, *you had actually seen 'em!* And smelled the wonderful dope-oil-hot-engine smell. And when Griffin and Mattern or Post and Gatty flew across the front pages of your paper, you could picture that cockpit, sniff the gasoline and castor oil and airplane dope, and squint through the vibrating isinglass windshield against the sun high up . . . and you flew *with* them. You were *not* 17,000 feet away on a beach at Cape Kennedy, watching a strange tube powered by a fantastic arrangement of Roman candles you couldn't understand, handled by three supermen you had only seen on television.

At the Winston airport, with grease under his fingernails, smudges on his knickers, and his hair tousled, Smith Reynolds was a familiar sight. He had an interesting face that could have a rather stern look to it at times. His mouth appeared tightly drawn, the skin above it stretched close around the flare of the nostrils and cheekbones. A no-nonsense fellow.

But Smith's Indian-like face obviously hid something less than a humorless interior. When word had come out shortly after Christmas of 1929 about his first premarital encounter with a wealthy young lady from another powerful North Carolina family, most of the good old boys all up and down the rigid North Carolina social scale had to have a quiet chuckle for themselves.

The story got better with the telling. And the embellishments were numerous. But basically it seemed to come down to the fact that sometime late of a November evening in 1929 old man Joseph Cannon, who owned and ran the mammoth Cannon Textile Mills of Concord, North Carolina, corralled his daughter Anne, plus Smith, a chauffeur, and a private policeman, and drove the group to York, South Carolina, the first town of any size below the North Carolina border. There he had them married in a midnight ceremony by a sleepy justice of the peace. The social niceties were brief to nonexistent. The good old boys slapped side. Old man Cannon fumed. Smith Reynolds's money didn't mean a goddamn thing to Joe Cannon. Anne was distressed, nervous, apprehensive, and unhappy. Smith was sullen.

From the beginning, the chances that the marriage of Smith Reynolds and Anne Cannon would work out were not very good. There was not much they had in common — except tough, rugged, and overbearing men as fathers.

There was an awkward period of speculation, rumor, and gossip when the marriage was first announced. Then North Carolina society closed ranks and decorously took them into its routine — certainly just as easily as they would have accepted any other average young couple from a shotgun marriage who were slated to inherit $20 million to $30 million between them.

Social activities were a problem from the start. Smith moved easily enough through a small group, but was ill at ease and often appeared awkward in a large one. He had missed the polishing social experience of college. And though he liked to drink well enough, he didn't care much for the parties that necessarily went with the drinking. He spent all the time he could with his plane, his flying, puttering around at the Winston-Salem airport, or talking with the pilots, the mechanics, and the hangers-on. His affable manner in airport company brought very little reward at Winston dinner tables.

Smith and Anne lived together indifferently at first . . . and then clearly let it be known they were occupying separate rooms. Anne told a few close friends that Smith continually swore at her. On top of all that — and maybe at the root of the swearing — Anne was going through an uncomfortable pregnancy. When a daughter was finally born, she was christened Anne Cannon Reynolds.

By the spring of 1930, Smith had confided in his brother, Dick, that he knew it wasn't going to work. Anne hardly cared. She and Smith had lived together for only a few months of their stormy marriage. He was surly and nagged her incessantly, so that she was "terribly nervous and upset all the time." Anne could not be blamed if she wanted out at the end of 1930. And by then, Smith Reynolds had met the young woman he wanted to be the next Mrs. Reynolds.

5

From "Varsity Vanities" to Rock-hard Broadway

LIBBY HOLMAN HAD MOVED with surprising ease from just-one-more-pretty-face in the mass of pretty faces that descended on Broadway each season to a highly paid Broadway star. Her success came from a fortunate combination of luck and timing, aided by a fierce drive, a measure of talent, a distinctive voice, and, finally, the help of some show business veterans who were prepared to take a chance. Yet Libby had always been lucky and had often been at the top of the less ambitious and less competitive things she had chosen up till then. So perhaps the rapid rise on Broadway surprised her less than it did others.

But it was still unplanned. When she had started for New York, Libby had come fresh from graduating from the University of Cincinnati. She had intended to enter law school. In the late 1920s, that was a radical enough career for a pretty young girl. But Libby's father, Alfred Holman, was a lawyer in Ohio, and a good one. He had encouraged Libby — somewhat jokingly at first. But when she continued to show interest in the law while in her senior year at Cincinnati, he urged her on enthusiastically.

There was good rugged lineage in Libby's background. Her father's grandparents had come from Germany in the 1850s and were of solid, respectable Jewish stock. Her mother was Rachael Workum, one of six daughters among the seven children of David Workum and Elizabeth Hart Workum. David Workum's parents were Dutch Jews who had met in New York in the early 1800s, married there, and had come to Cincinnati in 1829 from New Orleans.

In exactly the same years that David Workum's parents were born in Holland (1792 and 1798), his wife Elizabeth's *grand*parents, Benjamin Cohen and Rachael Shenon, were born in England. They made their way to New Orleans — by way of North Carolina — with three children. One of their sons, Jacob, was mortally wounded in a North Carolina regiment at the second Bull Run. The Cohens' daughter married a promising New Orleans merchant, Isaac Hart. And it was their daughter Elizabeth who was Libby's maternal grandmother. Libby's great-uncle Alexander, the third Cohen offspring, made a distinguished record as an officer of Louisiana infantry, fighting in the Virginia campaigns and winning several battlefield promotions. Seventy-five years later Libby would be whispered about as "the Yankee Jewess" who had come to be the mistress of a great North Carolina estate. But perhaps her line boasted a deeper Southern tradition than did the background of many of those who gossiped about her.

As Libby grew up in the easy 1920s in Cincinnati, there would rarely have been occasion to mention the Southern background. As a little girl, she was something of a tomboy. Her mother tried to compensate with lessons for Libby in the more feminine arts: dancing, singing, playing a whole series of musical instruments. When company arrived, Libby's mother often insisted that Libby play the violin for guests — whether or not the guests wanted the performance. Libby would balk, sulk, then saw away at the violin, all skinned knees and elbows, until her mother capitulated.

In spite of an occasional embarrassment at being called to entertain in the parlor when she preferred to be climbing trees, Libby had a reasonably happy growing-up period in Cincinnati. There was a wonderful maid, Mattie, who spoiled Libby thoroughly and who always insisted on calling Libby's father "Mr. Hogan" in spite of almost daily correction for her first five years there; there was somewhat higher caste in working for "old line white folks" in Cincinnati, rather than Jews; Mattie couldn't know of the bleeding and dying at Bull Run and the Virginia Campaign.

Mattie provided Libby with a second mother — though there was apparently little lack of motherly attention in the Holman household; sometimes her mother just hovered too much. Libby dutifully went through Cincinnati's Hughes High School, where she began her interest in dramatics. She graduated with a record that qualified her for the University of Cincinnati. When she received her Bachelor of Arts degree in June 1923, in addition to graduating with honors, she had made quite a record for herself in interclass athletic meets and the ladylike Greek Games held by the coeds, had been a principal in the sprightly "Varsity Vanities" show, and had directed the university's 1922 "Junior Show." In April of her senior year, the University Players had presented a musical comedy, *Fresh Paint.* When the *Cincinnati Times-Star* previewed the show, Libby was one of three featured players — and one of the most experienced ones. She already had several performance credits with the Cincinnati Art Theatre, and when the actor Richard Bennett came to play *He Who Gets Slapped* at the Cox Theatre, Libby landed a role for one week. But all that was extracurricular. She seemed most intrigued by the order and authority of her father's law work.

The New York City that Libby Holman arrived in, fresh from the exciting green enamel and maroon plush of a Pennsylvania Railroad Pullman car — that great American magic carpet to adventure — was the wonderful city only a few New Yorkers remember.

The old Pennsylvania Station was an awesome stage for a newcomer to step out onto. The great gray glass-and-black-girdered train shed seemed to brood in perpetual twilight, a giant cathedral built to pay homage to the power of a city. Next, the formidable waiting room, filled with echoes even when it was silent, stood ready to finish off the courage of the awed traveler who had entered in some panic from the train shed. Its escalators, delivering incoming passengers on up to the Seventh Avenue level, could seem like a processional to the sacrificial altar of the city.

But if you could take all that, then you were soon catapulted out into the wonderful horn-honking cacophony of what was regarded by New Yorkers, with no concern for modesty, as "the greatest city in the world."

Libby's ride downtown to the young ladies' residence near Washington Square probably would have taken her down at least a stretch of Fifth Avenue. Even today it is a most impressive street — and in the late twenties it was shining with a pride and luster that was hard to match. Rococo Parisian-looking, open-topped double-decker buses in cream and green and red livery, with bold brass headlights and curving back-stairs, trooped sedately up and down the avenue. The train of taxis mixed among them would have been more numerous and more color-ful than any Libby had ever seen; in those days every taxi fleet had its own distinctive two-toned or three-toned "house colors." More often than not, the cabs were shined like limousines and might appear to be just that. Many of them had a "town car" design, in which the cabbie sat out front in an open seat that could be closed off in bad weather with a convertible canvas roof. The open-air design was conducive to frequent and spirited ripostes with other drivers; it was only later, when the driver was enclosed, that he turned his famous hackie wisdom, spleen, and advice onto the customer in the back seat. A wonderful array of auxiliary vehicles — some virtually unique to New York — created something of the atmosphere of a parade. Department stores vied with each other with smart motorcycles that had sidecars — or tiny trunks set over the cycle's rear wheel. Visored and putteed drivers manned these steeds to rush expensive purchases to the stores' most important customers. Wonderfully ponderous, pug-nosed, snorting trucks crisscrossed the avenue (they were not allowed up and down it), driven by a smartly clicking chain-drive mechanism that looked like some giant bicycle sprocket. Tradesmen's vans were stately and dis-tinctive, emblazoned with impressive, just-invented heraldry, with the whole highly polished to serve as traveling advertisements.

And the entire parade was kept moving by white-gloved policemen, raised, as befitted their authority, above the melee of it in steel towers that stuck up in the middle of the avenue and sported a battery of blinking lights and smartly clacking semaphore arms.

Up and down the avenue, the doormen — and most Fifth Avenue stores had them — were resplendent in epaulettes and brass-trimmed military caps. The doormen all seemed as tall as grenadiers and wielded as much power over their turf as any of the policemen.

Out in the city that Libby had come to conquer, the terrible poverty of the Lower East Side, of Hell's Kitchen, of Harlem, of the Bowery areas was kept visually at arm's length. Much that is prime New York territory now — the United Nations area, Turtle Bay, the Upper East

Side — was taken up with warehouses, slaughterhouses, slums, docks. Manhattan Island was much as a black evangelist described it: "A long piece of land with a lot of rich folks crowded down the center and a lot of poor folks stretched up either side."

But there was little reason to venture into the territory of these poor folks. Libby's world would have been centered more or less between Washington Square to the south and Eighty-sixth Street to the north — with an occasional sporting trip to the Harlem jazz spots; it was the fashionable thing to do. Legitimate theaters dotted the area from Thirty-fourth Street to the high Fifties. A good balcony seat was less than one dollar. And a fine dinner before or after the theater could be had for about $2.50.

Thanks to all the introductions that Libby had come armed with, the invitations came quickly and easily. She was a pretty, personable young thing — with the added advantage of a quick mind. Her way was paid to most of the places she went to. She went often and stayed late. Smart little speakeasies and "private clubs," which could be entered with a freely obtained card and where you could get a terrible meal and passable liquor in a porcelain teacup, were down half a flight of stairs all over town. Drinking, Libby soon discovered, was fashionable. It also gave a nice warmth. Drinking made it easy to put off difficult things "until tomorrow."

The Columbia University Law School — a long subway ride away at 116th Street and Broadway — became an ever-receding destination and all the easier to put off when she found there were archaic age requirements for entrance, and she was some months too young. She would have to wait a bit.

Because she had come to New York with all those good introductions from those helpful, influential Cincinnati people, because she was young, bright, and attractive, because she had some time to kill before Columbia would accept her, she had gradually taken up with a fast-moving young New York crowd that was often on the edge of show business. As Libby moved through the rounds of their parties, she began to discover the value of her husky singing voice. It was regarded by others as quite distinctive. The huskiness dated back to an unskilled tonsil operation in childhood, and she disliked her voice — and had, since the first bratty little boy in the neighborhood kidded her about it.

Some catty New York friends dismissed it as "a small voice." But later one Broadway critic heard it as thousands of others would: "dark, throaty, insinuating." Libby at first was only resigned to it, but then she recognized it as a real asset: "I don't mind making ugly noises with it, if they communicate what I intend."

During that first fall when she was in New York she met, quite by accident, a young Southern newspaperman whose independence to-ward life — and toward her — was immediately challenging and ap-pealing. Because others gravitated toward her when she made but little effort, she, in turn, was drawn to those who seemed capable of indiffer-ence. She would first work hard to win them — and then, having done so, would often throw them over and go on to the next conquest.

So the Southern reporter's diffident response was an intriguing chal-lenge. She had met him when taken by a weekend host in Westchester to check on some casual job of his, being done in a small suburban printshop that specialized in the artfully constructed monograph of the amateur historian, the handsome privately printed book, the personal memorabilia. The young reporter was puttering around, waiting for a friend who owned the place. The reporter and Libby spoke briefly while her host tended to his errand. The meeting of the two was at first like so many other such occasions; he couldn't remember fifty years later what they had said, except he remembered they didn't seem to have much to talk about. A few where-are-you-froms. A few do-you-knows. But for the rest of his days he *did* remember vividly "a gorgeous creature with hair piled up all over and gold flecks in her eyes."

The Southerner was free to cater personally to Libby's needs in the months that followed. But he had no great impetus to demand things from her; he was busy with his work. And Libby was clearly going to be somewhat complicated to become involved with. She often demon-strated her hot temper, her mercurial moods. She was a talented oddity compared to most of the girls from the South he had been urged to look up in New York. And her drive to be on the musical stage was at full speed.

Libby had by then moved uptown to the Studio Club, a somewhat drab but highly respectable residence for young women aspiring to the arts. It was a fixture of West Fifty-seventh Street, a street that still maintains its strong artistic overtones. The club had an acceptable address, known to be bohemian enough to satisfy those who were looking for some of the trappings of the theater and art world but who were not yet geared for Greenwich Village. From its location at the southeast corner of Seventh Avenue, and Fifty-seventh, Carnegie Hall, with its floors of melodious studios above the auditorium, glowered over the neighborhood like a sedate old dowager aunt. Aeolian Hall, run by a piano company, stood nearby, as understated evidence that commercial interests could coexist fairly comfortably with the performing arts — at least that far north of Sheridan Square. Fifty-seventh Street, from Fifth to Eighth avenues, was shouldered with music shops, piano and organ stores, art galleries, portrait studios, rehearsal halls, and the charming little coffee shops and restaurants that offered the sort of rubbed-down, well-used, well-loved decors that were acceptable to the artistic temperament, while posting charges for a cup of tea and a club sandwich that would have been every bit respected along the elegance of Fifth Avenue.

The young Southern writer finally responded to one of several invitations she had given him to come have dinner at her "club" — "anytime; you don't have to call ahead." When he sauntered into the Studio Club, he was ushered by somebody's grandmother (in a shiny black dress and a white Puritan collar that would have done credit to Hester Prynne) into a room that looked like the hallway of an austere English parsonage. Then suddenly he was moved into a brightly lit and near dead-white dining room that held 150 chattering and clearly ravenous young ladies, also in white, attacking broiled fish, diced potatoes, creamed onions. And suddenly all staring at him! The almost blinding white-on-white-on-white effect was right out of *The Cabinet of Doctor Caligari!* Though he was a veteran — covering labor riots, train wrecks, and Saturday night cuttings — he found himself petrified, until Libby's nonstop conversation and reassuring chatter took him through the rest of the dead-white dinner.

Afterward, they strolled in the soft night air to the Central Park Zoo, sat on a wall near the Monkey House, smoked almost a pack of cigarettes, and talked in a relaxed fashion for the first time. He decided then that there were many things about the voluble aspiring actress that appealed to him.

A week or so later, he called her again for dinner — this time declining the virginal white ambiance of the Studio Club dining room. They went to a small restaurant in the East Fifties, then after dinner walked down to the East River, which at the time was not separated from the East Side by today's roaring Franklin D. Roosevelt Drive. In the early thirties, there was a pier for coal barges at the foot of East 58th Street. It stood deserted at night. The young reporter and his date strolled out onto it to relish the lights of the river. It was a handsome setting.

The two were talking intently when they noticed two policemen walking out onto the pier. The young couple was expecting nothing more than a casual greeting — but the policemen suddenly turned aggressive. Flashlights flared in their eyes, rough hands frisked them, running harshly over Libby's full figure, and lingering. "We're checking morals," one of the policemen growled out. Some remarks were passed that made it clear the police thought they had encountered a racially mixed couple. They glared at Libby. "What are you doing way downtown here, girl?" Then whatever look had misled them was suddenly gone in the harsh white beam of the flashlight. There were mumbled withdrawals — but no apologies. Libby started to lash out. She was furious! Her friend tried to calm her. They got back to the Studio Club, both rather shaken by the incident. Their first time on the wrong side of the law.

In a year or so, they would meet again in Paris. And after a long night of partying, they ended up again along the river's edge, arms tight around each other, talking, smoking. Two gendarmes on bicycles passed on patrol, asked for identity cards. Libby had nothing; she bristled for another incident. There was a Gallic shrug from one gendarme. "*N'importe pas.*" Apologies to madame for disturbing her. Libby relaxed. No, she insisted, *she* was the one who should apologize. But no, they responded, it was *for them* the duty to apologize. Alphonse and Gaston. Libby insisted *she* had broken the law. Finally her laughing Southern friend led all four of them to an all-night café for a bottle of wine. . . .

Later Libby spoke over and over of the difference. And then the rage at the New York incident came back over her until she shook, sobbed, pounded her tightly clenched fists.

It was somewhat frightening. The fierce and instant anger.

But that fall of 1928 in New York, the try for the stage was what consumed almost all of her. It promised glamour, recognition, a chance to exercise a creativity that would never be able to surface in law school. And nothing else seemed very attractive.

After a long round of walk-ons and road shows, Libby landed a part in 1928 in Vincent Youmans's musical *Rainbow.* She played an outcast in California during the Gold Rush days. Also in the cast were Charles Ruggles as a mule skinner and Brian Donlevy as a captain of dragoons. Libby's part was quite small — but she was winning enough in it to attract some attention. And that attention was sustained enough to earn her a real chance in a new sort of musical revue that was being planned.

6

The Dark Purple Menace of Libby Holman in the Blues

IN ADDITION TO all those elements of luck and good timing that may combine with real ability to deliver a successful show business career, Libby Holman owed much of her rise to the talents of a young New York composer-lyricist team — Arthur Schwartz and Howard Dietz. They brought the Broadway "revue" to its most elegant form on the American musical stage. And in the process, they swept along several notable theatrical careers in their wake.

Until the late 1920s a Broadway musical was thought of largely as escape for the tired businessman. By tradition, it revolved around a series of not-necessarily-memorable tunes, interwoven with the routines of a reigning comic or two. This would all be tied together with as large a number of pretty girls as the producer could afford, in costumes as scanty as he could get away with — all parading down assorted stairs and through assorted archways in that wonderful rocking, dromedary motion of plumes and trailing skirts and swelling breasts that Flo Ziegfeld seemed to have invented. The fact was that the rocking, dromedary advance was the only walk a highly crested showgirl could manage — and still keep all that millinery from falling into the orchestra pit.

Toward the end of the 1920s a producer named Tom Weatherly and a similarly innovative partner, James Pond, started putting on small Sunday night "entertainments" at the Selwyn Theatre on West Forty-second Street. These were light, fresh, different variety shows, almost collegiate in their offhandedness and their cheerful violation of all the

Broadway rules. The songs were gay and simple. The skits were effort-less, bright, and seemingly impromptu. No big budgets or big reputa-tions were riding on the shows. Everybody had fun. Particularly the au-dience. The good word got around.

Weatherly, encouraged by his success and by what he had heard and seen of a bright little English production called *Charlot's Revue* that was also pleasing Broadway just then, joined with William Brady, Jr., and a wealthy, quixotic sometime producer named Dwight Deere Wiman to turn "Sunday night at the Selwyn" into something more permanent. *The Little Show* was to be their first something.

To supply most of the words and music, Weatherly, Wiman, and Brady decided to stack their chips on some sort of musical score that would be clearly different from the big musicals. Their aim was partly innovative. But mostly they couldn't afford lots of chorus girls and boys. In the freewheeling manner that characterized much of the rest of their production, they discovered Howard Dietz in a saloon.

Dietz had been standing at the bar in a West Forty-ninth Street speakeasy and had overheard them talking in voices well oiled by whiskey about the plans for their new show. They outlined the revue to everyone who would listen in terms that to Dietz sounded artfully con-structed to launch a sleepy dud. Weatherly and Wiman were loudly debunking the Ziegfeld rhinestones-and-tights approach. The show they were planning they called "topical and artistic, a witty travesty on the leitmotif. . . ." Critics wouldn't even be able to spell it, Dietz thought; "leitmotif" was like the Broadway definition of satire: what closed on Saturday night.

Dietz kibitzed from the bar rather imperially, since they were ad-dressing just about anybody in the room. He felt he had some hard-earned experience behind his criticism. Though his nine-to-five job was publicity man for Metro-Goldwyn-Mayer Pictures in New York, he did have a couple of legitimate Broadway credits to his name: he had been on the fringes of several small musicals that had gone by without much acclaim, though today they enjoy stronger reputations. He had contrib-uted lyrics, portions of lyrics, song titles, and song situations to *Dear Sir, Oh, Kay!, The Merry-Go-Round,* and *Poppy,* the last having brought W. C. Fields his first starring role. His chief encourager in all this had been the young but startlingly successful Jerome Kern. So Dietz, from his post at the bar, gave them the benefit of his Broadway credentials and his gratuitous advice: forget "the witty travesty on the leitmotif." Apparently all that his caution did was to come through as reverse salesmanship. Weatherly invited Dietz to be his lyricist for $100 a week, an advance against one-half of one percent of the show's gross.

To Dietz one-half of one percent of a speakeasy pipe dream was hardly the sort of thing to rush out and quit M.G.M. over. But then Weatherly and Wiman showed they were not totally barroom pipe dreamers. Already signed were three lead people: Clifton Webb, known around town as a "soigné interpretative vaudevillian," who was developing the waspish stylishness that would make audiences love-hate him until his death. Then there was an unusual dry-witted comic named Fred Allen, who was also earning a good Broadway reputation. In an era of somewhat predictable stand-up, one-line comics in the vaudeville tradition, Allen's routines took the time to develop a person-ality, and it was a personality that found lots of sympathetic audience responses. Here was a man — skeptical, questioning, intolerant of the world that seemed organized to frustrate him. He suffered lots of de-feats — as had his audience. But there were occasional great and just Allen victories, with a real sense of revenge thrown behind them. The audiences were right with him in those hard Depression days.

The third person signed by Weatherly and Wiman was relatively new to Broadway. But her style was beginning to be recognized as "distinctive." She was Libby Holman, who had won those first good no-tices singing in *Rainbow.* She had also appeared in *Merry-Go-Round,* doing some Dietz lyrics. He knew her slightly as an enthusiastic, though sometimes unpredictable performer who liked to wander nearly nude around her dressing room. She attracted a lot of visitors.

But the real clincher to Dietz, as he stood propped up with more and more difficulty against the bar, arguing with Weatherly and Wiman, was the fact that they also had an agreement with young Arthur Schwartz to do the music for the show.

Dietz had not met Schwartz at that point. But five years before, Dietz had received an over-the-transom letter from Schwartz on a law firm letterhead, asking if they could collaborate. Bennett Cerf, a Columbia classmate of Dietz, was a mutual friend and had suggested that Schwartz write. Schwartz wanted to quit the law and be a composer.

Dietz had been interested and flattered; Schwartz had compared him in the letter to Lorenz Hart. But Dietz was also somewhat euphoric about his own recent "collaboration" with the meteoric Jerome Kern, and he wrote Schwartz at the time that they had better wait.

However, with Weatherly's energy and Wiman's money in hand, with Clifton Webb, Fred Allen, and Libby Holman waiting for something witty to sing and say, the time for collaboration seemed to have arrived. The next day lyricist Dietz had tracked down composer Schwartz and they had sealed their partnership. It was a casual beginning to one of the really fine and lasting twentieth-century American lyricist-composer teams. Then with a wad of expense money from Wiman, the two of them had holed up in the first of a series of hotels to write a score for *The Little Show.*

They coaxed that score out of their pianos from hotel suite to hotel suite in a gradually descending economic spiral as the money ran lower and as they were evicted from one place after another because of complaining guests. But slowly all the elements of a successful collaboration began to fall into place for the two. Schwartz would usually do the music first, with some general idea of the sort of lyrics that would go behind it. Then Dietz would start the words. Sometimes what Schwartz first conceived as a ballad would become, along the way, first blues, then a witty patter song — before ending up as a lover's lament.

Temperamental, demanding Clifton Webb wanted some special music, some "suave romantic frustration" that he could perform in a top hat, white tie, and tails. Schwartz tried, and threw out, several things — then recalled the melody of an old song that he and Lorenz Hart had written for the summer show at an Adirondacks boys' camp when they were both counselers there. For the camp show it had been called "I Love to Lie Awake in Bed" and it catalogued the pleasures of reflections after a day at summer camp: a placebo for homesick campers. Dietz put new words to it, they changed the tempo slightly, and it became the haunting "I Guess I'll Have to Change My Plan":

> *I guess I'll have to change my plan.*
> *I should have realized there'd be another man.*
> *Why did I buy those blue pajamas*
> *Before the big affair began?*

My boiling point is much too low
For me to try to be a fly Lothario.
I think I'll crawl right back and into my shell
Dwelling in my personal hell.
I'll have to change my plan around,
I've lost the one girl I've found.

It was just what Webb wanted — the first of what Dietz came to think of as Webb's many "solo flirtations" with a theater audience.

Wiman and Weatherly thought the sultry Libby Holman needed some special material, too. One of the pit musicians had composed some earthy he-done-me-wrong music. The producer thought they could use it in a macabre sketch, which would end with man-about-town Webb strangling Holman, who played his two-timing mulatto lover. Dietz put words to it — and it became "Moanin' Low," later a Libby Holman theme song.

The rest of the score seemed equally fresh and winning to all those who had worked so hard to put the show together. Kay Swift and Jimmy Warburg supplied the long-lasting "Can't We Be Friends?" Sketches were contributed by Dietz, Allen, George S. Kaufman, and Marya Mannes. Those inside tried to be professionally skeptical in order not to get hopes too high. But the show seemed to be shaping up promisingly. All of which made the flop, which came on the show's first-night tryout in Asbury Park, New Jersey, hard to understand.

Something about the alchemy of the first-night audience had been decidedly wrong. The second night in Asbury Park, the disappointed cast was hardly more than dutifully going through the motions. The curtain went up to a skeleton house. The word had gotten around, and only a few who had been stuck with unredeemable tickets had finally come, intending to recover at least something for their money. After a chilly beginning they began to respond with a little polite applause. Then it became cautiously spontaneous. Then it burst out for one after another of the hoped-for show-stoppers that had floated by to such a lethargic reception the night before.

The several other Asbury Park performances that followed, with a rouser on Saturday night, proved the second-night reception was no fluke. And when *The Little Show* started back up the Jersey Central tracks toward Broadway, all hands were cautiously hopeful they had a chance for a real hit.

On April 30, 1929, *The Little Show* opened at New York's Music Box Theatre. The first reviews were friendly but hardly overwhelming. Critic William Trapp had the dubious distinction, when the show later turned out to be known as "a classic of revues," of having written a first-night report commenting that the show "would be a great deal better with a real singer or two and, perhaps, an outstanding musical number."

But fortunately for the cast, several of the critics thought otherwise. Charles Brackett, writing in *The New Yorker*, said that "Libby Holman halts proceedings with two of the torch songs which are her specialty." Brackett found "the macabre setting for Miss Holman's song 'Moanin' Low' . . . a whole compact melodrama." Even Brooks Atkinson of the *Times*, often acerbic and hard to please, felt that "most of the wit, humor, and intelligence that somehow escaped the musical stage has settled down pleasantly into *The Little Show.*" The "dark purple menace of Libby Holman in the blues" delighted Atkinson.

The success of *The Little Show*, 321 performances, spawned a sequel, ingeniously titled *The Second Little Show*. It turned out to be amiable enough — but not successful at the box office. Dietz and Schwartz took part, but Webb, Allen, and Holman did not. *The Second Little Show* opened in September 1930 and ran for only 63 performances.

Then along came producer Max Gordon, who believed in sticking with a winning team. He had a new revue in mind, hired Webb, Allen, and Holman, and then persuaded Dietz and Schwartz to do the lyrics and music. That's when *Three's a Crowd* was born. An extensive tryout tour was arranged to give the cast plenty of time to shake down for New York. But in Philadelphia, the last stop, Libby Holman was still having trouble with her big number, "Body and Soul," which should have been a sure show-stopper. Discouraged, she sulked in her dressing room, drinking bootlegged bourbon, with one of the show's posters taped to her door, the *Three's a Crowd* billing altered in a shaky feminine hand to read: "Clifton Webb and Fred Allen in *Two's Company.*" Dietz, who had almost given her up as hopeless, arranged for a special voice coach to come down from New York to work with her. The coach and Libby experimented increasingly desperately with all sorts of deliveries and tempos. But it wasn't until the last night in Philadelphia that the number seemed to go right.

On October 15, 1930, the show opened in New York; for good luck, at the Selwyn, where the Sunday night revues had been so successful. When the reviews came in, there was a bit of carping at first. Robert Litell in the *New York World* complained that "the throat-tearing basso contralto of Libby Holman, which can be so exciting with the right kind of song, deserves something better than 'Yallar' or 'Body and Soul.'" And John Mason Brown in the *Evening Post* complimented Libby for doing a good show in spite of what he called "the disaster" of her opening number; it was the now-standard "Something to Remember You By." Robert Benchley of *The New Yorker* apparently saw the same show most of the audience seemed to see: "Miss Holman's voice is even more far-reaching in its effect than last year and her elevation to stardom has given her a new quietness and poise which do nothing to detract. I do not think that her big number, 'Body and Soul,' is a very good song; it was imported from England quite a long time ago and has had its edge worn off by several hundred saxophones. In fact, none of her numbers is as good as 'Moanin' Low' or 'Can't We Be Friends?' but Miss Holman herself makes up for whatever unfavorable imbalance there may be."

When Libby slowly undulated into a glittering purple spotlight on the darkened stage (the audience thought the serpent-like sliding of her feet ahead of her was meant to be seductive, but it was really a measure of caution on Libby's part because of her extreme nearsightedness), and when she slid huskily into "Body and Soul" — the first-nighters knew they were in on the start of another long Broadway run.

> *My heart is sad and lonely.*
> *I sigh for you, for you, dear, only.*
> *Why haven't you seen it?*
> *I'm all for you, body and soul.*

As the show settled down in the fall of 1930, *Three's a Crowd* pushed along a few unknowns: Portland Hoffa, who would team with Fred Allen with great success, dancer Tamara Geva, and Fred MacMurray, who played a young sailor to whom Libby sang "Something to Remem-

ber You By" in a French waterfront setting. Dietz and Schwartz had inherited that number from a British musical where the song, with different lyrics, had been titled "I Have No Words" and was sung by the
leading comedian. Dietz was first asked to supply new comic lines.
When he gave them a working title of "Something to Remember You
By," Schwartz thought that was too good for a comedy number and offered to do a romantic melody with Dietz doing new romantic lyrics.
They settled by playing the original music more slowly, with Dietz's
new words telling a touching story of parting lovers. It became one of
the most memorable moments in *Three's a Crowd* with Libby Holman at
the helm.

> *Oh give me something to remember you by*
> *When you are far away from me, dear,*
> *Some little something meaning love cannot die*
> *No matter where you chance to be.*
> *Though I'll pray for you,*
> *Night and day for you,*
> *It will see me through like a charm,*
> *Till your returning. . . .*

When the "second reviews" were written later in the fall, as was the
custom then, Libby Holman's career had already encountered its most
pivotal event: earlier that year, when *Three's a Crowd* had been having its
pre-Broadway tryouts in Baltimore, she had been introduced to Smith
Reynolds. She was not overwhelmed. For one thing, he was almost too
young — not yet twenty, and quite shy. And she was a Broadway-wise
twenty-four.

He was persistent. And Libby was kind. But she was also busy chas-
ing success. *Three's a Crowd* was due for an extensive road tour. And she
felt she had more to do than trying to draw out a shy young North
Carolina boy who might better have been in the warm, brotherly em-
brace of a Carolina fraternity house.

7

"Just Two Ordinary People Deeply in Love"

IN THE SUMMER and fall of 1930, while *Three's a Crowd* was in tryout, Libby Holman had two persistent men trying to change her life: Nick Kempner, director of *Three's a Crowd*, was trying to mold her into the star of a Broadway hit . . . and young Smith Reynolds was trying to persuade her that being a star did not mean she could not also be his wife.

It was complicated for the first man because Libby was not a completely pliable pupil and she had little professional training. It was complicated for the second man because he was already married and could not have taken on Libby had she accepted him.

To compound the difficulty in the case of Libby Holman and Smith Reynolds, she was being hurled along by the urgencies of an expensive show, counting down for a Broadway opening. And Smith, the son of a millionaire, had been raised from the beginning to show his true nature only very cautiously, as a protection against opportunists.

And so, with all the complications and the passions and the urgencies — with the artificial environment of show business all around and no families present on either side, there was little time for Smith and Libby to know each other at any point in that rather harassed courtship.

When Smith's older brother, Richard, had first introduced the pair in Baltimore, they had had a few dates, hardly anything glamorous, often following rehearsals and performances. Libby was usually exhausted after her day in the theater. And the age difference was often awkward — more so for Smith than for Libby. She had experienced enough success by that time to feel relaxed and at ease in most situations — sometimes so much so that to Smith she appeared condescending. He was trying hard to make her like him, and was alternately elated when he appeared to be succeeding . . . and moody when he did not. When he wasn't succeeding, it was often that Libby was just tired. She was beginning to like him — though she didn't completely understand him. Something told her she wanted to help: a "mother's instinct," perhaps, that she showed so often later. It has never made for the best marriages.

After their first few dates in Baltimore in the spring of 1930, Libby took a vacation from the show for Easter week and headed for Florida for a brief rest. Smith had gotten into his plane and followed her there. The time spent together in Florida was better. He told her a little about himself. That he had been married since the fall of 1929. That he had lived apart from his wife almost all the time. That he had a daughter born shortly after their marriage. That he was moving toward a divorce. That getting it would probably be difficult.

Still, Smith at twenty was already an accomplished aviator, and his flying charmed her — though she was a little frightened of it. The flying was dashing and romantic. And it was nice to be going with a young man who had plenty of money to use as he wanted, including following her around the country.

Some fond letters were exchanged after her return to Baltimore from Florida after Easter week in 1930. Then in summer she had been given some more time off when the hot-weather doldrums dictated closing the show and giving the cast a rest in anticipation of the New York opening in the fall. Libby had gone to the south of France to see her young newspaperman. Smith followed her.

"Smith asked me to marry him that first summer, almost right after he had met me," Libby said later. "I said no, I didn't think I should marry him because he was so young. And, of course, he hadn't his divorce yet and was still married. I told him I thought he had better wait a while. Besides, I was in the theater and didn't think it was fair to marry while still in the theater. He first agreed to that, to wait five years. Then he came to see me and said, 'You go on in the theater, Libby. I need you now. I never had any love in my life and I want someone like you, and as soon as I get my divorce I want you to marry me. I have been alone all my life.' " It was then, Libby said, they suddenly felt "a great love for each other."

They saw each other often through the fall of 1930, after *Three's a Crowd* opened, and during the winter and spring of 1931. In the summer of 1931, Libby and Smith both took houses in Port Washington, New York, on the north shore of Long Island. It seemed at first a gay vacation time. Tallulah Bankhead, a glamorous new friend of Libby's, was nearby. The three would often go walking together — at least part of the way; Tallulah insisted on being followed by her Rolls and would retreat to the back seat for any slight uphill stretch, then she would rejoin Libby and Smith on foot for the downhill or the flat.

There were lots of good parties and a good crowd. Everything should have been perfect. Here were two gifted and financially secure young people "taking houses" and idling away their summer in a fashionable Long Island resort community, at an age when most of their contemporaries were grinding in the library stacks at summer schools or sweating at summer jobs to earn some fall tuition money . . . at a time when millions of Americans at any age were out of jobs, on breadlines, not knowing where meals or mortgage money or help could come from. But there were also the first black clouds in Port Washington. They should have given Libby a clue to the sort of storm that could brew.

Smith had come to her Port Washington house one day, with a glazed and distant look in his eyes. She thought at first he had been drinking. But he assured her he hadn't. Pacing around the living room, he pulled out a gun, pointed it at the windows, aimed, said nothing. Libby asked him to put it away. No, it was perfectly all right, he reassured her; the gun was empty. He twirled the cylinder, handed it to her, insisted she pull the trigger. She didn't want to. "I don't *understand* guns," she protested. Smith moved behind her, laughing, and reached affectionately around her with both arms, grasped her gun hand firmly, squeezed her finger on the trigger. There was a blast and kick as the gun went off!

Smith laughed. "I'll be damned! It must have gotten jammed before. I was sure it was empty."

"You told me you knew so much about guns!" Libby was furious! The bullet had drilled a neat hole in the wainscoting of the living room. In addition to the scare, it meant that someone had to come in and patch the hole before the house was turned back to its fastidious owner. Libby started to lecture Smith on guns when she had calmed down a bit. She was afraid of them. They were obviously not safe. He could have shot her if the gun had gone off when he was first waving it around!

Smith seemed contrite at first. But as Libby kept coming back to the thing, he turned angrily on her. Damn it, he *had* to have a gun. He was afraid of kidnappers! There was kidnapping going on all around the country. "They" would come get him sometime when he wasn't ready for them . . . *if* he wasn't ready for them. And maybe he couldn't pay the ransom and maybe even his guardians wouldn't. Then what?

"Do you want my life always to be in danger?" he shouted at her. "Do you want *your* life in danger?" He sulked and was ready to storm out of the house when she calmed him down and changed the subject.

Later, she too began to wonder about Smith's fear of kidnappers. Several times when they were at his house in the evening, he had leaped off the couch — sometimes at most inconvenient moments — snapped off all the lights, then crept to the window with his gun waving. But as far as she could tell, there was never anything there. "Smith, I'm going to throw that gun away," she threatened. He cursed the people "out there."

"It won't make any difference if you do. I can get other guns. I've had guns since I was a baby, and I'm not going to get my ass shot off or kidnapped just because you don't like 'em."

That summer in Port Washington he told her he had gotten several notes threatening his life. People had called up his house, he said, and asked where he was — but would never leave a message. Then later there would be a call and a threat. He told Libby he even used to put a dummy in the bed, then wrap himself up in newspapers and sheets and sleep under the bed — with his gun clutched in one hand — until the first light of morning. There were two weeks at the end of the summer, she said, when he was so frightened he would not even leave the house to go for golf or tennis or to the beach, all the things they had enjoyed so much together earlier. Once when Libby tried to urge him out, he said that the night before he had heard voices in his front room, that he had jumped out a back window and run two miles to the police station.

But when he got the police to the house, they could find no trace of a forced entry. No trace of people. Nothing. They seemed annoyed at this rich, nervous young man. Libby only got him out a few times after that, and his gun was constantly with him, alongside him on the seat in the car, wrapped in a towel at the beach, cocked on the bedside table when they settled down for the night or any portion of it. In the end, Smith and Libby had a towering row, and he left Port Washington sooner than he had planned.

In late August of 1931, Smith had begun to make some news himself. He had purchased a flashy Savoia-Marchetti amphibian for $90,000. It was a versatile airplane with a proven long-distance flying record and was equipped with a number of advanced safety and navigational features. On August 27, the Cunard liner *Berengaria*, sailing from New York, had recorded for passage the reservation of Smith Reynolds for a trip to England. The reservation specified that there would be several trunks of equipment as well as certain "personal baggage." A few minutes after three on the afternoon of the sailing, Reynolds's Savoia-Marchetti amphibian had circled the ship at her North River pier, headed into the wind, landed gracefully off the head of the pier, and then taxied to the side of the liner. Removing his helmet, Reynolds shouted up to the surprised deck officers that the plane was his "personal baggage" and he wanted to be taken aboard. To the eternal credit and calm of the English — eccentricity being a highly respected quality among that citizenry — a crane was swung out, and soon the amphibian was snugged down on the foredeck of the ship. It was a happy time for a wealthy young man to be alive.

Smith told astonished ship's news reporters he was headed on a round-the-world flight. The *Berengaria* would take him to Southampton. He would then fly from England to Paris, down to the Mediterranean, along the coast of Spain and across to Africa, down the African west coast to Cape Town, around the tip of Africa and north to Aden, to Arabia, and to Persia . . . then on to India. The trip was a relatively ambitious one for a twenty-year-old pilot — even a pilot with as much experience as Reynolds. But he had plotted out as big a margin of comfort and safety as he could. His brother, Dick, was already in Europe with his private freighter-yacht. His plan was to stay ahead of Smith with fuel and supplies. Smith planned to take a reasonable time with his flying. He was not trying to break any records, just take a "grand tour" with his new airplane.

But Smith's leisurely flight hardly had a chance to get mapped out from his south England base when he had to return to the United States early in the fall of 1931. "Because of sickness," he told reporters. The excuse hid a lot of intensely personal business. On October 5, 1931, Smith flew Anne Cannon Reynolds to Nevada for her to establish residence in that state on a ranch near Reno. He saw her settled and then immediately flew back north. He expected a divorce to become final in mid-November. Also shortly after he returned to the United States, Smith had invited Libby for her first short stay at Reynolda House, his family home in Winston-Salem. From then on, they had seen each other almost every day.

Smith's devoted pursuit made a deep impression on Libby at this point. "I was starting on the road," she recalled later. "While rehearsing in New York I would see him. Then we played in Newark — and he would come out at night and bring me back. Then we played in New Haven, and he came up there to see me. Then to Washington and Baltimore, and he came to both those places. And then we went to Philadelphia, and he came . . . and then we played Pittsburgh. He was always there."

In Nevada, Anne Cannon Reynolds put in her six weeks' residence but was distressed about the divorce, nervous about the procedures for it, and her health had gotten bad. She was so ill when the final hearing was scheduled that she could not appear to testify. She settled for a $500,000 trust fund to be set up for herself and another of a similar amount for her baby daughter. By layman's terms, these were handsome settlements indeed. But with an eye to the money that Smith Reynolds would eventually come into, they were quite modest. All she wanted, she said, was something fair and adequate, considering his circumstances and hers. She had gotten it, in return for a promise that she would make no further claim for herself or her daughter on Smith Reynolds or on his estate. She was glad enough to give that promise, in order to get away and start a new life.

With the divorce becoming final, Smith followed Libby's touring swing through the Central States. And he did some research on local laws. Libby remembered that "the week preceding the twenty-ninth of November, he went down to Monroe, Michigan, because by Michigan law you have to publish banns five days before you are going to get married. He found out that the State of Michigan was the only state you could be married in when you were under twenty-one without consent of guardian."

And so had come about on November 29, 1931, in the drab surroundings of Justice of the Peace Fred Schoepfer's house in Monroe, Michigan, the wedding of "Zachary Reynolds" of New York City to "Elizabeth Holman," also of New York. The j.p.'s wife remembered later that they were "just two ordinary people deeply in love and asking to be married." She thought nothing further . . . until a neighbor who had been called in as a witness figured out who Libby was. But a Zachary Reynolds was nobody either of them had ever heard of.

In the hectic months that followed the marriage, Libby struck out in one direction, and Smith in another. As Libby explained later, they were both saddled with complicated plans. A honeymoon wasn't one of them.

Smith sailed for England on the S.S. *Paris* on December 1, to get back to his plane. On December 27, he took off for France, giving the headlines a quick flare when he landed — after crossing the channel — at Châteaudun for the night (and was unreported), rather than proceeding on to Le Bourget near Paris as planned. By early January he was in Lyons, planning to take off on the Africa-Asia-India-China leg. Libby's U.S. tour contract didn't end until the last week in February 1932, then she caught the first boat she could for Hong Kong.

The reunion in Hong Kong in April had been a delightful one. Smith's plane had been forced down with engine trouble at Fort Baird, about 250 miles south of Hong Kong. The problem had been unfixable at that point. He had hitched a ride to Hong Kong on an oil company's coastal tanker sailing up the China coast. Libby had found out when he was to arrive and had arranged to hire a junk to go out and meet the tanker in the harbor. She had fixed herself up with a complete Chinese outfit — and with makeup her round face assumed a suitable Oriental appearance. When Smith's tanker had come plodding into the harbor, he was surprised to see it paced by a ratty Chinese junk with a pretty, wildly waving Chinese girl on its deck. When Libby climbed aboard the tanker, he had choked with emotion at her stunt and with his delight at seeing her. There had been a relaxed couple of weeks together seeing Hong Kong. Then they had finally booked passage on April 22 for Victoria, British Columbia.

They had boarded the Canadian liner, a magnificent white "Empress" ship with three prestigious buff funnels, the night before sailing. As much as Libby had loved her brief taste of the Orient, there was something reassuring to a girl from Cincinnati, Ohio, about picking your way through the somewhat frightening cacophony of a Chinese steamer shed and then — after walking thirty feet across a scrubbed teak gangway — finding yourself in all that English-wrought peace and serenity. Starched white-coated and flush-cheeked stewards moved through the companionways. Muffled chimes from somewhere around a corner announced some leisurely change in departure routine. The confident we-own-the-Empire atmosphere was everywhere.

They had settled into their cabin and begun to unpack. By the ritual of ocean travel in that more gracious day, there would be no dressing for dinner that first night before they sailed. Smith suggested they go up, have a drink at the bar, and then if things did not look too promising they could head back ashore and link up with a gregarious Australian they had done some extensive bar-hopping with the night before. Libby said she would bathe and get ready.

The long, leisurely, steaming bath was luxurious. When she stepped out of the bath and into the cabin, Smith was gone. Not unusual. She would dress and search him out in the bar.

Half an hour or so later, with the last pin in place, with her full lips glistening a bright red, bag and gloves in hand, she headed for the cabin door.

Some tentative struggle with the handle. Damn! Jammed. No matter. Call the steward.

Libby punched the steward's buzzer. At first perfunctorily. Then with increasing annoyance. Then with some panic. Then she found the note from Smith.

I want you to stay here.
I will be back about 11.

She was furious. She didn't even have anything to eat! And the steward had obviously been instructed not to answer!

Outside the porthole, Hong Kong harbor was making its own abundant noises. Junks and sampans moved by. She called out, waved, pantomimed. The Chinese on the boats smiled, laughed, waved back, giggled. She felt ridiculous. If she yelled loudly enough, someone on the promenade deck two above would eventually hear. They would come for her, all right. And then there would be the embarrassing questions. She would be the butt of humor from behind dinner napkins for the whole trip. And Smith would be furious. She was beginning to be apprehensive about his black moods.

Tears rolled down and streaked the carefully applied makeup. She slumped on the bed. After a while she got up and rummaged around in one of Smith's bags and found a flask. By the time he came back on board about midnight and unlocked the cabin door, Libby was sound asleep in an alcoholic daze with all her clothes securely on. In anger, she had upended a whole canister of dusting powder in his bed. He laughed, climbed in on top of it with all his clothes on too, and slept boozily and peacefully. When they woke up the next morning, the liner had left Hong Kong out of sight astern.

That morning they repaired somewhat uncertainly to their deck chairs, stonily silent. Then the first barbs. Then the salvos of anger. Then they went down to their cabin to make love and repair the damage. Libby tried to understand his jealousy; he told her to take it as a compliment. As they made love/peace, seemingly without much pleasure and certainly without much satisfaction, she tried to concentrate on the compliment.

As she told it, for several days the voyage went more smoothly. The rancor of the night-before-sailing incident receded. Then one evening Libby had gone on deck to look for Smith, when he had failed to come down after dinner as promised. When she overtook him pacing the boat deck, she had tried to explain to him how worried she had been. He had been sulky most of the afternoon and had complained on two occasions that she didn't love him. He started in on it again. "No, you don't love me. I can't make you happy."

According to Libby, suddenly he was leaning against the rail with his revolver to his head. She had never seen anyone do that in real life. She was terrified. If she touched him, that might make the damn thing go off. She stood very quietly just a few feet away from him at the rail and began to talk as soothingly as she could. "Smith, please be logical, be reasonable; put that thing away."

"You don't really care whether I kill myself or not, because you can stand there so calmly," he said. The gun was leveled at his ear. All the time, she was thinking: "Be calm with people like this. If you make a sudden move you might startle him." She tried to move a little closer. She wanted to ease the gun away from his head. Gently. Gently.

"Smith, I want you to understand that if you want to kill yourself I want you to kill me, too. I don't want to live without your love."

She claimed then that with one swift motion the gun was at her head. She said she knew later that what she did next could have caused him to shoot, but she said her reaction was instinctive. Her hand flew up, knocked the gun away. And she put both her arms around his neck and buried her head against his shoulder. She expected a shot.

Then it was all over, she said. The gun had vanished into his pocket and the two of them stood sobbing at the rail, arms around each other. Neither mentioned the incident for the rest of the trip, but from then on everything was even more strained. They docked in British Columbia and started east by train the next day.

A couple of stopovers had been scheduled by the Hong Kong travel agent, so they could see something of the West. It had seemed a good idea back in Hong Kong to try to stretch the honeymoon time out as long as possible, but the incident aboard the "Empress" liner had dampened their enthusiasm. Libby now had a feeling that if they could get back to New York as soon as possible, maybe things would settle down a bit. Perhaps they had been thrown on their own too much too soon, after the emotional problems leading up to the divorce and the odd and frequently interrupted courtship. Now there were no show-business commitments waiting to sweep her up at the othe end. And New York was where most of the good things had happened. Maybe they could happen there again.

A stop-off at the luxurious lodge in one of the big national parks was the last side trip on their schedule before they would board the train for Chicago and New York. They had enjoyed what Libby thought was a good day, horseback riding and hiking. After a couple of drinks before dinner on the terrace of their apartment, Smith had gone to lean on the rail of the terrace, with its command of a majestic view — when he suddenly wheeled on Libby, his revolver in his hand again, waving it insanely toward her, toward the lodge, toward the sky. "Damn it! We can't go back. They'll all know you don't love me!" Libby said she was trying to love him very much. It had been a very long day. She was tired. Bothered with cramps. And the hiking in the late afternoon had left her aching already from the unusual demands on her muscles.

"Goddamn it yourself, Smith!" She was on her feet, her cocktail glass knocked to the wide, rough planks of the porch. She advanced the three steps to Smith all in a rush. It was his turn to be startled. She had always tried to reason with him before. She grabbed at the gun in his hand. It was not a very well coordinated grab, but Smith was not ready for it. She snatched the gun away, her hand around the cylinder. She wheeled around, stomped back toward her chair, shifting the gun to her other hand. Then she whirled to face him and shook both fists. Trembling!

"Don't you ever do that to me ever again, you son of a bitch!"

There was a blast from the shaking fist that held the revolver. The gun fell from her hand, sounding almost as loud as the shot.

Then again tears. The clutched bodies. And the dinner ultimately missed . . .

A few days afterward, they were back in New York. At first a relief for Libby. Then complications. They were staying at the Ambassador Hotel on Park Avenue. But after a row with the manager, who thought they were unmarried and living together, Smith had to reveal that they were indeed married. Libby was relieved. And the New York press was delighted. Once it was known, Smith seemed intensely proud of his wife . . . and from that point, according to Libby, he seemed to become intensely possessive.

Smith was six years younger. In his tight society, a woman six years older was probably almost as wise and knowledgeable as a maiden aunt. She was a lover — but also instructor, and adviser.

Smith complained that he often felt "uneducated, unpolished, unfinished." He was. Most of the additional schooling, the tutoring, the special instruction he had received after leaving Woodberry Forest had really been designed to satisfy the antitruancy provisions of North Carolina law, rather than to provide a useful training and polish.

The shortage of formal education had hardly mattered in Smith's daily life before. Smith's glamorous reputation as a flyer had carried him in the less sophisticated North Carolina gatherings. Then there was the acceptance that money gave even the roughest conduct; it could be overlooked. In Libby's New York circles, however, his lack of social grace and ease was magnified by his basic shyness. Shyness had clearly turned out to be a problem in his marriage to Anne Cannon also; a more cautious young man might have thought the shyness could rear again tragically if you picked as a mate a glamorous Broadway star. But Smith had ignored the warning.

New York life soon got as complicated as before. Libby's theatrical agent wanted to angle for a few singing engagements in some of the select New York spots that were considered showcases for her sort of talent, to keep her in the eyes of producers and directors while waiting for the next Broadway opportunity. Her publicist started to funnel out copy about the demand for Libby's presence at champagne suppers, all-night dances, weekend house parties on Long Island, her likes, her dislikes, her bons mots, where she ate, her favorite dishes, what she wore, the witty things she said. In the hands of the publicist, her university record at Cincinnati easily became in the columns a Phi Beta Kappa key and a near-miss at a Rhodes scholarship. The publicist easily linked her romantically with people she had never met. It all enraged Smith.

Cutting out Smith from the pack did not seem quite enough for her, either. She appeared to want to monopolize all the other men, too. Which made the rest of the women at any party predictably jealous. Kay Wilson, another young Southern actress who had come to New York at about the same time, remembered Libby at some of those parties:

> She had a rather unique beauty that was quite apart from what the fashion magazines might say was currently beautiful. Her eyes and her hair, which she tended to wear in strange and wild fashions compared to the rest of us, were most striking. And she seemed to be able to eat and drink all she wanted to without worrying about her figure. We all felt frightfully

sorry for young Smith when she annexed him. She seemed capable of eating him up totally. She was certainly a tough gal. I was often at odds with some of my friends who liked her quite a bit, even though they were terribly jealous of her. I never wanted to see any more of her than I could help. But she was in great demand. And if you wanted to go to the parties, you were sure to run into her.

At one time or another, Libby had succeeded in alienating the wives of several of her producers, directors, and composers by injecting her flirtations into the already supercharged anxiety of shows in preparation. It often seemed as if she wanted everything her eye surveyed, whether or not she could handle it. One contemporary, whose husband became so infatuated with Libby that it later caused their divorce, remembered the singer as becoming "quite fascinated at the time about me being a Southerner, too. She was curious about so many aspects of Southern life — including, it turned out, Southern husbands. Notably mine."

Toward the beginning of June, 1932, Libby found herself in an ideal position to pursue her new curiosity about Southern life. Smith decided they would spend the summer in Winston-Salem. They arrived after a romantic all-night drive through the mountains of Virginia. Perhaps it could be the start of a whole new life.

8

"I Have Written the Book on the Tobacco Business"

WE AMERICANS SEEM to secretly love the majesty of wealth and pay a quiet deference to it. Regardless of our belief that the worth of a man is his essential moral worth and that we really like him for what he is, there is a mesmerizing attraction about the very rich. By the summer of 1932, Libby Holman had spent a good bit of time among the very rich. In turn, Libby had been in the position of someone whom even the very rich often felt in awe of. Her smile across a crowded cocktail party meant a good deal. She met dozens of new people every week . . . so if, three weeks later, she could come up with your name and some shred of personal recollection, that bestowed on you a bit of glitter-by-association. The girl was famous. The fame was important, even to the very rich.

Libby was a handsome woman rather than a classic beauty. Her face was round, pleasing, and almost innocent — in what used to be thought of as a Midwestern sort of way. Her mouth and her hair were perhaps her most memorable features; her mouth was often painted in the exaggerated Betty Boop style that was popular then; her hair — invariably described as "raven" — was usually dressed in a manner extreme enough to catch attention. Sometimes it was slicked tight around her head in a style considered Latin. Sometimes it frizzed out almost to the Afro of today; *that* was supposed to suggest wild abandon. Her voice was one you remembered. When she sang to you . . . or talked to you, you remembered.

Yet even though Libby was clearly no slack-jawed Ohio hayseed, her entrance into Winston-Salem in 1932 and her introduction to the power and presence of one of the wealthiest and most influential families in North Carolina must have been something of a sobering experience.

To go to Reynolda years after the influence of the Reynolds family has been somewhat watered down in that rather grand "company town" is *still* an experience.

Libby came first by car (though the visitor today will probably come by plane, perhaps landing appropriately enough at Smith Reynolds Airport). If you come by car, you will approach the city via one of several scenic highways. Interstate 85 runs east and west and passes near the mammoth R. J. Reynolds tobacco factory. If you come up from the north, you may drive down something labeled on national road maps as North Carolina Highway 67, but it is known through most of Winston-Salem territory as "Reynolda Road." On the way you will pass the entrance to Wake Forest University (moved by Reynolds money to Winston-Salem from Raleigh, 100 miles away) . . . the Reynolda Presbyterian Church . . . Reynolda Gardens . . . the Reynolda Art Center . . . and finally, on the left, a magnificent, stately park that encloses a great estate. A North Carolina historic marker says:

REYNOLDA HOUSE
Built in 1917 by the founder of the Reynolds Tobacco Co. Dedicated 1965
as a center for the advancement of arts and higher education.

You are clearly in Reynolds country. The name can be oppressive by its repeated appearance. In central North Carolina it has long been a symbol of raw power, vast wealth, political force — and sometimes quiet intimidation.

This estate, the seat of the late R. J. Reynolds, was closer to a vast fiefdom than even most people in North Carolina and Winston-Salem realized at the time.

R. J. Reynolds, Sr., was regarded as something of a character in his own family and was the source of countless, often circumspectly told stories outside it. As a boy, R. J. had helped hide the family horses from marauding Union cavalry during the Civil War. But he had been too young for active service until the cause of the Confederacy was obviously lost. By the close of the war, he was already considered mature for his years. Before the 1860s were over he had been sent off by his father on his first tobacco-selling expedition, helping to peddle the family crop.

The stories about R. J.'s early years are so numerous and have been told so many times that it is hard today to determine which ones are true and which ones were simply R. J. lore, aggrandizing his image as a self-made man. But according to one favorite tale, he started off on that first selling trip in his late teens with a wagon full of tobacco into the competitive lowland territory to the east of Winston-Salem . . . and in a week he had collected a lifetime-full of rebuffs from the thorny storekeepers who weren't prepared to do business with "a young squirt." Whereupon, so the story goes, young R. J. took off in the opposite direction into the mountains, where he could be sure the competition was *not* going. In four days he was supposed to have sold his entire consignment of chewing tobacco — for barter. He returned — much to his father's dismay — with a wagon full of peas, corn, hides, tallow, moonshine.

After a strong dressing-down from his father, old Hardin Reynolds, young R. J. was then given the task of selling the whole damn lot of barter goods at auction, just to clear it out of Hardin's tobacco "factory." When the auction brought in about twice as much cash as the retail value of the original tobacco consignment, Hardin was, first, surprised, second, a little chastened, but, third, not so chastened as to let the boy do it again. Nevertheless, R. J. was launched into the tobacco business and his technique of trying "the unusual" more often than not brought him success and a new leg up in a tough competitive business. The power and the money came along surely. Big money. On many occasions later in life when he reminisced about the early days, R. J. would claim: "I have written the book on the tobacco business; the others only have to follow when I'm gone."

Although he continually liked to spread the story that he had grown to wealth from a low start as an "ordinary factory hireling," the truth, as his brother Abram would often take the trouble to point out, was that R. J. had had a good many advantages along the way: some college and a good business education, with financial backing thrown in from the rest of the family. But there was definitely more charisma to the rags-to-riches stories, and R. J. particularly liked to foster the belief among his own poor, illiterate, or semi-illiterate workers that he had come from the humble background and had been illiterate until late in life.

Literature and the liberal arts subjects had always come hard for him; it was discovered later he had an "ocular defect" that enabled him to see in effect only a single letter at a time. As a result of this reading difficulty, he turned into something of a mathematical whiz at school and college when he found that, even seeing them just one at a time, he could handle numbers well. He threw himself with all his energy into his business activity where horse sense and figures seemed to make the difference. R. J.'s physical size, coupled with his later wealth and power, made him an intimidating adversary or valuable ally.

He did not seem to have had the time or the inclination to think of marriage until 1905, when he was fifty-four. At that point, he courted and carried off Katharine Smith, a distant cousin whom he had always enjoyed and often paid passing attention to. Katharine was thirty years his junior, a resourceful independent girl. These were characteristics that R. J. obviously admired, but which made Katharine's father say to R. J. when he asked for her hand: "But why don't you just marry Maxi [another daughter]? She needs a husband and Katharine can take care of herself." R. J. wasn't impressed with the logic. While other suitors sent Katharine candy and flowers, R. J. courted her with regular deliveries of milk. Katharine was not at all disillusioned: "It showed how he cared for me."

R. J. and Katharine had four children in fairly prompt order: Richard Joshua Reynolds, Jr., born in 1906; Mary Katharine Reynolds in 1908, Nancy Susan Reynolds in 1910, and finally a second son, Zachary Smith Reynolds, in 1911.

In 1916, R. J. started the construction of Reynolda House. It was designed by Charles Barton Keen, a Philadelphia architect who was undergoing great popularity among the very rich at the time. And in contrast to the rococo and ostentatious lines of so many millionaires' estates of the period, Reynolda was laid out in rare good taste. R. J. planned it not only as a home for his family and a gathering place for his brothers and sisters and their children, but also as the heart of a thousand-acre model village and farm, with a whole series of outbuildings and houses that would comprise a self-sustaining community of about a hundred people. There were to be stables, a dairy, smokehouse, blacksmith shop, post office, school, church, and homes for most of the estate workers. If the whole reflected a sort of European paternalism more befitting the lord of some English manor, R. J. came by it more naturally than some rich men just playing games. For years he had been more or less the "father" of his raft of brothers and sisters. He had trained several brothers in the tobacco business with an old-fashioned zeal and thoroughness that sometimes bordered on ferocity. But at the same time, he was experimenting with such visionary plans for employees as stock ownership and work incentives, innovations that would not be a part of business in general and the tobacco business in particular for many years to come.

To this ferocious-looking giant of a man, who had ignored marriage and an entrance into family life for so long, the transition to being the father of four lively children seemed apparently no more difficult than some of the dramatic turnabouts of the business that had made him a multimillionaire. A whole series of charming photographs exist of the Reynolds family on outings and picnics, in a harness rig, and in a magnificent open touring car. And Reynolda House today contains a loving "Costume Collection" with the wonderful clothes of Katharine Reynolds and her four children comprising an intriguing record of the life of this wealthy family. The children are a prominent part of the scene. Zachary Smith, being the youngest (he was named for Katharine Smith's father), was often held up proudly for the camera.

Smith was only about seven years old when Reynolda was completed in 1918. Nine months after moving into the house, his father died. In another six years, when Smith was thirteen, his mother died too.

R. J.'s estate was valued at $10,776,000 at the time of his death. And rumors were that the boy's share at twenty-eight should eventually be some $20 million. The money was to be kept in trust for him until then. Until he reached that age, his needs would be taken care of by an increasing allowance. In addition, R. J. had set up a rather visionary work-incentive plan for both his sons, whereby the family trust would match every dollar they made on their own by two dollars from the trust.

The Reynolda House that Libby Holman moved into with Smith

Reynolds in the spring of 1932 looked very much as it does today. A graceful winding drive swings east from Reynolda Road through some handsome stone gates, then north across a rolling approach that could be the fairway to a top-flight golf course. The publicly traveled Reynolda Road, off to the left of the drive and perhaps no more than 50 yards away at most points, is screened from the private drive by a careful arrangement of small shrubs and large trees. At first the house seems hardly there. But then it appears, low, rambling, understatedly rich and comfortable between rows of large trees that mask the substantial wings angling out gently from either side of the main portion of the house. The first view on driving in leaves the visitor with the somewhat disappointing impression that Reynolda is not going to be anywhere as grand as one had been led to believe. But as the drive approaches, it swings dramatically east, carrying the visitor across the sweep of great lawn south of the building with a quick glimpse of a handsome formal garden and fountain, then dips down into a deep grove of trees, to emerge in a graceful curve that lands the visitor at Reynolda's welcoming front door. Everything about Keen's architecture — the placing of the house and the gradual introduction to its grandeur — is artfully done. Perhaps it was because R. J.'s power was so clear in central North Carolina in the early 1900s that there was no need to build some elaborate edifice that said, "Here is the seat of a great and powerful man."

Today, the visitor enters a modest, tasteful entrance hall that would fit in any well-appointed large home in a comfortable suburb. This entrance was cut after Libby Holman's time and has the advantage of allowing the visitor to discover the majesty of the house in impressive stages. Off to the right is a paneled study. But the visitor probably will swing to the left into the handsome library, a commodious but not an overpowering room. And then you walk into the only room in Reynolda that is breathtaking: the living room, which runs the full depth of the house at that point, starting behind a spacious french-doored veranda and stretching back to a magnificent oval terrace in the rear of the house. The room is two stories high, with a broad interior balcony around all four sides at the second story level, looking down into the living room. The twin staircases to the balcony are the only vaguely Hollywood touches, as they rise up above and behind an enormous fireplace. The bedrooms open off the second-floor balcony and off the halls that run east and west from the balcony, like the arms of a flat Y.

At the extreme end of the east wing of the second floor is a wide, pleasant sleeping porch, removed from any noise of the living room but with a view of the small private lake to the north of the house, as well as of the entrance drive and the sweep of lawns that roll south in the direction of Winston-Salem. In that sweltering June of 1932, Libby and Smith settled in at Reynolda, adopting the relative cool of the sleeping porch as the first bedroom they could call their own.

From the outside it looked like a loving marriage — and an extremely glamorous one. "The young couple have been living an outdoor life since arriving," wrote one Winston-Salem society page reporter, "and have gone horseback riding numerous times. . . . They are seldom seen in the city, but when one is seen, the other is nearby on practically all occasions."

Smith seemed constantly attentive. He would hardly let Libby out of his sight.

9

He Was Losing Her

IN SPITE OF Reynolda's comfortable and well-trained staff, Libby's new role as mistress of the house was a rather large responsibility for a twenty-six-year-old woman who had never run anything much more complicated than an efficiency apartment in a New York residential hotel. The house was large. So it tended to be lonely. Libby solved that by promptly filling it up with guests.

The society columns of the *Winston-Salem Journal* recorded the comings and goings of various houseguests in the breathless, isn't-it-wonderful tone of society pages everywhere. Smith and Libby provided some useful casual copy during a social "off season"; most people that the paper was interested in had already headed for Sea Island or Pawleys on the coast — or Roaring Gap in the mountains.

June was not the ideal month to be in Winston. Traditionally there was little breeze. Too far from the coast. Too far from the mountains. When the parboiled thermometer finally got to its daily low, it was usually about five o'clock in the morning — just before the sun started to heat things up again. And nobody of any quality was up then — unless they were coming in from an all-nighter.

In the good parts of town at five o'clock in the morning, you could swing easily from block to block with the only noise being the sound of your tires . . . and the occasional dutiful and not-too-angry bark of a watchdog, grateful for the final cool of his belly-scoop, in the red clay of a backyard, that had been made at the peak of a hotter afternoon before.

The tires passed and the dog stopped barking and burrowed down into the scoop again . . . and upstairs his master rolled over on still-damp sheets for a couple of hours of sound sleep after the sweat of the night had gone. A few all-night lawn sprinklers pinwheeled their way invitingly around parched front lawns.

Out east in Darkie Town, the corrugated tin roofs still held in the rooms below them the last fetid ten degrees of yesterday afternoon's heat as if they were reluctant to part with it. In addition, the worn shutters with which many of the houses were equipped were kept latched tight — regardless of the heat — from dusk until well after sunup. Some of it was just habit, some of it was the idea that night air made you sick — just like sleeping with the moon shining on your face made you crazy. Some of it, if you could have tracked it down, went back to black Gullah ancestors on the Carolina coast — and before them, to Jamaica and Haiti Negroes — who knew the "jumbies" prowled at night. But jumbies could never get in through *closed* shutters. Voodoo stuff in Winston.

Downtown, the last of the night bugs were tempted down to crash into the blinding, enticing public service streetlights before they flicked off about five. Before long, a leisurely sanitation department sprayer with its impressive sprinkle redistributed the clay dust and the crumpled Baby Ruth wrappers. By seven, the early shift was coming in at the R. J. Reynolds factory.

Out at Reynolda, which all the early-shifters helped make gracious, almost nobody would stir for another couple of hours.

June at Reynolda had gone by rapidly in spite of the long, lethargic, hot, and humid days. Had gone by not always without incident — but perhaps the incidents were the results of the young couple's making the adjustments to living together for the first time. Though life at Reynolda House bore very little resemblance to the way most young couples started off their home life, it was the closest thing to reality Smith and Libby had ever had as a married couple.

But the friction was building again. Maybe it was too much company. Smith was proving to be an incredibly jealous man. He followed Libby almost spaniel-like through most of each day, sitting on the grass by the

This January 1930 wedding photo was taken in the imposing living room at Reynolda. Included: (1) sullenly handsome Smith Reynolds; (2) his first wife, Anne Cannon Reynolds; (3) Dwight Deere Wiman, New York socialite theatrical producer whose easy-come dollars would help finance Libby's first hit, *The Little Show,* in the fall of that year. *Wide World Photos*

Producing her best pout, and with her baby fat tightly corset-
ed, Libby posed for an early publicity still. She insisted the
bottom of the picture be cropped; her foot size embarrassed
her. *United Press International Photo*

With *The Little Show* cast of Clifton Webb, Libby Holman, and Fred Allen brought back together in *Three's a Crowd,* the show ran for 271 performances. But Libby had almost backed out during the Philadelphia tryout. *Culver Pictures, Inc.*

Smith Reynolds was glum in Seattle after his steamer trip across the Pacific with Libby. She claimed later he had almost shot her en route. *Wide World Photos*

This blurred snapshot, made in June 1932 at Reynolda, perhaps tells more than any perfect formal portrait. Second from left is Libby, showing off the gracious estate to her smiling sister, mother, and father. Smith glowers, highball in hand. He probably found out on this visit that he had married into a Jewish family. *Wide World Photo*

Shakespearean actress Blanche Yurka didn't quite fit among the big boozers at Reynolda. But prosecutor Higgins considered her perhaps his best witness; she'd been sober. "She could tell you a lot, if she would." *Culver Pictures, Inc.*

Though Reynolda was soon closed off by private security men, this photographer climbed a fence on Reynolda Road, sneaked through shrubs, and photographed a surprised flanneled-and-blazered houseguest — probably Walker — and the daughter of a Reynolds friend. *Wide World Photos*

Coroner Dalton thought he had settled the biggest case of his career — after a lifetime of moonshine shootings and Saturday night cut-and-slash. Then Dick Reynolds demanded exhumation of the body and a midnight autopsy. *United Press International Photo*

This photo was widely circulated after the shooting as showing the sleeping porch where Smith's body was found. However, it appears to be the virtually identical porch of the west wing — the opposite end of the house from the shooting scene, but right above the kitchen driveway and close to Reynolda Road. This was one of the few places where a photographer posing as a delivery man could sneak in for a close-up of the house. *Wide World Photos*

Artful landscaping masks the size of Reynolda House, which gracefully follows the contour of the rolling estate. The sleeping porch occupies the second floor corner in the center of the picture, with the spent bullet emerging from the windows facing the sun.

Cocktails before the barbecue were served on this spacious rear porch looking down on Lake Katherine, named after Smith's mother. Then the guests trooped down the steps for the barbecue site at the south end of the lake. Shortly before he was shot, Smith stood at the edge of the porch looking out into the darkness when he heard the watchman's dog bark and saw a grass-stained and disheveled Libby — followed by Walker — guided in by the watchman's flashlight.

foot of her chair as she sunbathed in the garden, crowding in close beside her on the sofa as they gathered with their guests in the living room
for cocktails or a drink after dinner. Although Smith had not been in
Winston-Salem for any length of time for almost six months by the
time he brought Libby down, it was *Libby* who was the novelty. Almost
for the first time in his life, the handsome young millionaire-to-be was
not the one being fussed over. All the attention — particularly the male
attention — went to Libby.

Sometime in the early part of June, Albert Walker, another Winston-Salem boy and a longtime friend of Smith's, had stopped in on his
way back from "Mouth of Wilson," a popular mountain fishing camp
frequented by Winston people, on the North Carolina–Virginia border
to the northwest. He had heard Smith was back and wanted to welcome
him home. The two were glad to get back together, pounding and
thumping each other in boyish enthusiasm and falling into the almost-
Negro dialect that Southern males often curiously adopt on convivial
male occasions.

Smith proudly introduced Libby to "Ab" Walker. Walker stayed for
dinner, went home that night to his parents' home on Country Club
Road, also in Winston-Salem's fashionable northwest section, to pick
up some clean clothes, promptly returned, and moved into a guest
room on Reynolda's second floor. In that Depression year, Ab Walker
was one of several million young men who didn't have a job. But he
had a friendship with Smith Reynolds. Within three or four days,
Smith had hired him as a secretary, a man Friday, and as an assistant to
help plan Smith's next long-distance flight. Ab Walker could not type
or take dictation, could not fly, knew none of the principles of navigation, could not send or receive radio code. But he was there. And he was
working.

With Smith following Libby and Walker following Smith, the inseparable two became an inseparable three. And in a few days, Ab Walker
was accepted as a familiar member of the household and one who
moved easily and intimately through the family quarters on the second
floor of the house at any time of the night or day.

It was a right convivial second floor. Reynolda was hardly formal.
And if the hallways in the second-floor wings had not run off at slight
angles from the two-story living room, you could have looked from one

end of the second floor to the other, a distance of very nearly the length of a football field.

Ab Walker had occupancy of Smith's "old room," not thirty feet from the sleeping porch the young couple now occupied. In that hot June weather, with the master and the mistress about the age of a couple of college seniors, and with an odd lot of scarcely older houseguests and hangers-on coming and going, the second most stately home in North Carolina easily gave the atmosphere of one big fraternity house-party.

Libby's accustomed morning-to-predinner attire was one of several striking knit bathing suits, occasionally with a skirt wrapped around or a robe thrown over. Having felt it adequate to receive New York backstage visitors in her dressing room practically nude, Libby moved about the upstairs halls of Reynolda House often as little clothed. A young New York dancer who many years later was invited to Libby's Connecticut home remembered that the singer still had the most beautiful breasts she had ever seen. Libby was rarely shy about displaying them. And they would not have gone unnoticed on Reynolda's second floor that summer of 1932.

In the cast of characters at Reynolda, Walker's role at first seemed to have little definition, little substance. He was colorless. His father was a highly successful Winston-Salem land speculator who was considered worth more than a million dollars, though most of that worth was in land not easily negotiable. The Walkers took pride in their comfortable house, a sedate and insulated distance west of the downtown area. Young Ab Walker had been through high school with little more distinction than Smith. He had weathered some college when Smith had not. He showed little promise for the land speculation business. He was no businessman. No salesman. No scholar. No athlete. When he moved into Reynolda, about the only thing he showed promise for was what he finally did: run as messenger.

Yet, both Libby and Smith developed a strange trust in him. Libby said she sometimes worried about Smith's "escapades," but then said later she knew that "if Mr. Walker was along, he wouldn't let Smith do anything rash."

Given Walker's nonexistent secretarial and aviation skills, it was natural perhaps that he would become mostly a conversational companion for the two Reynoldses; there was not much else he could do for his money — except be a pleasant fellow to send into town on errands, or go for the mail, or make telephone calls for party arrangements, or chauffeur guests to and from the railroad station and the airport. And be a hand-holder.

On Sunday, July 3, there had been a row between Smith and Libby. And Smith needed his hand held. Among the guests at Reynolda that Sunday was Blanche Yurka, a distinguished dramatic actress from New York with some notable Shakespearean roles to her credit. She had come to Winston about a week before, to give Libby lessons in dramatic technique. But that may just have been handy camouflage for the reason she really wanted to be there: to attempt to interest Libby in acting in — and backing — a rather heavy European drama that Blanche Yurka felt was just the right vehicle for Libby's intended debut on the "serious stage."

Deciding whether or not to do the Yurka play was going to be something of a problem to Libby. Like many performers who have won great fame in one field, like the comedian who really wants to play Shakespeare, Libby, at twenty-six, secure in her rise to prominence as a musical comedy and revue star, was nagged by the desire to see if she could accomplish more. Though she had been a hit in each of her shows, the critics usually mentioned little more than her unusual voice and delivery. Rarely was anything said about her acting ability. Though this was hardly surprising when you considered the scene-stealers Libby had played opposite, it did annoy her. And some of her less charitable theater friends insisted on calling her voice "an interesting *little* voice" and her performance "a pleasant *small* talent." In the back-biting world of show business, there was always a way to see that those comments got back to Libby. So, with a certain doubt in her mind, Libby was tempted to try to show up her critics. Except for the encouragement of Blanche Yurka, the urging to try a heavy dramatic role was mostly coming from within. Producers and directors were reluctant to risk so much on what might be only "star vanity" — even in that day, when mounting a show was far less of a financial risk than it is today. So while Libby had two or three interesting musical offers pending that summer, there was nothing proposed for the sort of dramatic work she thought she needed to really test her talents.

Blanche Yurka's encouragement appealed to her. Miss Yurka's fondness for the particularly sad Slavic play she had brought to Reynolda may well have gotten in the way of her professional evaluation as a dramatic coach at that point. But she insisted the play was an ideal showpiece for the smashing introduction of Libby as a dramatic actress. Her insistence had already caused a fairly high-decibel argument between Libby and Walter Batchelor, Libby's agent, which would later send the agent stomping out of Reynolda and back to New York. But Blanche Yurka kept right on her course. The script — without any mention of Libby's participation — had been exposed earlier to several producers, none of whom was enthusiastic. Nevertheless, Blanche Yurka reasoned that if a star of the caliber of Libby Holman was interested, then perhaps the play would look more promising at the box office. Blanche Yurka seemed to believe in Libby and the play. It took a lot of faith. One theatrical critic who had seen the play abroad called it "thoroughly depressing."

Libby's role would be that of a prostitute with a heart not exactly of gold. There were only three other major characters: an ex-convict who had become a cabaret entertainer, a wealthy young architect, and the architect's wife. The cabaret entertainer is in love with the prostitute . . . and when the prostitute picks up the architect (who is having domestic problems) and takes him to her apartment, she is surprised there by the cabaret entertainer, who kills the architect in a rage. The prostitute and the cabaret entertainer dispose of the body, placing it in the street, to make it look as if the man had fallen to his death from a building. They leave all the man's money and jewelry untouched. Then they arrange to find the body — whereupon the architect's wife, in gratitude for their kindness, gives them all the money on the body. . . .

So it went. Though the play had been highly successful in eastern Europe — it represented a questionable puller with tired New York businessmen.

Sunday afternoon Blanche Yurka and Libby had been reading the play back and forth, taking all the parts themselves. Walker had tried to listen, but he became both bored and confused. He knew absolutely nothing about acting, the stage, and certainly nothing about Czech drama. Smith was equally bored, clearly feeling sorry for himself, and jealous that Libby was giving so much time to the play and to the handsome blonde drama coach.

The four of them were sitting on the screen porch, sprawled across the collection of comfortable chaise longues there, all languid in the afternoon heat. Blanche Yurka wore a low-backed sun dress, freshly starched by the Reynolda laundresses; she was enjoying the good life, which was a good bit different from the way she lived in New York. Libby was in a tight white knit swimsuit that eschewed the traditional "modesty panel" that dropped down across the crotch in most 1930s swimsuits. Walker and Smith were in tennis clothes, and all were trying to keep cool with tall drinks of iced tea.

At one point in the droning dialogue, Smith moved to the floor at the foot of Libby's chaise, propped his back against it, stretched out his legs along the floor and raised an arm languidly, letting it drop along Libby's bare thigh. Without stopping her reading or glancing at Smith, she brushed his arm aside. Not with annoyance. It was simply a distraction. Smith did not move. But his face tightened, and his body seemed to go rigid. He sat that way for perhaps five minutes. Then he slowly uncoiled from the floor and left the room. No one paid any attention. The reading went on.

"If he comes here again," read Libby from the script, "what shall I do?"

Blanche Yurka provided her line. "You must receive him. And you must look your best . . . your most modest. That is important."

"What do you mean? You mean I am not modest?"

It droned on. Outside, the big Reynolda lawn tractor chugged along sleepily, trimming the grass.

Walker began to doze in the heat.

At supper that night, Smith was in a black mood. Afterward, Smith had called Walker aside and asked him if he would come along with him downtown. Smith had a bottle in his hand. He said he was planning to "get the hell out of Reynolda." They piled into Smith's coupe and took off fast, the way Smith drove everywhere.

No questions were asked when they checked into the Robert E. Lee Hotel. The night clerk knew Smith, saw the two had no other luggage except a small overnight bag that obviously contained whiskey. He knew only that they needed some ice, ginger ale, and sandwiches. Coming right up, sir! There was certainly no question about Smith Reynolds running up a tab at the Robert E. Lee.

They had been given a double room with a "parlor," the kind of quarters usually assigned to traveling salesmen who needed to spread out their lines to show to the local buyers. Salesmen's rooms were clustered on the lower floors of the Robert E. Lee — and were purposely somewhat off to themselves so the "trade" and any attendant noise wouldn't bother the regular guests.

Smith and Ab didn't bother anyone. They just got royally drunk. One knowledgeable local man, who had occasion to check up on such things, said they entertained only one set of visitors in their rooms that evening: two prostitutes who had checked in earlier from Norfolk. The celebration was nevertheless reasonably quiet. Smith and Ab checked out shortly after seven Monday morning when the early-rising salesmen were paying up and getting on the road. They were back at Reynolda before anyone was up. Walker was hung over pretty badly and headed back for bed. The first thing Smith did was to tap lightly on Libby's door. She was still too sleepy to take in an apology. All he could do was crawl in beside her.

Later that day he sat for a long time in the sun at the foot of Libby's lawn chair as Libby and her agent discussed various offers for shows, other than Yurka's play, that might be possibilities for the fall. Smith knew as much as any man his age in the country about airplanes and engines and flying — but all the Broadway stuff seemed to be going by him too fast. Most of it he didn't understand. He did realize one thing, however: Libby's world was a world he could never be at home in, never be part of. He had offered her all of Reynolda, but that wasn't enough. She was already impatient to get back to New York. He was losing her. She didn't seem to want to talk about it with him. She just wanted another party. Just like Anne Cannon and all those people from his first marriage.

10

One for the Road

IT WAS TO BE a small party with just a few close friends attending. Except for Libby and Blanche Yurka, most of those who would be present had grown up with Charlie Hill around Winston. Libby had planned drinks on the rear terrace, which looked to the north and was well shaded from the late afternoon sun by towering trees, then a barbecue down by the artificial lake that curved around the bottom of a pleasant hill about two hundred yards behind Reynolda House.

The party guests started to arrive about 6:30. At Libby's suggestion, Walker had chivvied each one with several telephone calls to make sure all were coming. It was still fiercely hot and sultry. They parked their cars off the sweeping drive and were ushered immediately back to the covered terrace. To reach the barbecue site, a visitor either walked from the rear porch down over the clipped sloping lawn, or took one of several paths through the woods that led east from the house past a tennis court and several small outbuildings artfully hidden in the woods. The party would be well hidden from the house. At the eastern end of the lake, water flowed in from a dam fed by a stream coming out of the woods. There, Reynoldses had built a swimming pool and a small, open summerhouse on top of a formidable stone dressing house and pump house for the pool. Alongside the summerhouse a stretch of ground had been leveled into a terrace and garden. It was a quiet cool spot. Though it didn't get much breeze because of the surrounding woods, the garden had the advantage of being in the shade for all but a few of the peak hours around noon. The shade, the pool, and the lake nearby made it one of the most pleasant spots at Reynolda that hot evening. A barbecue grill had been set up at the edge of the lake, and two black cooks were busy grilling big racks of ribs, cooking sauce, fresh ears of corn, and beans, and heating pans of cornbread.

The cold drinks on the rear porch were welcome relief. A visitor to Reynolda today on a hot July afternoon can sample the inviting cool of that same porch; it seems to shut out most heat and noise, although Reynolda Road, a busy thoroughfare, is only about a hundred yards to the west of the house at that point. Enjoying their drinks there, in addition to young Charles Hill, were Charles Norfleet, another young Winston-Salem bachelor; Mrs. William Vaught, a lively young lady who went by the nickname of "Babe" and who had driven down that morning for the party from the mountain resort at Roaring Gap; Miss Virginia Dunklee, a pretty, bored young Winston debutante, Lewis McGinnes, an aviation friend of Smith's who had just installed some night-flying equipment on his plane; James Shepherd, who came without a date but who intended to be Mrs. Vaught's companion for the evening; and Billy Shaw Howell, a Charlotte radio salesman — and the only real outsider — who had been brought along by Shepherd.

The party would celebrate more than Hill's twenty-first birthday. Libby and Smith had decided to leave Reynolda in the late summer to set up housekeeping in a New York apartment. That night they planned to tell everyone about their first "home," which they had just leased at number 7 Gracie Square, a fashionable building with a fine address, which overlooked the East River, the quiet green of Gracie park, and the house and grounds of Gracie Mansion, the official residence of the mayor of New York. Libby was eager for Smith to enter New York University, where he wanted to take some conventional college courses, in addition to aeronautics and more of the mathematics needed for celestial navigation. To help him prepare for this first formal schooling in years, Raymond Kramer, a young New York University graduate, had been at Reynolda for about two weeks, tutoring Smith. Though being in New York City would allow the Reynoldses to spend more time with each other — particularly if Libby decided to do the play Blanche Yurka wanted her to do, Smith could already see Blanche Yurka's play was going to be a problem . . . and Blanche Yurka, too. So the Charles

Hill birthday party approached on July 5, with the Reynolda household in some disarray — but perhaps not much more so than many other American households on far more important occasions.

The evening seemed successful in the beginning. The barbecue was superb. The woods around the lake had cooled down somewhat, while most of the rest of Winston-Salem sweltered. Around 10:00 P.M., after the meal was finished, the temperature where the party was being held had dropped pleasantly enough to encourage even the heavy before-dinner drinkers to take another stiff one.

In the group at the barbecue, all the old friends knew each other's jokes, escapades, high triumphs, and dismal failures. Libby was an outsider and had come late. With style and reputation. But late. In addition, some of the Winston crowd were waking up to the discovery that their beautiful hostess was a Jew. It shouldn't have troubled her. It had happened before. And after all, she came from a family as "old" as any there. She had won her fame on rock-hard Broadway when all that Winston crowd had been thinking of was senior proms and country club tennis tournaments. She was also the mistress of Reynolda, something quite a few young ladies in Winston-Salem had secretly hoped they might have a chance to be. And maybe that was part of their envy.

That night Libby surely drank too much. Some of it, perhaps, was done in the cause of being the gracious hostess. But most of it was simply because she liked her liquor. She was also drinking because she was uneasy, nervous, a bit frightened. Winston-Salem was a big show too. And there were times since she had been there when she had the distinct feeling she was flopping.

Smith was becoming worried about his guests' noticing his wife's heavy drinking. But at that point, the person most distressed about it was someone Smith wasn't concerned about impressing at all: Plummer Walker, a Reynolda maid who had worked on the place since a month after Smith was born. She had taken care of him when he was little, consoled him when his mother died, seen him through dozens of childhood bruises, cuts, barked knees, bee stings, bloody noses, and upset stomachs in the night. Now she had charge of the east wing upstairs bedrooms, which included the sleeping porch where Libby and Smith slept. She was helping out at the barbecue in place of another servant, who had the Fourth of July weekend off.

Plummer Walker was from the old tradition of Winston-Salem black servants. *She* was the one who had adopted the Reynoldses. She didn't think of it as being hired. It would have taken a substantial amount of money to convince her to work for a family if she didn't care to "adopt" them. And the goings-on at the lake were not what she liked to associate with the Reynoldses — particularly with Smith. She knew he raised a little white-boy hell sometimes, and she had seen him come in full of whiskey sometimes, and she'd had to do some unpleasant cleaning up after him. But she would always defend him to the other servants — only one of whom had been at Reynolda as long as she had; Mr. Smith wasn't raised to be bad . . . wasn't raised to be dirty. That was just growing-up tomfoolery. After all, she had practically raised him herself.

That night she felt sorry for him. He sure wasn't having much fun. Mr. Walker and Mrs. Reynolds were cutting up pretty bad, and Mr. Smith and everybody else couldn't help but see it. So Mr. Smith was just plain glum. Plummer was worried that her young boss didn't seem to take to the party, didn't get into it. He just followed Mrs. Reynolds with his eyes — like he was trying to hypnotize her or something.

And he wasn't eating nothing, much as he loved that barbecue. Plummer had tried to fix him a plate.

"No, Plummer. I haven't got up any appetite yet. But I'll be over directly and get me something to eat." Then he went back to following Mrs. Reynolds with those eyes. Then there was Mrs. Vaught.

She had strutted into Reynolda that evening like Princess Pure Delight, Plummer thought. She acted like she owned the place and the party and everything. She sure made it clear she looked down her nose at Mrs. Reynolds. And the more sassy Mrs. Vaught got with the men, and the more she pitched her little biddy voice up high to get the attention of the men, the more Mrs. Reynolds just had to do it better. And that went for the drinking, too. Plummer had seen some of those white girls around Winston try to throw down the hard liquor like the boys — and somebody usually had to clean up after *them.* But that Mrs. Vaught had been drinking pretty hard since about 6:30 and didn't seem to show a sign of it, except that little high voice got shriller and she was talking nonstop.

And then Mrs. Vaught and Mrs. Reynolds told everyone they were

going to have themselves a drinking contest. Plummer had seen Mrs.
Reynolds do some drinking, and she had an idea Mrs. Vaught was
going to lose. So then the ladies said they were going to have a singing
contest on top of their drinking contest, and Plummer *knew* Mrs.
Vaught was sure going to get beat, because Plummer had heard Mrs.
Reynolds sing, and that lady could *sing.* Sang like a regular colored girl.
Deep. Smooth. Lowdown. Mrs. Reynolds *knew* what she was doing at
singing.

There was a big stump right in the middle of the barbecue setup
where a dead tree had been sawed off about two, three feet up to make
a sort of table. And about that time, Mrs. Reynolds hopped up on it.
Well, she didn't exactly hop up. She tried to climb up, but the pants of
her lounging pajamas were just too tight. A lot of the people had
stopped to see what she was going to do — and as she lifted up one
knee to try to get it on top of the stump, there was a loud ripping, a silence, and then a lot of laughing. One of the men had come over as
Mrs. Reynolds groped around her bottom in funny style like she was
trying to find the rip. And then the man sort of half-lifted her up and
helped her get on the stump. She teetered around up there, and Plummer thought she was going to fall.

"Somebody hand me up my little drinky-jug!" Mrs. Reynolds
reached out both hands to the crowd, snapping her fingers in a come-
on. Like she was some nigger street dancer; Plummer felt ashamed for
Mr. Smith. Crazy lady.

A couple of glasses were handed up with some catcalls, and Mrs.
Reynolds took one in each hand. Then she took a drink from each.
More catcalls and cheers.

" 'Moanin' Low'!" somebody shouted.

" 'Something to Remember You By'!" came another voice.

" 'Body and Soul'!" Mr. Walker shouted.

"Yeah," another man's voice. " 'Body and Soul.' Yours, baby!" Male
laughter and some women giggling.

Mrs. Reynolds made a big pouty face, kind of making her lips flat;
the sort of face that Plummer had seen her making a couple of times
before in the dining room when Plummer had walked in with a dish.
The talk had always stopped at those times — and would only begin
again, low, when Plummer had passed the food and left the room. Then

usually from the kitchen she could hear them all laughing. She always wondered if they were laughing at her.

Up on the stump, Mrs. Reynolds made that pouty face again and then started to sing in that deep man's voice of hers:

> *Ain't got you to care for*
> *'Cause you'll never care for me.*

And then she stopped and look sort of questioningly at the people. Plummer was disgusted; Mrs. Reynolds was imitating colored people. Mrs. Reynolds didn't talk like that and she didn't say "ain't."

"No, no," came several voices. " 'Body and Soul'! 'Body and Soul'!"

Mrs. Reynolds looked at both glasses she held, then took another pull from each. The young people cheered and then quieted down. She began to sing.

It was one of her New York songs, and Plummer had heard her sing it a couple of times before in the living room to the piano as Plummer was clearing away after dinner. Plummer knew that when she wasn't messing around, she was really good.

The people were very quiet when she sang. And when it was over they clapped kind of quietly. They're all pretending that they're a lot more sober than they really are, Plummer thought.

Some more shouts, but softer now. "More! More!"

Now Mrs. Vaught was sidling up to the stump like she was going to sing. Mrs. Reynolds sort of pointed one of the glasses at her and laughed, like she knew she had gotten the best of Mrs. Vaught, and then she started to do a little dance step and looked like she was getting ready to clap and couldn't with the glasses in her hands, and leaned over to put them down on the edge of the stump. That was when she seemed to fall forward, real slow, like one of those slow-motion people in the newsreels, and she said a loud *"Uh-*oh" and she fell right into Mrs. Vaught, who was just starting to try to get up on the stump. And then they both went down in sort of a soggy heap on the ground. But not hard. Just collapsing in that slow-motion way. Everybody laughed. And Plummer was more disgusted — mostly for Mr. Smith, that Mrs. Reynolds would act that way.

She looked at Mr. Smith and he looked disgusted, too. He put down a bottle of beer he had and walked over to Mrs. Reynolds and lifted her up. A little rough. And he moved her away from the stump where everyone was laughing and looking down at Mrs. Vaught, who was still there, lying on her back and laughing. Plummer couldn't tell what he was saying to Mrs. Reynolds, but he sure wasn't satisfied. Mr. Smith liked for things to be straight, in spite of the fact that he liked to do a little hell-raising. Then Mrs. Reynolds kind of shook him off and walked back to where all the people were helping Mrs. Vaught get up.

So Libby drank too much. So did Smith. And Walker. And most of the guests. There was a good bit of good-humored pawing. Hugging. A stroll off into the dark. Laughter. Then a hurried self-conscious move back to the main group. A few stayed away longer.

Smith got more and more moody as he drank. Libby, in contrast, tended to become more and more vivacious. She moved from one twosome to another as a good hostess should, with a pat on the shoulder here, a hand squeezed tight there, a brief kiss on the cheek in another group, an offer to get another drink, a drag on someone's cigarette. When Libby didn't come back to Ab Walker's group often enough, Ab would rise somewhat unsteadily from his seat and follow her for a time. Their shadows occasionally disappeared from the cheery outlines of the barbecue fire. Though most of the other couples were too intent on the music, the drinks, and the laughter to count noses, an occasional glimpse would have shown Libby and Walker drifting back out of the darkness with a smile, a last pat, laughter. Smith noticed.

Sometime shortly before eleven o'clock, the canoes came in off the lake and the party began to break up. There was a slow movement up the hill toward the house. Smith was one of the first to head back. When Libby and Walker finally started up the path, a good bit later, there was laughter behind them from two adventurous couples taking a sobering plunge, giggly nude.

Though several of the guests did not look in great shape for driving, there were the pleasantly intoxicated good-byes at Reynolda's front door, then the sounds of uneven acceleration as the drivers took off down the winding drive with a bit too much gasoline and alcohol. Through the french doors of the living room, where several of the remaining party guests were having one for the road, the headlights of the homeward-bound cars could be seen tracing graceful curves as they snaked toward the front gate. Kramer, Smith's mathematics instructor, who had not been invited to the party, had been in his room most of the evening. But he had gone out for a walk about eleven-fifteen and had met Smith wandering around the grounds. Kramer thought Smith seemed unusually somber considering the partying. Kramer had noticed a strange car approach the house from the north side on the back drive, the road normally used by servants and delivery people. The car had come on hesitantly, backing and trying to turn at one point, as if confused about which way to proceed. Then it had stopped near the house and doused its lights. When Kramer told Smith, thinking Smith might be awaiting a lost, late guest, Smith seemed unusually agitated. He had run inside the house for a large flashlight and headed toward the drive, waving it ahead of him. The car had started up, backed around rapidly, and headed out the way it came, not switching on its lights until it was almost out to the highway. Smith, seeing Kramer on the way back, slurred out a curse and said the intruders worried him. Kramer headed on to bed.

The party had been miserable as far as Smith was concerned. He hadn't wanted to have it in the first place. And Libby had seemed to want to embarrass him in front of his guests. Drinking so much. Slopping all over Walker, arms around the little bastard and all that loud stage laughter. Now she hadn't come up from the lake when the others came. And Walker was just coincidentally nowhere around either. He could fire that little son of a bitch! But Libby was something else. The others were probably talking about Libby behind his back. Having a fine time swapping those rumors from New York about her black blood. Being Jewish explained the mulatto look to him — but finding *that* out hadn't helped either.

Babe Vaught had also made him mad. Egging Libby on with their crazy drinking contest. Was Vaught reacting to all the smart-ass comments going around town about Libby being Jewish? Or was she just being another little Junior League sour-grapes snot? Now Vaught was drunk, too, and pretty soon she would probably throw up all over the living room or something. The last he had seen of her was when Shepherd had hustled her off in his convertible. Maybe she would get sick all over Shepherd's seat covers instead. Serve him right.

Smith flopped on a lounge in the living room. Still no Libby. Babe Vaught came tripping back in from her ride in Shepherd's coupe, looking not much better than Libby had when he had last seen her. She promptly collapsed on one of the living room couches. When Smith grudgingly offered her a bed for the night, she rose unsteadily and made her way upstairs. He started to help her — but damn it, she could find a room for herself.

Out in the back drive behind Reynolda's kitchen, watchman Fulcher's old Hupmobile flivver was parked. He had retrieved a sandwich and a Ball jar full of lemonade that his wife had fixed to help cool him. Then he had gone down into the basement under the kitchen, where it was cooler and where his dog was tied so it would be out of the way of those crazy kids' cars. He had been around Reynolda long enough to be used to the antics of all those rich people.

Fulcher's pattern was to arrive on the premises ready for duty about eleven or so on an average evening. "Ready for duty" meant accompanied by his ravenous crossbreed watchdog at the end of a frayed rope, with a couple of meat sandwiches, a thermos of coffee or a jug of lemonade or new cider — and a reasonable intention of staying awake. In Reynolds Company terminology he was an "outside man," meaning not that he worked outside but that he boasted no long time as a Reynolds employee.

He had just settled down with his sandwich when suddenly his dog sat up, stiffened, and began the low, irritated growl that usually preceded barking. Then he busted loose with the barking. Fulcher wrapped up the sandwich with a sigh, untied the dog, hushing it with a rap on the snout, and started out into the yard. He saw the madam come walking up the road that came toward the kitchen.

The dog started up again. "Shut up!" Fulcher jerked hard on the rope and cussed him; Mrs. Reynolds didn't care much for that dog, he had already found out. She had a mighty curious walk on her as she came out of the dark. Walked just the way he reckoned he walked when he had had a lot to drink.

The dog was still growling kind of mean when she came up to him.

"This dog won't bite you, ma'am," he said. Then the damn thing reared up on his hind feet — he was as tall as the madam was — and started straining at the rope. But now his tail was wagging. She sort of grinned and walked up beside Fulcher and put her arms around the dog. The fool dog was slobbering all over. Jesus!

"You'll get your clothes dirty, ma'am."

She just looked at him sort of dumb and went over and sat down on the running board of the car. She still didn't say anything. Just grinned.

She sat there for a minute, then got up and started on through the yard for the back porch, and she came to a wall, a low wall across the path. She stepped up on the wall kind of shaky and she hesitated. Then she stepped back down and sat on the wall and slumped like she'd give out. Fulcher could see that her white britches were a mess, with grass stains heavy on the knees. Britches usually looked funny on a lady, but he decided they looked pretty good on her, no matter how funny she walked.

"You can't go around here in the dark, ma'am. Don't you want my flashlight?"

She said yes, and Fulcher handed it to her and then walked behind her around to some steps over the wall, showing her the way and telling her which way to shine the light, which was bobbing all over the damn place, just like her.

They got halfway around through the shrubbery and from somewhere out behind them Ab Walker hollered at Fulcher. He sounded back down the road where Mrs. Reynolds had come from.

"Be still, Fulcher! Shut down that dog!"

"I got someone here," Fulcher answered him. "The madam."

Walker hollered out, "Where you at?"

And Fulcher said, "I'm here!" And Walker came puffing in out of the dark, in his bathing suit. Looking drunk and dumb-eyed.

And then they saw ol' Smith.

Smith was up on the circular porch. "That you, Fulcher? Where the hell are you going?"

'I'm coming on around to the porch."

"What's the matter with your dog?"

"He just barked at the madam when she came up in the yard a minute ago."

By the time they reached the lawn off the circular porch, Walker was standing in the circle of light that the madam played first on them and then all over.

Smith came down off the porch steps. Didn't stand there a minute. Never said a word. The madam kind of looked up at him and smiled, and he took her up by her left arm sort of sharp and marched her back up on the porch.

When Fulcher felt he had seen them all safely back inside the house, he went back to sit on the running board of his car and try to finish his sandwich. He wanted to be handy in case Smith called. The boy had sure looked mad. He'd be feisty tonight about the place. He seemed to think someone was going to come in and tote it off.

By 12:30, though the downstairs was lit up, most of the lights in the house had gone out upstairs. The partying looked over, and Fulcher felt it was safe to settle down to the routine for the night. At maybe quarter of one he was back in the basement room under the kitchen when he heard what might have been a shot. Damnfool kids!

Leaving his dog tied, he came out to the edge of the yard, listened — then went around toward the end of the house nearest the lake where the living room and all was. He stood in the hot, still air, but didn't hear a thing, except somewhere in the house one of those English clocks struck the quarter hour with its little singsong. Hell, if he could hear that, he figured, he could hear if anyone was making trouble. Plenty of times he had stood back there in the basement yard, which was almost at the tip of the west wing and had clearly heard them singing and laughing up there in the east wing.

Maybe it just wasn't nothing much. It had sounded kind of small anyway. Maybe he shouldn't pay no more attention to it. The boys would often stand in the door with their guns and shoot around. Maybe it was something like that. Wouldn't pay no more attention to it. He'd had enough nursing for one night.

They had all been drinking too much. And ol' Smith was looking mighty strange. It was hard to get into that boy's mind. Then that damn fool Walker, who had just moved onto the place, was busy throwing his

weight around, shouting out orders: "Be still, Fulcher!" "Shut down
that dog, Fulcher!" Maybe that's what you had to expect from rich kids.
Anyway, he wasn't going to pay any attention to Walker. He checked
his watch again — then started off down toward the lake on his one
o'clock rounds.

11

"He Shot Himself, for Chrissakes!"

ACTRESS BLANCHE YURKA had been enjoying herself immensely at Reynolda — until that evening. But early in the party, when they were still having their second round of cocktails on the big rear porch, she sensed from the escalating bonhomie of the Winston crowd that she was soon going to feel somewhat out of place.

The actress was a striking blonde — a bit physically overpowering to some small men, and possessed of the same husky, disarming ebullience that Zsa Zsa Gabor has since made famous. It rankled Blanche Yurka that she would already have had two or three men dancing attendance on her at such a party in New York — even though she was then forty-five. The Southern boys seemed to look right past her. Not rudely. A nice enough smile on introduction — but then they moved right on. Anyway, they were all terribly young and unsophisticated. And with a few drinks in them they were all beginning to talk like the local black people, for goodness sakes.

When the guests gathered up their third round of drinks and headed for the lake, Blanche Yurka had caught Elizabeth's elbow and said she had a headache; she would only go down to the barbecue for a little while. She had thought Elizabeth would pout and beg her to stay. But there was only a smile, a pat, a peck on Blanche Yurka's cheek, and a "Sorry, darling." Then Elizabeth was gone, hurrying off to the lake to catch up with the others. The heat seemed to settle down closer. Blanche Yurka began to feel she really was going to have a headache.

She watched them all disappear, a little sorry now that she was taking herself out of the party, then headed upstairs to her room in the west wing. She took a long cool shower, dressed in the most informal outfit she had brought along, then went briefly to the lake.

It was hard for her not to feel out of place with all these young people. She did her duty as a guest, talked animatedly, canoed briefly, then returned at the first chance to the house. She read a bit, before dropping off to sleep in the late-falling summer dusk, with the radio for company, tuned to some dance music from a hotel in an American city she had never heard of.

She was wakened by voices from downstairs, two men talking in a rather animated way. It sounded as if they were in the kitchen or the pantry, under her bedroom. It was dark and she could not see the time. Perhaps the remains of the party had moved to the kitchen for a late snack. She listened for a minute and wondered if it were Smith; maybe Elizabeth was there too. Then the voices subsided. But if Elizabeth were still up and some of the boring local people were gone, it might be fun to join them. Elizabeth still owed her a little party, she felt. She got up and slipped on a dressy black robe that she thought was particularly flattering to her — one Elizabeth liked quite a bit — then she headed down the stairs, at the end of the west wing, that led to the kitchen.

Opening the door to the kitchen, she found lights on but no one there. She went out through the pantry and dining room, both brightly lit, into the living room. And there she saw Albert Walker in his bathing suit.

"Isn't anybody around?"

"No," he said. "They've all gone. I'm just locking up."

His voice was slurred and he looked bleary. A very unattractive young man even when he hadn't been drinking, the actress thought. He certainly dogged Elizabeth's steps these days, too. Blanche Yurka felt cheated that there was no after-party. She walked back upstairs to her room. Walker was still moving aimlessly in the living room when she got to the top of the stairs and glanced back down at him.

Her room seemed a good bit hotter than downstairs. The outside was quiet in the heat, as if nothing moved for fear of making it hotter. The only sounds were the almost inaudible swish of the big lawn sprinklers ratcheting back and forth out front. She pummeled her pillows, angry that she had missed Elizabeth when she had been looking forward to a nightcap and a little good after-party gossip. She realized that the radio station she had been listening to had signed off, and she reached out and twirled the dial for something else. There was only growing-then-fading faraway music. And static. Elizabeth had told her that late-night static meant thunderstorms coming. She certainly hoped there would be one to do something about the heat. . . .

She realized she had been asleep again, though she did not know how long, when she became conscious of a hysterical voice, a woman's. She got up quickly, went to the window, and listened for a moment.

The voice trailed off, swallowed up almost as if it belonged to a person being pulled beneath the water. It seemed to come from the other end of the house, but she could not tell if it had come from outside or in. She pulled on her robe again and hurried down the second floor hall toward the balcony that surrounded the living room. When she got there and looked down, there was Walker again. She wondered if only a few minutes had gone by; he stood much as he had before. Still in his silly bathing suit. She noticed for the first time that he had quite spindly legs.

"I heard a voice," the actress said. "Someone crying. Hysterical. That's how it sounded."

Walker looked at her for a long moment. She was about to repeat what she had told him, thinking he had not understood, when he ran up the stairs.

"I'll go see what's the matter."

She didn't have a chance to tell him where she thought the voice had come from. He was on the second floor then, heading at a run down the hallway opposite the one Blanche Yurka had come down — heading toward the end room that Elizabeth and Smith occupied. Was that where it had come from? Had Walker heard it, too? Blanche Yurka remained standing at the balcony.

A wail, stretched high and long, came down the far hallway. The next thing she saw was Walker and Elizabeth dragging a body of a man out of the darkness at the end of the hallway.

And then she could see that it was Smith!

Walker had his arms under Smith's shoulders. And poor Elizabeth was struggling with his feet. Poor, slight Elizabeth! She was sobbing so much she hardly seemed able to help, and Smith's rump was bumping along the floor. Blanche Yurka rushed forward, pulled Elizabeth away. "You poor dear!" Then she took Smith's feet.

"My God, Albert! What happened?"

"He shot himself, for chrissakes!"

Walker was backing toward the stairs, pulling Smith after him in a series of jerks.

Elizabeth wailed again.

It was a wonder they didn't all tumble down together, the actress thought, as Walker backed off the top riser; suddenly all the weight went to him, as Smith's body was tilted down with the steps. Walker stumbled backward. Elizabeth shrieked. And as Walker tried to lift Smith's head and shoulders so the body would be more on a level, Blanche Yurka found she was staring straight into Smith's face. His eyes were open, looking up at the ceiling so they mostly showed white. His mouth was slack, with a brownish ribbon of spit running down his chin. High on his right temple, just where his hair began, she thought she could see the bullet hole. She was surprised how neat and round it was. Almost like a beauty mark — but a deep maroon. No blood came from it. Strange. So that was what a bullet hole looked like.

Elizabeth, clumsy in a flowing negligee, pushed past Blanche Yurka to help Walker with Smith's head — and almost toppled them all again. When they finally laid him down on the living room floor, they were all panting. Walker glistened with sweat, and the actress realized she must, too. Smith was surprisingly heavy, though he was not that big a man. "We need some of the men." Blanche Yurka suddenly felt drained.

"Nobody here, damn it. All gone."

"I don't think just the three of us can get him into a car."

"We sure as hell better. Come on, lift! You're a big broad."

Blanche Yurka flared. She felt like slapping the little prig! Poor Elizabeth had collapsed to a sitting position on the floor. Smith's head was in her lap. She was trying to brush back his hair, pawing at his forehead between sobs, staring at the wound in his temple. She moved the other hand under his head to shift it slightly, and when she lifted that hand away it was covered with blood. She looked at it dumbly for a moment, as if it belonged to someone else.

"Oh, Jesus, he's cold! He's dying! How could this happen to me!"

Elizabeth struggled to her feet. Smith's head dropped roughly to the floor. Her negligee was crimson with smears. Walker knelt down and got another hold under Smith's arms.

"Come on, goddammit, all of you. We got to get him there!"

Somehow they lifted Smith up again and carried and dragged him out the front door, to where his sedan was parked under the canopy leading to the front door. Walker backed himself in through the rear door, pulling Smith in by his arms. The other two lifted his legs and pushed. It was awkward. Walker cursed them both for what they were doing — or weren't doing. A deep gurgle came from Smith's throat, and he coughed — a liquid, drowning cough. Walker dropped Smith's arms, and the women, startled, let his legs fall.

"Oh, my God, he's going to puke!" Walker groaned. "For chrissakes, Smith, don't puke!"

And then they had him in the car. Walker pushed Blanche Yurka into the back with Smith. "Now hold him and keep him from falling on the fucking floor!"

"But where do I sit?" Smith was crammed all across the back seat.

"Jesus! How do I know! Sit on the goddamn floor. The guy's dying!"

She squeezed into one end of the back seat and got his head on her lap. She would probably be as bloody as Elizabeth when they got there.

Blanche Yurka did not see much of the ride to the hospital. Some of the time she had her eyes closed. Walker drove terribly fast. Elizabeth cowered in the corner of the front seat, clutching at the handhold on the dashboard and begging Walker to slow down each time they screeched around a turn. At one point, they heard a siren up ahead, and Blanche Yurka almost hoped it was a police car that would arrest them all. Anything to stop them before they were all killed. But the siren screamed by them going in the opposite direction and faded into the night from where they had come.

Her eyes were shut tight and her fingers were clenched deep into the flesh of Smith's shoulders when they finally pulled up at the front entrance of the hospital.

12

"They Had Been Spending a Quiet Evening at Home"

LOCAL Winston-Salem newspaper readers got little clue on Wednesday morning to the drunken party that had been going on at Reynolda. Or the circumstances leading to the shooting. Or the wild postmidnight ride to the hospital. The story had developed pretty late for a morning paper that was essentially made up by ten the night before, and could take little change — short of the assassination of a President — past midnight. So the first shooting story was little more than a bulletin, something gleaned from one of Walker's wild calls from the hospital. Walker was quoted by reporters only as saying that he had been closing up the house for the night when a shot was heard.

WINSTON-SALEM JOURNAL

WINSTON-SALEM, N. C., WEDNESDAY MORNING, JULY 6, 1932

Smith Reynolds Shot In Head;

Condition Serious

The out-of-town Wednesday afternoon papers were somewhat clearer about what had happened. And by the end of the day on Wednesday, when East Coast editors had had a chance to think about both the social and circulation aspects of the case, more than two dozen top reporters were on their way to Winston-Salem from various Eastern cities to dig in.

Smith Reynolds had been pronounced dead at 5:25 A.M. Before the day was out, Dr. W. N. Dalton, Forsyth County coroner, announced that the death was suicide. It was the sort of pronouncement that would certainly disturb a prominent family. Why would the young, expectant son of a distinguished family, soon to come into a vast fortune, married to a glamorous Broadway star, commit suicide?

"They had been spending a quiet evening at home," the staid authoritative *Winston-Salem Journal* reported to its readers when it ran an "extra" on Smith's death. There was no mention of the birthday party, the numerous guests who had eaten and drunk with Smith and who might have been witnesses to the moroseness of a suicide on his last evening alive. In fairness to the *Journal* staff, there had been little time to dig into anything.

That public relations genius of the thirties, Ivy Lee, would have been useful to the Reynoldses at that point. He would have moved to lay the drinking party flat out on the table for starters. Then it couldn't pop up as a surprise later. As it was, when details of the drinking came out — as mild as they were in relation to what was going on in any number of other homes in North Carolina that same night — they suggested an orgy.

The reporting by the *Winston-Salem Journal* for the first two days after the shooting was perfunctory and hardly investigative. It failed to underscore some rather flagrant omissions in the statements of officials investigating the case that must have been the heart of many a heated city room discussion elsewhere in the country.

On Friday, July 8, roughly forty-eight hours after the death of Smith Reynolds, a lead editorial appeared in the *Journal* that seemed to chart a safe position:

> The coroner regards the tragedy as a suicide, and the almost absolute lack of evidence pointing in any other direction suggests that any further investigation that may be made will not alter the verdict of that official.

The editorial then paid tribute to Smith, which he deserved in many ways. But at the same time, the paper may have been doing him the greatest disservice by not pressing harder to find out just how he died.

In that same Friday paper, the reporters assigned to the case (and the editor in charge) should have wondered why, almost forty-eight hours after the death of one of Winston-Salem's most prominent young citizens, the sheriff of Forsyth County still had been permitted to interview only one of the three people who had discovered Smith wounded — and why, in that time, several major witnesses were still being shielded from questioning by one excuse or another.

The paper first reported that Libby and Smith had been found together on the sleeping porch — though it was already quietly rumored they had been occupying separate rooms in the last few weeks. The porch was diagramed, described. The arrangement of the furniture. The position and extent of the bloodstains on the porch. Stories mentioned a bloody towel found stuffed behind one of the french doors of the sleeping porch and a .32 caliber "Italian automatic" found on the floor near the head of the bed.

THE RALEIGH TIMES

| TEN PAGES | RALEIGH, N. C., THURSDAY, JULY 7, 1932 | MARKET EDITION |

Couple Lying On Bed When Shot Was Fired

Sheriff Transou Scott surely knew how things worked in the Reynoldses' "company town." Though he may not have been the most technically qualified man in Winston-Salem to pursue the investigation, he seemed to be the only one willing to, at that point. Ignored and angry, his self-respect hurt, Scott stiffened. With a good many influential people seeming ready to gloss over anything unpleasant or conflicting or confusing just to get the case out of the papers, Scott began doggedly to worry each confusing, conflicting statement in turn.

He was already discounting any help from Mrs. Reynolds. Her doctor, William Johnson, continued to assure Scott that she was under heavy sedation, "prostrate with grief," and could not be questioned. Yet two initial statements from her had been passed out to the sheriff.

And already they conflicted. She announced first that she had been in the bedroom adjacent to the sleeping porch when she heard a shot from the porch and ran there crying that "Smith had shot himself." Later she passed out a second statement that she had actually been on the sleeping porch with him at the time he was shot. The difference was vast. In one instance she had simply heard a shooting. In the other, she could have been a witness to it. What did she think he was? A dumb country moonshine cop?

There were also conflicting statements from Albert Walker. First, he told the papers that he had found Reynolds stretched out on top of Libby when he entered the room. Then he had changed around, too, telling Scott he first saw Mrs. Reynolds not on the sleeping porch, but running hysterically down the second floor hallway, coming from the direction of the porch. Walker, by his own admission, was one of the nearest principals to the shooting. And since he said he had been one of the first on the scene, he was going to be relied on for some vital testimony. And it was already contradictory.

The Reynolds clan was gathering. James. S. Dunn, an uncle, one of the first senior members on the scene, told the press he could not figure out why Smith might have committed suicide, since he was in high spirits with many plans for the future. Mrs. Charles Babcock, one of Smith's sisters, was flying in from New York with her husband. She would arrive late that evening. Mrs. Henry Walker Bagley, a second sister, was also on the way. R. J., Jr., Smith's older brother, could not be reached immediately. He was somewhere off the southern coast of Africa on his freighter-yacht, making a pleasant two dollars from the estate for every one he earned, under the terms of the old R. J.'s will.

There was, of course, a good bit of speculation about what would happen to all the money that was rumored to be coming Smith's way. And even though Libby was mentioned only in the most conventional legal sense as "the widow of the dead man," the unspoken implications of Libby's windfall were already there between the lines. It did not matter that Libby Holman was, by all common standards, comfortably well off, in the first flight of a career that could keep her living well for at least a dozen years. The money concerned now was *millions.* Plus she was an actress; that implied a fortune hunter. Plus a few insiders knew she was a Jew; that implied, in the South, a certain canniness.

Libby's friends and family also started to gather to offer what support they could. Mr. and Mrs. Alfred Holman told reporters in a brief and tearful interview as they were leaving Cincinnati that they were totally mystified at events in Winston-Salem; they had visited Smith and Libby only a month before and found them fine, with Libby saying that for almost the first time in her life she was "supremely happy."

So with Smith's two sisters flying in with their husbands, with R. J., Jr., more or less unlocatable, with the Holmans of Cincinnati moving sedately toward Winston-Salem in a Norfolk and Western Pullman car, and with almost everybody else at Reynolda incommunicado, there wasn't much else for reporters to do at that point except speculate.

By the end of the day on Friday, the town was blanketed by reporters, headed by top crime writers from a dozen Eastern papers and the wire services. Fulton Lewis, Jr., who came into Winston by private railway car from the then-powerful Universal Services was the headliner.

A postmortem examination that was reported to have been performed didn't seem particularly helpful. It apparently failed to determine whether the bullet had been fired from a distance, or at close range, or whether the gun had actually been in contact with Reynolds's head.

Sheriff Scott, however, was responsible for the story that was getting the most talk of all. Angered at how all the society types at Reynolda were blocking his investigation, he let slip word of the three searches of the sleeping porch during the night — before the gun was finally found on the fourth search, in plain sight. Where the gun had hid in the early hours of Wednesday morning, who might have taken it, how it might have been tampered with, and who placed it back in the room were all questions that were getting a lot of street-corner speculation.

Strangely enough, the Reynolds family then began to make some moves that indicated they were somewhat less than enthusiastic about the prospect of the sort of thorough investigation sheriff Scott seemed to be going for: R. E. Lasater, the company man who had been at Reynolda the night of the shooting and who was one of Smith's guardians, agreed to talk to reporters. It could be assumed that Lasater's statement was more or less an official one: Lasater said there was no evidence to indicate that Smith Reynolds was the type of person to commit suicide.

WINSTON-SALEM JOURNAL

❖ ❖

WINSTON-SALEM, N. C., FRIDAY MORNING, JULY 8, 1932

Thinks All Evidence In Case Points To Suicide

W. N. Reynolds Reaches Winston-Salem From Cleveland

Unable to Offer Opinion Just Now

Has Not Talked to Widow; Sisters Believe Smith Killed Self

Nevertheless, he thought he could state now that the family was satisfied that all evidence pointed to suicide. He assumed that would be the end of it. Reporters questioning Lasater could get little more; in Winston-Salem you didn't press too hard when a high official of the R. J. Reynolds Company said the interview was over. And even the brash out-of-towners were somewhat overawed by the mystique and power of the Reynoldses' reputation. So when the local men began to make "thank-you-Mr.-Lasater" noises, the hard-nosed reporters from the *New York Daily News* and the *Chicago Tribune* found themselves folding their yellow copy paper and backing toward the door, too.

At Reynolda, the gawkers and the curious clustered about the heavily guarded gate of the estate and saw a few visitors enter. Dr. Johnson, Libby's physician, came and went without speaking to reporters. The rumor was that Libby was still under sedation, being attended by her actress friend Blanche Yurka and almost no one else. The Holmans of Cincinnati, along with Mrs. Myron Kahn, Libby's sister, arrived and were hustled through. The crashers were turned away by armed Pinkertons.

Smith's funeral was scheduled for Friday, with burial in Salem Cemetery. Nobody outside a few members of the family and certain handpicked county officials had been told, but a coroner's inquest had already been scheduled to take place at Reynolda on Friday afternoon, immediately after the funeral. Because of its private-property setting and the surreptitious manner in which the inquest was called, what it came down to was the coroner apparently assembling a closed hearing to investigate what was possibly a capital crime. That was clearly against the law in North Carolina.

13

"Under the Influence of Alcohol to a Rather Marked Degree"

THE FUNERAL ON Friday afternoon was a family affair in the main house at Reynolda. Any attempt to hold it outside the estate grounds would have quickly turned into a press circus.

Libby attended, heavily veiled, leaning on her father's arm for support. Often her shoulders could be seen shaking softly. Several times she seemed near fainting. But she went through it all. Walker was a pale and shaky pallbearer. The eulogy was the story of Smith's talented aviation career, snuffed out in its prime. The substance of what the minister was saying had been written also by the *Winston-Salem Journal* in its lead editorial that day. The paper lauded Smith as

> intelligent, animated by abounding energy, a descendant of stock remarkable for business achievement, certainly there must have been a great future ahead of him which he screened forever.... It is not too much to fancy that many a time he may have longed for a simpler place in life....

Elsewhere in the paper, the *Journal* implied it would look favorably on a verdict of suicide. But a few of those closer to the situation showed the first cautious doubts. Coroner Dalton told of finding fragments of a bullet on the sleeping porch and was trying to trace its trajectory. He ended his statement to reporters by leaving an intriguing crack open in the investigative door: even though he acknowledged that the death "was thought to be suicide," he reminded the newspapermen that an inquest could still be held at the request of the sheriff or any member of the family. He implied that an inquest was uncertain — yet he already intended to hold it within a few hours. In secret.

The sheriff was guarded in making any new statement. But he could not understand why the Reynolds family would not be eager to push hard for a solution of just what had happened. Scott didn't appreciate the secrecy of the upcoming inquest, and he resented the fact that it was being held inside Reynolda.

WINSTON-SALEM JOURNAL

❖ ❖

WINSTON-SALEM, N. C., SATURDAY MORNING, JULY 9, 1932

Secret Inquest Here

Officers Hold Albert Walker For Testimony

Friend of Reynolds Taken Into Custody Upon Orders of Coroner; Mrs. Libby Holman Reynolds Says Mind Was Blank From Monday Until Wednesday Night; Recalls Flash In Which She Heard Reynolds Call, Saw Him With Gun and Saw Him Fall; Newsmen Barred From Inquest

Albert Walker, of Winston-Salem, a friend of the late Smith Reynolds, 20, who was fatally shot at his home in Reynolda early Wednesday morning, was being detained by officers last night as a material witness to circumstances surrounding Reynolds' death.

The arrest of Walker was one of two developments in the case yesterday. At a secret inquest called by Dr. W. N. Dalton, Forsyth county coroner, Mrs. Libby Holman Reynolds testified that her mind was a blank from Monday night until Wednesday night with the exception of a brief interval in which she recalled having seen her husband with a gun in his hand, having heard him call her and having seen him fall.

Sheriff Transou Scott said last night that orders to hold Walker were issued by Coroner Dalton. When talked with by newspapermen, the coroner referred them to Solicitor Higgins, who with Assistant Solicitor J. Erle McMichael assisted in the inquest.

Assistant Solicitor McMichael said the move was made merely to prevent intermingling of witnesses prior to completion of the coroner's inquest which was begun yesterday afternoon and recessed until this morning.

Walker was placed in the county jail shortly after being taken into custody. Later in the evening, however, arrangements were made for him to spend the night at a local hotel and he was transferred there by Deputies Sheriff H. A. Morris and A. C. Bavender. The arrangements were made

But at least a formal interrogation — even a secret one — would get a few questions answered, would get something on the record.

The coroner's inquest came to order in the book-lined library about thirty minutes after the burial. A six-man coroner's jury had been assembled that morning and had "viewed the body," though the wound was well hidden by a skillful mortician. Then they adjourned until 4 P.M. The coroner's jury was composed of one J. P. Simmons, Avery Transou, W. T. Alspaugh, William Pfohl, E. C. Goodman, and J. Wilbur Crews, all white Anglo-Saxon males — and universally a bit long in the tooth. Court stenographer Hardin Jewett transcribed the record. The questioning was started by the assistant district attorney for Forsyth County, Earl T. McMichael.

Because of the surroundings of the Reynolda library and the deference the coroner's jurymen, the sheriff, and the assistant district attorney obviously held toward these rich, powerful people, the inquest started with the air of a rather stilted game of charades: "guess what I'm after — I can't say." The coroner's jurymen were singularly uneasy, often losing the train of the questioning as they tried to stare unobtrusively about them at the handsome room with its fine early American landscapes and its walls of superb books in finely tooled leather bindings. A few days later the *Journal* tried to re-create the scene when it finally heard about the inquest: "The coroner's jury began its deliberations in an atmosphere of drama more gripping than that of the stage the Broadway singer forsook to marry the wealthy youth who was found mortally wounded in his luxurious mansion here last Wednesday." Perhaps fair appraisal.

The house was elegantly quiet. Occasionally a servant passed through one of the other rooms, or some member of the family came through the front door and moved assuredly up to the second floor. The guest rooms were all filled with the family members who had come back for the funeral. Off to the west, an occasional car could be heard traveling down Reynolda Road. But for the most part, the loudest noise was the quiet patter of a sprinkler rotating on the lawn outside . . . and the rattle of the estate's big lawn mower far down at the end of the front lawn.

To be heard first was Dr. Hanes, who would testify to the efforts to save Smith's life.

Hanes was an impressive man with an impressive background. None of the coroner's jurymen knew him personally, but they all knew he was a powerful and influential man around Winston-Salem, in addition to his status in the medical community. Hanes described the situation when he first arrived at the hospital. He told of the complex procedures that had been used in the operating room, and he said that in his opinion there was little the doctors could have done that they had not done. Because the questions asked him and the answers he gave had a critical importance and were not made public at the time, those points of his testimony that appear here are verbatim, just as it was taken down that hot July afternoon. The questioner, McMichael, may have been unconsciously searching for a verdict of suicide at first.

McMichael: Just tell His Honor what you did and what you found.

Dr. Hanes: I think it must have been about one o'clock that my phone rang and I was told from the Baptist Hospital that a Mr. Reynolds had shot himself. Or Mr. Reynolds was shot. Or at any rate was injured, and at the hospital, and to come at once. So I did. And when I arrived at the hospital I went to the operating room and on the operating table was Smith Reynolds. He was dressed in a blue shirt, a blue sport shirt, as they are called, a soft-collar shirt. I don't know whether he had his trousers on or not, because he was covered with a sheet. The sheet was very bloody, of course, and he was unconscious. On the right temple there was a contusion, a swelling as large as a small orange, with a puncture wound of the skin in the middle of the swelling. Just back of the left ear, then, was another wound, just a puncture wound of the skull and scalp. We examined very carefully at the time with a very good light, Dr. Valk, Dr. Johnson and I, seeing if we could determine which was the point of entrance and which the point of exit of the bullet. We found around the wound on the right temple slight evidences which we attributed to be powder burns, not marked, very slight, just on the edge of the wound, a blackening of the edge of the wound which it seemed possible to us at the time were powder burns. The wound at the point of exit showed nothing, merely a puncture wound of the skin; the hair was not seared or scorched, but just covered with blood.

McMichael: On the right side was the hair scorched?

Dr. Hanes: The wound was not within the hairline; the hair was very scanty over the raised place and must have been cut pretty short, because there was very little hair around the wound. We could not determine that the hair was scorched or burned anywhere around the wound at all, but the hair was very scanty; it wasn't clotted or matted, anything of that kind.

McMichael: Can you give the jury an idea of the angle from the point of penetration to the point of exit, followed in the brain?

Dr. Hanes: Yes. If one would place their hands here, just above the right temple at the hairline, and the other finger at a distance of about two inches back of the left ear, one would have about the way the bullet penetrated. . . .

McMichael: The part of the brain that would have been penetrated by the bullet in the course that it took, would that affect the muscular action of Reynolds?

Dr. Hanes: Well, without having actually examined the brain it would be difficult to say because the damage of a bullet passing through the brain is largely due to injury to blood vessels; the hemorrhage that follows is the thing that does the damage, not so much the penetration of the bullet itself. Generally, though, one can say that the bullet in its course passed below the motor area of the brain, but it possibly would have gotten into the lower motor area in its passageway.

Though the coroner's jurymen had all sat on cases involving violent death before, the calm, textbook description of the wound seemed to draw a terrifying picture by its very matter-of-factness and its relentless detail. Several jurors stirred squeamishly in the hot room.

Dr. Hanes was pressed for his opinion on the proximity of the pistol to the wound — a point that would become a major, and disputed, issue later. Dr. Hanes, at first, seemed quite sure of himself.

Dr. Hanes: I should think it would be reasonable to conclude from the fact that the skin was so slightly powder-burned that the muzzle of the pistol must have been resting almost, if not quite, on the skin itself, or close to it. The greater the separation from the skin, the greater the powder burn.

McMichael: Up to three feet, I understand.

Dr. Hanes: Yes, until you get away to where the powder does not burn at all.

Then Dr. Hanes *volunteered* some information that had damaging potential.

Dr. Hanes: I think it might be well to state the condition that night of Mrs. Reynolds and of Albert Walker.

McMichael: Did you examine him over at the hospital or after you got back home?

Dr. Hanes: Well, we were all there together. Understand this was a matter of some five or six hours there at the hospital altogether. It was my opinion, and is still my opinion, that Mrs. Reynolds was under the influence of alcohol to a rather marked degree.

McMichael: How about Mr. Walker?

Dr. Hanes: I think he was, too, in the same condition.

McMICHAEL: Did you notice any odor or any indication from the examination of Mr. Reynolds that he had been drinking?

DR. HANES: He had. Both Dr. Johnson and I confirmed that.

McMICHAEL: Doctor, the jury wants to know if the gun was placed directly or in close proximity, as you have testified, to the right temple, in firing position, whether or not the bullet would have ranged down or would have ranged straight across.

DR. HANES: Well, now, of course — I am just giving you an opinion, such as you would have yourself. It would depend entirely on the angle at which the gun was held. A difference of only a slight degree in the angle would make quite a difference in the trajectory of the bullet. I saw no reason to suppose that the gun, held against the temple, would not have followed the trajectory that we found . . . it could have followed that trajectory.

Albert Walker, whom McMichael called next, looked a good bit steadier than he had on the morning after the shooting when sheriff Scott had first questioned him. He presented himself as a saddened old friend of Smith's.

McMichael had heard about the Sunday night drinking party at the Robert E. Lee Hotel that Walker and Smith had run off to.

"Was any statement made at the hotel, Mr. Walker, or was there any information on your part that you knew any reason for Mr. Reynolds leaving the house abruptly like that to go to the hotel?"

"Well, late yesterday afternoon I learned from Mrs. Reynolds why he left. . . . During the reading of the play in the afternoon, she told me she went to place a hand on Smith's leg, and he moved her hand away. . . . That started an argument."

Sheriff Scott, sitting beside the jurymen, was furious. Here was this kid Walker saying that *he* had talked with Mrs. Reynolds Thursday afternoon — when she was still supposed to be in too much of a shock to see the sheriff or anyone! She was refusing to see him — but here was Walker popping in and out of her bedroom whenever he damn well pleased!

Walker didn't look at Scott. He continued to answer McMichael. Libby had told him that she was surprised at Smith pushing her hand away. Smith was the one who always needed lots of attention. She said something about that to him — and he flared. He accused her of being the one who had shunned *him; she* had drawn away. According to

Smith, either she had pulled back and had shoved his hand away — or he was crazy, and he was going to see a doctor. During the night of drinking at the hotel, Walker said, Smith had told him again and again of his fear that he, Smith, was going crazy. But then next morning when they got up, rumpled and hung over, there was nothing more said about it, and they had returned early to Reynolda. The first thing Smith had done was to go to Libby's room to apologize.

Other than keeping Smith company when he was drinking, McMichael wanted to know what else was involved in Walker's job. His answer gave the coroner's jurymen both an intriguing look at life at Reynolda and a drab view of his dogged, faithful role as Smith's man Friday. The birthday party seemed a big moment for him, and he bustled with responsibility:

> Mrs. Reynolds had me phone the guests for six-thirty. I have previously told them seven or something later than that. But she had me phone them and see that they were all coming. . . .
>
> When the guests arrived, I ordered up the barbecue and everything . . . and I went to the downstairs bar and brought the whiskey and the White Rock and the glasses. . . .
>
> Towards the end of the party, I remembered Mrs. Vaught's shoes. She wore a pair of shoes with her bathing suit, and she left them out on the lakeside of the boathouse. And I drove down to get them. But I tried to get back as quick as possible, while looking for Mrs. Reynolds at the same time. . . .
>
> In the past few nights I had always locked up the house . . . after the party, I continued to take my time and kill time locking up the house. . . .

And so it went. He really seemed to have tried to give his new employer some useful service, doing all the things a millionaire's son needs to have done for him. Walker described how he had been "consulted" by Smith on Charlie Hill's desire to have Smith sign a $1,500 note so that Hill could buy a plane of his own from a man in Troy, Ohio. He ran errands to the bank and to the railroad station and to the airport. He reported on a rambling assignment to get Smith a French grammar book so he could study the language for the flight. No job too small. No job too large.

Now, no job at all.

14

"Wasn't He Accusing You of Being Intimate with His Wife?"

UNDER McMichael's unhurried questioning, Albert Walker attempted to describe what had gone on during that party night. He prefaced his recollection of the party by running over the arrangements for the barbecue, seeming to be rather proud of having handled most of the details of the party. When McMichael showed some surprise at the substantial amount of whiskey and "home brew" that Walker was able to lay in in that Prohibition summer, Walker protested that he just wanted to be ready. Walker then volunteered that before they went any further, he wanted to put down the rumor that there had been nude swimming at the party. He and Mrs. Vaught, he said, had been the only ones to get even as far as bathing suits that sultry evening. A couple of the jurors exchanged looks. The other story was better.

Then McMichael decided to investigate another interesting rumor he had picked up. He had heard that there had been long periods during the party evening when Mrs. Reynolds had been conspicuously absent from the group down at the lake. "Do you recall that situation, Mr. Walker?"

Walker seemed reluctant. "Well, I remember missing her." He paused. "But that was only the latter part of the night."

McMichael wanted specifics. What time had she been missing?

Walker blossomed into his gopher role: "That was after I made a trip in a canoe to tell everybody who was out in the canoes to come up to the house. And then I came up to the house and found Mr. Reynolds and this friend of Jim Shepherd's sitting in the reception room."

Walker said he didn't want to raise the question of Libby's absence in front of Smith's guests. "But sometime after that — not so long after — I asked where Mrs. Reynolds was. And Smith said, 'She is roaming around on the outside.' We got up and went back to the pantry to talk, and I asked him to let me go out and look for her. He said, 'No, I don't want you to. If she is not in here after the guests leave, I will go out and look for her. I think you should stay here, Ab, being as the guests haven't left.' "

Smith sounded too accepting for a man who had a reputation for an extremely jealous personality. McMichael felt he was onto something. "Was Smith disturbed?" Again Walker paused. "I would say he had a rather worried look, yes."

Walker said he made one more trip down to the lake, looking for those shoes Mrs. Vaught had left behind — and then took a swing around the grounds, hoping to find Libby. McMichael was interested in the rumor that Smith had seen Walker kissing Libby. What about that? Walker flushed: "The early part of the evening, Mrs. Reynolds was — well — very tight. . . ."

"You mean under the influence of whiskey?"

"Yes, sir — and she threw her arms around my shoulder and leaned down and whispered to me — something pertaining to Smith loving her."

"Was that at the boathouse, Mr. Walker?"

"Yes, sir, in the early part of the evening. And it wasn't long after that until they both came up to me. And Mrs. Reynolds said, 'Did I kiss you?' And I said, 'No, of course not.' Later when Mr. Reynolds and myself went back into the pantry at the house, he said, 'I want you to get it straight that I wasn't accusing you of anything!' He said, 'I saw what happened.' "

"Did he say, Mr. Walker, that he wasn't accusing you of anything? Or that he wasn't accusing you of being *intimate* with his wife? Which words did he use?"

"I don't know the words. All I know is the thought of what I am trying to say."

"That he wasn't accusing you of being intimate with his wife? Is that correct?"

"That's right. He wasn't accusing me of that."

"When Mrs. Reynolds leaned down and whispered to you, what did she tell you?"

"I don't remember the exact words. But she said, 'I don't believe Smith loves me,' or something to that effect — in a very light tone."

McMichael was finding Albert Walker a little hard to figure. The vision of the glamorous Broadway star falling off balance over this callow, nineteen-year-old North Carolinian, just returned from a month of worm-digging and fly-casting at a Mouth-of-Wilson fishing camp, was not easy to accept. Was Walker such a big stud? Did he *remember* it right? Did he *tell* it right? "What was your condition along about this time of the evening, Mr. Walker?"

"Usually when a crowd had been there, I drank pretty heavy," Walker admitted. "But this night I had engaged a tutor and was going to meet him at nine o'clock in the morning, and I went down to the party with the full intention of staying on the wagon. . . . I had this bottle of beer and then one drink up at the house."

"Then," said McMichael, "you would say you were practically sober?"

"Yes, sir. Not only for the reason of that. The party didn't look like it was being very successful on account of Mrs. Reynolds disappearing." Walker had brought himself back to McMichael's concern. "Did Mr. Reynolds accuse you at any time that night of disappearing at the same time she disappeared?" McMichael asked.

"Oh, no," Walker answered. It didn't ring with much conviction. Walker's recollections of the evening were bound to be regarded with some caution. McMichael had already heard that he had been heavily intoxicated at the hospital. And Walker had testified to taking "seven or eight drinks" in "the general run" of other evenings.

Walker testified the last guest had left about midnight. Smith had been downstairs with him at that point. They had been sitting in the living room, with a good view of the balcony . . . and of the hall that served the east wing bedrooms. Then, according to Walker, Libby appeared at the balcony and beckoned. Smith got up and climbed the stairs, disappearing with Libby into Walker's bedroom. Walker could only speculate that they had gone into his room to "study the globe" there. The bedroom had been Smith's room before his marriage, and there was a large globe of the world still in it. Walker — from the living room — said he could hear them talking, saw them come out again. Libby retreated down the hall to the sleeping porch. Smith returned downstairs.

According to Walker, Smith stayed down for about ten minutes. Then he began to behave very strangely. Walker related the conversation:

"When Smith left me to go upstairs, he said something like, 'You needn't bother about leaving a door unlocked, Ab, I won't be back' — or something like that. He said, 'I'm coming back downstairs but then I'm going out and I won't be back.' "

Didn't that seem a bit strange? McMichael wanted to know. Walker didn't think so.

"But then came a part I can't get straight in my mind . . . the order of it — this last talk before he went upstairs. I can't exactly remember the interval, the order of things . . . but he had given me his wallet. And I placed it behind the cushion of the sofa. And someone walked in, but I can't get that straight. . . ."

Had Smith argued with him then? McMichael asked.

"No. He just said, 'You can have that' — the wallet — said it in a way that I took it to mean since I hadn't been paid for a week that it was my pay. I tried to joke it off with him, saying 'Thanks' and tossing it around." Then he said Smith had gone back up.

Walker said he had lingered downstairs locking up the house, hoping Smith would come back down to talk it out further. Smith had been upstairs for the second time for about ten minutes, Walker said, when Walker heard something disturbing. "I heard Miss Yurka calling for me. She was coming from the west end of the house."

"You didn't hear a shot?"

"I heard what I thought at first was a shot. But then it went through my mind, 'That is not loud enough for a pistol shot.' "

"Did you hear a woman scream?"

"Miss Yurka called me and said she heard someone scream — and immediately after that I heard someone scream."

"Mr. Walker, when did you first see Mrs. Reynolds?"

"I immediately started running to the sleeping porch, and Mrs. Reynolds met me on the balcony — on the stair side — and she fell across a little stool there at the side of the hall. And she said that Smith had shot himself!"

"What did she have in her hand? Anything?"

"She didn't have anything that I remember. I am quite sure of that, because I leaned over her and shook her and she was just crying and hollering — and she told me Smith shot himself."

"Then what did you do?"

"I immediately ran in there and found Smith on the bed."

McMichael asked all the coroner's jurymen to move upstairs to the hall off the bedrooms. They crossed the magnificent living room and up the imposing stairway at its rear, moving respectfully in the manner of people walking quietly through a church.

McMichael wanted the jurors to see where Miss Yurka had stood, where Walker's moves had taken him, where he first saw Mrs. Reynolds. They flattened themselves up and down each side of the hallway — like tourists — as McMichael paced up and down asking his questions.

Walker told how he took one quick look in the sleeping porch, saw that an ambulance was needed, and ran downstairs to phone. Then he said he raced back up to the sleeping porch. He looked more carefully at Reynolds then, he said. The young man was lying on one side of the bed, face down, with his head toward the foot of the bed and his legs partially over the side near the head of the bed.

"When you got up here, Mr. Walker — from the time Miss Yurka called until you got up here — how much time expired?"

"I was at a run when I met Mrs. Reynolds and stopped and shook her and asked her what was the matter."

"This was just a second or two?"

"Yes, sir."

"You say you remember that he was lying face-down on the bed, head toward the foot?"

"Yes, sir, because the first thing I saw was the hole in his head."

With Walker the first person to encounter Libby Holman at that crucial moment, McMichael thought whatever Libby might have sobbed out in horror would be an instinctively truthful statement. What had she said?

"She said she was sleeping out here on the porch," Walker testified. "But I had the impression previously she was in her own bed. But she told me she was out here and she waked. And at the same time she heard a pistol shot and Smith crying, 'Lib!' and at that he fell right across her."

McMichael couldn't forget the stories about Walker's strange and agitated conduct at the hospital, insisting that he be driven back to Reynolda. Why was Walker so eager to get back? Hadn't Walker said that he was afraid the police would search his room? Walker denied that; he had simply wanted to clean up all the glasses and the whiskey, and retrieve Smith's wallet; in addition, the house was wide open; "there was no telling who would enter."

If Walker was vague on some points, he was amazingly precise about conversations he had heard before and after the shooting. Walker said that before Smith had gone upstairs for the last time he had rambled on about his plans with Libby for New York in the fall. Walker thought from what was said that Smith was dreading it: he would be all day at school and Libby wouldn't get away from the theater until maybe one or two o'clock in the morning if they were rehearsing. Smith complained that they would never see each other.

"He was afraid something was going to break up this happiness of his," Walker said. "Mrs. Reynolds had asked him if he wanted her to give up the stage. And he had said, 'By no means.' He told me that was the last thing he would ever want her to do."

"Did you say this to the sheriff, Mr. Walker? 'Well, the whole truth of the matter is Smith just thought too much of that woman.' "

"Yes, sir."

"Did you say later that there was something about this affair you couldn't tell and that you would carry to your grave?"

"Yes, sir. I said that — but it was in a state of mind . . ."

"Why did you make that statement at that time?"

"I have no idea why I made that statement. There were personal things that were said that would have no bearing on this. But I will answer any questions you ask me."

Libby's slippers in Walker's bedroom and her sweater in Walker's bathroom seemed to need some explanation. Walker didn't have any. They were "just there." McMichael pressed for more logic. "Can you give us any reason at all why, if she was in there — in your room — with her husband, she should leave her bedroom slippers in your room, under your bed?"

"I have no idea," Walker answered innocently. Then an afterthought: "Mrs. Reynolds was very tight."

"Mr. Reynolds wasn't?" Walker said no.

"Didn't Mr. Reynolds look after his wife when she was drunk as best he could?"

"That was the first time I have ever seen her drunk," Walker fired back.

McMichael persisted: "Didn't she drink all the time?"

"No, sir."

"Day and night?"

"*No sir!* She worked practically ten hours a day, in the morning at the piano with Mr. Vardell. In the afternoon with Miss Yurka at dramatics."

"Will you say now, Mr. Walker, why you made the statement that there was something you would 'carry to your grave'?"

He paused so long before answering that McMichael was getting ready to repeat the question. Finally: "I don't know. You have to remember in that interview with sheriff Scott I had been up all night. I had collapsed at the hospital and had been carried away from there. And the interview with Mr. Scott was hardly two hours after I had left home. I just don't know why I said it."

"Mr. Walker, did you know Mrs. Reynolds was a Jewess?"

"No, sir."

"When did you find out?"

"I *never* knew she was a Jewess."

"Did Smith know it, Mr. Walker?"

"I don't know, sir."

"Did you ever hear Smith express his opinion, or make any statement in regard to people of the Hebrew race?"

"*No, sir.*"

"On Sunday night when he talked to you at the hotel, didn't he tell you he had just learned that Mrs. Reynolds was a Jewess?"

Walker seemed to waver. "No, sir. He did not."

"At no time since you have known Mrs. Reynolds has she ever said she was a Jewess?"

"No, sir."

"At the hotel that Sunday night, didn't you ask Smith why he wanted to spend the night down there?"

"I never asked Smith anything pertaining to his life or anything. If he wanted to tell me, I was perfectly willing to listen."

"You didn't interrogate Smith at all?"

"After the conversation had started, I asked him some questions . . . sure."

"But in your conversation down at the hotel, did he ever tell you why he went there to spend the night away from Reynolda?"

"Yes, sir. He said he was insane. He said he was going to see a doctor the next morning."

"Well, was he insane, Mr. Walker?"

"Not to my knowledge."

Ab Walker wasn't an illuminating witness. And he was so hopelessly involved that as fast as one facet of his relationship with Smith Reynolds was clarified, another came under question. McMichael made one more attempt to unravel the confusion about Walker's missing gun, and in the process Walker made a rather surprising admission: ". . . I placed my gun beside my bed in the drawer. I looked in there once before and remembered seeing it in there. But the next morning when I was up there with the sheriff, I saw my gun wasn't there. I think it was a German Luger."

McMichael thought they were all very casual about guns — even for North Carolina in the 1930s, when handguns in bedside tables and the glove compartments of cars were almost essential pieces of equipment.

"Up until you saw that gun today, the Italian automatic, you thought Mr. Reynolds had killed himself with the gun normally kept in your room? The Luger?"

"Yes, sir."

"You thought that was what he and his wife went into the room to get?"

"That's what I thought *he* went into the room to get. Yes, sir."

McMichael had hit on an interesting point. Walker was now saying that when Smith and Libby went to the room occupied by Walker, Walker already suspected that Smith was looking for a gun. Earlier Walker had said the visit there was to "look at the globe."

He asked Walker a few more questions, then led them all back downstairs. At this point, McMichael excused Walker — but warned him to remain outside. There was a brief whispered conversation with a couple of the sheriff's deputies, and then the deputies went out too. Young Walker was just beginning to savor the relief of the long questioning's being over when the deputies hurried him to a car in the drive. He was not under arrest, the deputies explained. But he was to be lodged in the county jail as a material witness, to keep him from "intermingling with other witnesses."

The niceties of this nonprisoner legal status must have escaped him. To reporters who glimpsed him as he was driven at high speed through the Reynolda gate, he *looked* like a man under arrest. He felt like it. He had never been in jail before.

Reporters waiting at the Reynolda gate had no trouble figuring out that an inquest had been held in secret when they then observed McMichael, sheriff Scott, and the six jurymen leaving late Friday afternoon. Several reporters who buttonholed Scott later had then had time to think about something besides their anger at being held out of the story; such a secret proceeding in a criminal case was illegal under the laws of the State of North Carolina. They told the sheriff they were going to go after an injunction to get themselves admitted.

Considering the kid-glove treatment that had been given so far to almost everyone connected with the case, Walker's detention was a sign of some progress. But wire-service reporters hardly had time to get out their leads on Walker's being in the lockup when Smith's two sisters, Mrs. Babcock and Mrs. Bagley, interceded with the sheriff. Walker was removed to the Robert E. Lee Hotel under guard. For a material witness, the living was better. But there was no question about bond. *He was in custody.*

The reporters pressed Scott for more details. Was the affluent young

Walker *really* a murder suspect? No, the sheriff insisted, just a material witness. Was Forsyth County afraid Walker would skip out? No, said the sheriff, it was just to keep him from talking with the other witnesses . . . and there *were* some discrepancies in his story. The sheriff claimed he had no suspects. He had, in fact, no evidence that Smith Reynolds had not taken his own life. But, on the other hand, he didn't have sufficient evidence that it was a suicide. Therefore, he felt he was obliged to continue the investigation, and Walker, at that stage, was crucial to it. Though Scott didn't make a point of it, after his frustrating visit on the morning after the shooting at Reynolda — where he couldn't interview two of the principals — the ability to have one other principal "available" was pretty tempting.

15

"It Is a Haze; It Is Blurred"

COUNTY SOLICITOR Carlisle Higgins, McMichael's boss, was a man who was trying to juggle a lot of responsibilities that week. He was deeply concerned with the investigation and preparation of a big fraud and conspiracy case, when the Reynolds shooting occurred . . . whereupon everybody in town seemed to swivel around and look to him.

It was pressure he would become accustomed to at several later points in his life. In 1932, Carlisle Higgins had already made a reputation at both the North Carolina bar and in the voting booths. He was a fiercely loyal graduate of the University of North Carolina, an avid sportsman, a crack hunter, a follower of Tarheel football — no matter how far it took him to travel back from the court's circuit to make a game. He liked the challenge and excitement of his job. Carlisle Higgins would handle some fourteen hundred homicide cases in the course of his career — but he would never get to the point of regarding the death of a man lightly. Yet the shooting of Smith Reynolds couldn't have come at a more inopportune time if he had to handle it personally.

By necessity, he had to delegate much of the hurried Reynolds inquest work to his assistant, Earle McMichael. The two men had little time to confer. And before long the investigation and the legal procedure that ran hand in hand with the Reynolds case seemed to get moving on conflicting tracks.

Important as was Higgins's conspiracy case, the snowballing demands of the Reynolds investigation soon made the business at Reynolda something he could no longer delegate. When sheriff Scott and McMichael began to turn up one conflicting fact after another and the newspapers began to ask some questions, Higgins knew he must get involved — and quickly. Late Friday afternoon, by the time McMichael had finished questioning Walker, Higgins had arrived at Reynolda to take charge. And Libby was to testify next.

Libby came down for the inquest attired in a long and elaborate negligee; it was suddenly as if the coroner's jurymen were intruding on a very private family scene. Libby slumped into the recesses of a large wing chair with her father and mother seated on either side. Those two sat stiffly and formally, Libby's father in a dark suit and vest in spite of the heat, a heavy gold watch chain prominent across his stomach; Libby's mother in a cheerful large-brimmed hat, as if she were headed for a garden party. The stiffness reminded Higgins of a couple on their first visit to a portrait photographer. Sunk in her wing chair between them, their striking daughter was like some butterfly pinned inside a shadow box. She sat motionless, except when she occasionally dabbed at her eyes with a handkerchief.

By the time Libby began to testify, the jurymen had had some time to become accustomed to their lavish surroundings. Now there was less uneasiness. In response to Higgins, Libby began to answer, slowly and in her low, husky voice.

She told about the leisurely, meandering auto trip down to Reynolda from New York. They had arrived about noon on June 6 — one month before the shooting — after their romantic all-night drive through the mountains of Virginia. They had spent most of the month of June at Reynolda, with the exception of a trip to Jacksonville, Florida, to buy Smith a new plane. There had been one weekend trip to Roaring Gap. Smith had flown to New York once briefly, on business. And they had had several visitors: the Holmans had come to Reynolda briefly. A friend of Smith's had come back with him from New York for a couple of days. And about a week before the shooting, Blanche Yurka had come down to coach Libby.

Libby described the good life at Reynolda; tennis in the morning, riding in the afternoons, leisurely drinks before dinner in spite of Prohibition. Then, with Higgins leading her slowly, she dropped the first of several surprises.

"Mrs. Reynolds, on last Tuesday, Tuesday of this week, did you spend the entire day here at Reynolda?"

"Yes — or I am told I spent the entire day here. But I don't remember. . . . I was asking Miss Yurka this afternoon if we had worked together on Tuesday, because I don't remember that day at all, from the time I woke up."

Higgins looked up from his notes. "You don't remember Tuesday at all?"

"No."

"You don't remember anything you did?"

"No, I don't know if I took a piano lesson. I usually took a piano lesson from Mr. Vardell."

"Do you remember what you did on Monday, the day before the party?"

"Yes, that was the Fourth of July. I remember *everything* I did."

The coroner's men sat up with a little more attention. Higgins wanted to make sure they got the point: "You remember distinctly and clearly, Mrs. Reynolds, what took place on Monday?"

"Yes."

"But you do not remember anything that took place on Tuesday — the day of the party and the shooting?"

"I don't remember anything that happened Tuesday — or anything that happened the next day."

"Mrs. Reynolds, were you feeling all right when you went to bed on Monday night?"

"Yes. Absolutely."

"And you do not recall getting up — waking up — on Tuesday?"

"No, I don't remember any of that day. The last thing I remember is Monday night, Mr. Higgins."

"So, as a result, you have no recollection at all of anything that happened after you went to bed Monday night until when?"

"The next thing I remember, Mr. Higgins — and it is just a flash — is hearing my name called and looking up and seeing Smith with the revolver at his head, and then a shot . . . and after that I don't remember anything."

The coroner's men were shifting skeptically. Higgins watched several of them exchange quizzical glances.

"Can you account in any way, Mrs. Reynolds, for the fact that you do not remember anything that took place on Tuesday?"

"No." She almost seemed to share Higgins's rather polite amazement that the strange loss of memory had taken place.

"You didn't take any medicine of any kind on Monday?"

"No, I don't think so. I never do. In the morning, I usually get up and go downstairs and practice the piano, and I have a lesson and we have lunch usually. And then we go out under the trees and work. But on Tuesday I don't remember any of it. Miss Yurka was telling me what we were working on that afternoon before the party — but I don't remember it."

"You didn't drink anything on Monday?"

Libby flared — and snapped out a "No!" But the suspicion of heavy drinking had already been firmly planted by McMichael's earlier question to Walker about Libby's reputation for being drunk "practically all the time."

"And the only recollection you have of Tuesday is the flash — as you call it — of your husband with a pistol?"

"That is the only clear thing."

"Do you recall, Mrs. Reynolds, exactly where you were?"

"Not clearly. But I am so used to sleeping on the porch I sort of imagine I was sleeping out there. That is all I know."

Higgins asked the inquest group to move upstairs to the sleeping porch. Perhaps he was hoping the sight would jog something from Mrs. Reynolds's blacked-out memory.

The french doors had been locked to protect the crime scene. Higgins unlocked one set of doors from the outside, beckoned those behind him into the room, and then went around the bed and opened the other set of doors from the inside. There was not room for all of them inside, but even those still in the doorways could see clearly.

It could have been a bedroom in a house closed for the summer. The bed had been stripped and was pulled out at an angle from the wall. Two small rugs were hung over chairs by the screened windows at the far end of the room. They had been washed and the floor still showed dark traces where they had been dripping. A piece of screen about one foot by one foot had been cut away near the top of one window. The filmy curtains had been loosely looped with each other so they would be clear of the floor. Chalk marks had been smeared at several points on the floor. And a large rug and the mattress carried big dark wet areas where someone had tried to scrub out the blood.

Higgins motioned Libby to a large wicker armchair that was pushed against one wall. With a courtly nod, he began to continue the questioning. Did Mr. Reynolds keep a weapon out there?

Libby acknowledged that there was usually a pistol on the sleeping porch. Smith kept it in a small marble-topped table on his side of the bed. "I used to sleep on the left side and Smith on the right side. And I would have kept the water over there on the left-hand table. And he kept the pistol there on the right-hand table, because we had been hearing footsteps and he was always worried. Often he would either get up and go to the window with the pistol, or else he would go downstairs and find the night watchman. Several times we heard those footsteps, and the pistol was kept right there." She rose, walked to the drawer in the table as she talked, as if she expected to still find the gun. She opened and closed it.

In an answer, she said she couldn't remember whether the pistol had been there on Monday night — her last lucid time. She turned away from Higgins then and looked slowly around the room — almost as if she were seeing it for the first time. Those inquest members who had followed into the room seemed to push back a bit, as if to give her space. She stared without any emotion at the scrubbed-out bloodstain on the mattress, then turned to speak again to Higgins.

"I remember the pistol to his head and the shot. I can't hear the shot now, but I remember — I don't know what it was; it was just — oh, I don't know; it was just like a terrible crash."

"Do you remember anything after that?" Higgins tried again.

"No," Libby insisted. "I do not. Nothing. . . . But Father said to tell you one feeling that I had afterwards, which was a feeling — it wasn't a mental picture of anything particularly clear after that flash — but I have this feeling that Smitty was in my arms and I felt his blood. But really it is a haze . . . it is blurred."

At every other point the haze closed in solidly. She didn't remember the conversation with Smith in Walker's bedroom which Walker had testified to. She had no idea why her slippers were under Walker's bed. Nor did she answer as if either fact was odd or needed explanation. The one and only blackout of her life seemed to have very conveniently shut out everything.

Higgins thought for a long moment and then began a line of questioning almost as if he were reluctant to do so.

"I regret to ask you this question, Mrs. Reynolds, but it may be material. Are you pregnant at this time?"

Libby seemed drained and weak. She sunk back into the wicker chair before she answered.

"I don't know yet. If I am, it is recent."

"It is recent and you don't know it?"

"Well, I have had one symptom."

"You have passed one of your periods?"

"Yes."

"How long past, please?"

"From June twenty-fifth."

To the citizens of Winston-Salem, Walker's detention was the only fact known about the afternoon of questioning — but that was a rather surprising development. The *Winston-Salem Journal* felt called upon, on the basis of what little they could get from McMichael, to do an abrupt about-face from its editorial of the day before. Prepared hurriedly for Saturday morning's paper was an editorial headed rather righteously (for a paper that had said the day before nothing more would be discovered) "Let the Truth Be Uncovered." Wrote the *Journal:*

> It is evident from even this small bit of testimony that . . . the public has not yet been given all the facts surrounding the death of young Reynolds. Much remains to be cleared up about all this.

16

Items to the Contrary

WHEN THE INQUEST was resumed on Saturday, it was no longer secret. But it was still "closed." The newsmen had petitioned a judge for admission, but had been turned down.

So they crowded around the only two entrances to the estate and harried the armed guards that the family had hired to keep them from infiltrating. They surrounded every car that entered. Peered inside. Tried to get pictures. Shouted at the occupants.

It was a wild scene. Most of the out-of-town newspapermen — and they were the tough, aggressive reporters from the Eastern big-city dailies — really had very little knowledge, that early in the game, as to who was who. So they depended on local reporters to identify car occupants for them. If nobody local was present, they would yell at whoever was in the cars, hoping to startle an identification. The photographers snapped away at any target, and assumed that anybody who came to Reynolda and was passed through by the guards was somebody important to the case. It was surprising how many times their cries of "Who are you?" brought back a startled truthful answer from a polite, dignified family member. Accustomed to the deference normally paid to a Reynolds, most of them had never before experienced anything quite like it.

Saturday was another hot, sticky day. But it seemed pleasantly cooler inside the library. Once again Alfred Holman sat at his daughter's side, still insisting he was there as a father, rather than as a lawyer. McMichael explained carefully to reporters afterward that Mrs. Reynolds had no legal need for a lawyer. Nor, he explained, had Holman acted as one. "He has no right to ask any questions. There are no accused and no defendants in this case. It is purely an investigation to determine all the facts with regard to the death of Smith Reynolds." McMichael did make it clear, however, that now Libby was getting the same sort of close isolation treatment that Walker was getting, since she too was a material witness. McMichael promised reporters that he had a guard posted at her bedroom door and that no one could see her in private, *without* the guard present. He was emphatic. Not even her father and mother could see her privately. Yet he really knew that Libby, at Reynolda, was effectively out of his jurisdiction.

Fulcher testified first on Saturday morning, and his testimony turned out to be something of a warm-up to that of the principals. Fulcher planted some questions in several minds with his simple, credible responses. The jurors then learned something from him of all the vigilante types around Reynolda with pistols in their bedside tables or dresser drawers ready to bang away at mysterious intruders in blacked-out cars. There seemed to have been a lot of guns on hand — not all of which could be found after the shooting.

McMichael found it curious that Fulcher had heard the shot, but no crying — while Miss Yurka, much farther away and even in the peaceful stages of beginning sleep, had heard the crying — but had not heard a shot. Who was right? Or were they both right? Had the shot that killed Smith and the hysterical crying that spread the alarm come not seconds apart . . . but perhaps fifteen or more minutes apart, the crying finally coming when Fulcher — first alerted by the shot — was then down by the lake, well out of hearing?

McMichael was eager to establish the exact time of those two happenings. The time was beginning to loom up as quite critical. Miss Yurka testified in a guarded way, but was quite precise about waking once to hear voices in the kitchen, going down and finding only Walker, then returning upstairs and back to sleep. She was equally precise about being wakened the second time by the hysterical crying, going to the top of the stairs and seeing Walker in the living room, asking him to investigate, and then seeing Walker and Mrs. Reynolds come "almost immediately" down the long hall, pulling Smith along, limp and bleeding.

Clearly Walker was the best person to have heard *both* shot and crying. Locking up in the living room, he was standing roughly halfway between Miss Yurka's bedroom in the extreme west wing and Smith's and Libby's sleeping porch in the extreme east wing. McMichael asked Walker back to try to resolve some of the conflicting testimony given by him and Miss Yurka.

"In testifying yesterday, Mr. Walker, you said that you ran to the top of the steps when Miss Yurka called you saying she had heard a scream."

"Yes. That's right."

"And you said you thought you heard a shot — but later decided it wasn't loud enough to have been a gunshot."

"Yes, when I was downstairs."

"And immediately Mrs. Reynolds came down the hall screaming that Smith had shot himself? Is that right, Mr. Walker?"

"Yes, sir."

Walker had no way of knowing that Blanche Yurka had testified something to the contrary. But McMichael was giving Walker every opportunity to change his story if he felt he had been mistaken at first. Nevertheless, Walker stuck firmly to his earlier testimony that Libby had run out of the room. Only then had he gone in, found Smith, and rushed downstairs to phone for the ambulance.

"Why didn't you go to the phone upstairs?" McMichael wanted to know.

"I never thought of it. The phone in the booth downstairs is connected directly with the outside. Upstairs you have to wait for an outside dial signal. I never thought of the upstairs phone."

Walker didn't know it, but McMichael was offering him an out; if he had used the upstairs phone, that could have been the reason why Blanche Yurka never saw him call for an ambulance.

In fairness to his witnesses, McMichael was trying to find a way for Walker's testimony and Blanche Yurka's to dovetail, some area where there might be understandable confusion because of the emotion at the time, the sorts of minor discrepancies that almost invariably occur when several people are describing what happened in a tense or dramatic or frightening moment.

McMichael decided to try some logic. Suppose Miss Yurka had been mistaken. Excited. Was her testimony suspect because of the excitement?

Walker seemed to know he was in trouble almost any way he answered that. "I don't know, Mr. McMichael."

"So you think Miss Yurka was mistaken?"

"Mistaken in what?"

"When she says Mrs. Reynolds did *not* come out and meet you both at the top of the steps."

"Oh, I am positive that Mrs. Reynolds came out first. . . . Mrs. Reynolds told me when she dropped down on that stool in the upstairs hall that Smith had shot himself."

"Yesterday in your testimony, Mr. Walker, and when you made your statement to Sheriff Scott, you never once mentioned that Mrs. Reynolds helped you carry the body."

"I am not conscious of the fact that she did, because I remember stopping on the steps and saying, 'Won't somebody help me!' "

"So now you say that your recollection is that she did *not* help you?"

"She might have attempted to help me; I don't know."

"I am asking, Mr. Walker, what your best recollection is."

"My best recollection is that going out of the hall, she attempted to pick up Mr. Reynolds' feet, but before we got anyplace, she let him down and started running, or doing something. I am not conscious of what she was doing actually. I remember very distinctly when I was on the steps, stopping and asking somebody to help me, and that Miss Yurka picked up Smith's feet."

Walker was confusing himself and the jurymen with his conflicting answers. They were aware of the time lapse between the shot, the crying, and the discovery of the wounded Smith. But if Walker was to improve his position, he had to establish that the shot that fatally wounded Smith had been fired at the time when he was talking to Miss Yurka. Yet her account contradicted his on almost every critical point.

"How much time elapsed," asked a juror, "between the muffled shot you heard and the time you met Mrs. Reynolds out on the steps?"

"I don't imagine the whole thing was a minute," Walker answered.

"Did you hear any scream before you saw her [Mrs. Reynolds] come out?" the juror asked.

"Not before Miss Yurka called me," Walker answered firmly.

The suspicion wouldn't go away. Why had the wide-awake Walker, perhaps fifty feet from the sleeping porch, failed to hear any screams — when Miss Yurka, sleeping maybe a hundred and fifty feet away, was *wakened* by them?

Sheriff Scott, McMichael's next witness, was as puzzled about some points as was McMichael. The most important of these was the path of the bullet. Assuming that Reynolds had shot himself while standing over Libby, as the singer testified, the bullet — after leaving the muzzle of the pistol at maximum velocity and passing through the relatively unresistant substance of young Reynolds's skull and brain — would have had to perform a series of almost billiard-ball maneuvers, caroming around the room in a seemingly illogical pattern, to have made the marks it did.

McMichael asked Scott to try to visualize at what point on the porch Smith Reynolds might have been standing if he were to fall on the bed as he was supposed to have: face toward the foot of the bed, feet toward the head. Scott guessed he stood near the head of the bed. Then McMichael quizzed the sheriff for an opinion on whether or not the bullet that traveled through Smith's brain could have left a bullet fragment on the bed, where one was found well *below* the line of fire . . . and still sent another fragment tearing through the window screen, well *above* the line of fire.

Scott's answers made it immediately clear that he was not prepared to be positive about just where or how Smith was positioned when he was fatally wounded. But the sheriff felt the evidence indicated Smith could not have been *standing*—as Libby had testified. Scott theorized that had Smith been standing at almost any point around the bed, looking down at Libby, then his face would have been angled down toward the bed . . . and a bullet going in his brow and emerging from behind his ear would have been traveling *away* from the bed and upward. As it was, the bullet had fragmented, leaving one piece down *in* the bed, the second piece on the floor beside it, with the last piece more predictably emerging near the top of a window screen.

Scott's testimony then touched on one other incongruity: the sheets, the mattress, and the covering of the box spring were all *thoroughly* soaked through with blood — the sort of soaking that normally would only be accomplished if the body had stayed bleeding on the bed for some period of time. Yet Libby and Walker had both testified they had started to move the body downstairs within a minute or two after the shooting — at which time, as Blanche Yurka testified, the blood was not spurting. Oozing a bit — but oozing so little that no stains appeared anywhere in the upper hall or on the stairs. Oozing in the manner of a wound that had been inflicted some time before.

The only other witness who might have shed some light on what happened on the sleeping porch that night had been housed in a room only a couple of doors away. That witness was Mrs. Vaught. But she was not much help. She admitted only to "two highballs," "some beer," and then a very sound night's sleep through all the rest of the tragedy. One of the biggest news stories in Winston-Salem history had happened outside her door — and she had nodded out on the whole thing.

Finally, with all hands exhausted, the inquest was adjourned until Monday. But not the speculation. Nor the debate on the legality of a closed inquest. The *Winston-Salem Journal*, having been needled by the secrecy of the Friday and Saturday inquest sessions at Reynolda, began to question the legality of all that had gone on in those sessions. A small page-one story written late Saturday afternoon — after a local judge had denied the paper's request for an injunction that would give its reporters entry to the inquest — took aim on the whole issue. The *Journal* had rounded up opinions from three attorneys, including two who were public officials. The consensus of the three was that a closed inquest was forbidden, both under the Constitution and under the laws of the State of North Carolina.

17

"I Want You to Go Out and Have an Affair"

ON MONDAY, almost a week after the shooting, the inquest was resumed, and reporters were finally present — but only as a result of protests from outside Winston-Salem that had been added to the *Winston-Salem Journal's* complaint. Higgins had opened the hearings, even though the judge had ruled he did not have to.

The day before, a venerable and respected lawyer, Frank Nash, former assistant attorney general of the state, had died. But the way he influenced the Reynolds case that day — "overruling" the local judge — was through a decision he had made some time before in regard to an earlier legal battle, *Knight* v. *North Carolina:* under the state law, a coroner's inquest must be public. Nash's name and reputation at interpreting the state constitution seemed to be the final word on the legal issue, regardless of what the local judge said.

The *Raleigh Times* sounded off shortly on the whole matter of the Reynolds shooting with a strident tone of Puritanism to its editorial voice — and some high-minded disregard for the constitutional issue of public hearings:

We do not remember another such bizarre probing into matters that should have been kept as sacred as the bathroom.

. . . It [the inquest] is essentially a preliminary investigation. It seeks the probabilities rather than the absolute facts of a death. . . . But it is entirely conceivable that what transpires in such an inquest might, to the ends of justice, better remain hidden.*

Certainly the spectacle of an evidently ignorant chorus girl being subjected to an intimate and revolting exposé of her sex life in marital relations can serve no possible good.

The only wonder is that this Libby person did not avail herself of her constitutional privilege of sitting mute on the witness stand. But, one supposes, the old hunger for the picture on the front page and the publicity of the sob-sisters held strong.

It was not one of that paper's finest hours. "This Libby person" seemed to be conducting herself with more dignity than the *Raleigh Times*.

When solicitor Higgins had cut off his questioning of Mrs. Reynolds late the previous Friday afternoon, she seemed near fainting at times, slow in her answers, and wavering in her attention. When she returned to the library at Reynolda on Monday morning, she looked more composed. Higgins led her gently into things, asking her about her first meeting Smith, their courtship, and their marriage. Libby painted a rather touching picture of those first days at Reynolda, in spite of the difficulties of their divergent careers. Smith had explained to her soon after they were engaged that, since each state had its own laws, North Carolina would probably not recognize his Nevada divorce and his remarriage; she might never come into any Reynolds money. Nevertheless, he had talked repeatedly about making a will, a subject she felt was morbid. She told Smith she hated the constant talk about money.

As it was, even on his $50,000-a-year allowance, Smith told Libby that money was short. He had lately spent a good bit of money combing the South and then purchasing the new plane (the old amphibian from the round-the-world flight had been sold in China). He said the new plane was really for her. "I was going to take up aviation, too," Libby explained, "and he wanted me to learn in something that wasn't as complicated as an amphibian."

She remembered that all had seemed to go well at Reynolda at first. There had been a fair amount of company, and lots of lazy things to do

* Deplorably bad advice for a paper to give on its editorial pages, since it is advising subverting the law. But the fact that it was published is some testimony of the heat the case stirred up.

between his studies and her work on the play — until that Sunday before Smith's death. The description of the friction that began then spilled out of Libby in one long rush, and it was significantly counter to what the coroner's jurymen had heard before:

Sunday afternoon Miss Yurka was going to read this play that Smith wanted to hear, because he was interested in it too, and we were in here in the library — and Smith and I were on that sofa; Smith was sitting up and I was sort of lying down with my head propped up. I had on a bathing suit because I had been out playing tennis or something in the morning. I was lying there and had the script of the play, and I was reading the part I was going to take and Miss Yurka was reading the other characters. It was hot and I was restless. At one time I changed my position to put my hand on Smith's knee — he was very sensitive and I had to be conscious all the time to be close to him and tell him that I loved him. He used to tell me all the time, "But you can't love me." He had a real inferiority complex. He would say, "You have gotten where you are by yourself," and I knew he was a very sensitive boy and I had to show him with every gesture that I did love him. I changed my position and put my hand on his knee, and he drew away, and I said something to him . . . and put my arms around his shoulders, and he said, "You shrank from me." I said, "Let's go upstairs," and we got up. I didn't want a scene. I said, "I didn't shrink from you; I never could shrink from you. I love you better than anyone in the world."

He got this shrinking business in his mind, and he said, "Libby, if you didn't shrink from me, I am crazy." I said, "Smith, can't you understand this? I was reading the script and may have gotten restless as I always do and was moving around on the sofa." I am terribly nearsighted, so I explained to him, "Maybe you made a gesture toward me and I didn't see it." He shouted, "Libby, if you didn't shrink from me then I am crazy! I don't see things that aren't true!"

It was a childish "you did — I did not" exchange. But according to her, it was not an exceptional one. She told Higgins they used to have arguments just as strange lots of times, with Smith imagining "all sorts of crazy things" that weren't true. Libby said she drew him upstairs to keep from embarrassing the others. They had talked there for about an hour and Libby said she tried to get his mind off the subject. But he had kept saying, "No, I have got to have my head examined."

Things had quieted down by dinnertime, she said, though the attempts at lighthearted conversation, in an effort to keep Smith and Libby fron tangling again, often flowed so inanely that it was almost as uncomfortable as the arguments might have been. When the meal was over and Libby told Smith that they were going to continue with their reading of the play and hoped for his suggestions, he walked out, saying he was going to town. Libby said she had followed and pleaded with him as he dressed to leave. But he was determined: "I am going to stay at a hotel tonight and go to the doctor tomorrow and have my head examined," he said.

"Don't you realize how silly that is," Libby said she protested. "If you want me to go to town, I will go with you. Won't you take me?"

She said she repeated her plea over and over and put her arms around his neck, crying: "I love you and you love me; that's the only thing that makes any difference in the world. You told me you never wanted to make me unhappy. . . . Smith, if you love me, you won't leave this house tonight!"

But Smith had left for the night of drinking with Walker. And the two Norfolk prostitutes.

Libby's comments about Smith's "black moods" prompted Higgins to question her further on that. Higgins was beginning to wonder how unsteady Reynolds's mental state might really have been. Here was Reynolds described by his family as being placid and happy only a day or two before the tragedy. Now Libby was calling him moody and suicidal.

Then Libby told Higgins the bizarre story of being locked in the ship's cabin in Hong Kong and described Smith playing the gun scene — in Port Washington, on the boat coming back across the Pacific, at the lodge in the national park on the way back to New York.

"Ever since I have known him, he has had a gun." Libby sounded resigned. He would threaten to kill himself, rant at her in his despair that he could not make her happy or live up to her expectations — and then she would take him in her arms, and all that would be shoved into the black back of his mind until another time.

Higgins tried to be polite about her unexplained amnesia, but his tone could hardly mask his skepticism. He had had a lot of experience with evasive witnesses over the years. He could usually spot them and bring them to book easily enough. But if hers was an evasive tactic, it was certainly a unique and effective one. He had never hit anything precisely like it. Mrs. Reynolds protested that she had tried to reconstruct the blackout time "backwards and forwards," but she said she could not remember one thing.

Higgins decided to try to take her through it a step at a time, as a memory jogger: "You don't remember dressing that day?"

"Mr. Higgins, I don't even remember getting up. I have asked Miss Yurka and Mr. Walker about it long ago, when I first gained consciousness. I thought if *they* could tell me what I did, it would click in my brain and bring it back, because I have never forgotten things like that. So they told me what I did — which all sounded natural to me because everything they told me I did, I had done before. When Mr. Walker told me I had taken a walk late that evening all around the grounds, that wasn't unnatural. I have done that lots of times before. And Ab said I got lost. And that is not unnatural. I have no sense of direction; I used to get lost lots of times."

She looked questioningly at Higgins — as if she thought he was going to debate her lack of direction. He didn't argue. She had already made the point to the jurymen of her nearsightedness. She was certainly positioning herself as a bad risk as a North Carolina country girl.

"I can't tell you that I remember this next thing — because I don't remember it either. But Ab told me that Smith and I went upstairs that night to Smith's old room, Walker's room. That wasn't unnatural either. Smith had all his papers, all his letters, his globe, his navigation things in there. And it is on the way to the porch. Many times we used to go in there together and sit on the bed and discuss things and look over the papers and the globe. . . .

"And if I felt like it, I would take off some of my things. And if Smith felt like it, he would take off some of his things. Many times we would wake up in the morning and Smith would say, 'Where is my shirt; where are those shoes?' And the first place I would go to look for them was back in Walker's room. And my clothes, too, because we would sit in there lots of nights."

Several of the jurymen shifted uncomfortably; with all those clothes beginning to come off.

"Lots of times Smith had taken me back to that room and sat and talked to me — and then said he was going downstairs to get some water or something, and I would lie down and doze off. That wasn't un-

At the time of the shooting, the glassed-in first floor sun porch was totally open and a covered entrance-way stuck out from the house where the center french doors are. In this garden Fulcher, the watchman, still not knowing what had happened, waited for the estate manager to come after seeing Smith's car roar off to the hospital.

This would have been the last view of Reynolda house Smith would see. Searching for Libby after he had been out wandering on the grounds in a rage, he moved un- steadily through this door that opened into his bedroom suite from the upstairs hall and, hearing voices from the porch straight ahead of him, stepped out to find Libby and Walker. The bed would be to the left of the open french doors at the rear of this picture.

Alfred Holman walked head-high among the courthouse loafers at Winston-Salem. As he watched the Reynolds family's fears of scandal, an idea to save his daughter formed in his mind. *United Press International Photo*

With Libby in hiding before her surrender at Wentworth, photographers ransacked every photo morgue they could find. This publicity reject was published — but looked nothing like the "grieving widow" who came to court a few days later. *Wide World Photos*

Judge J. N. Stack (left) poses at Wentworth with bright, politically savvy Carlisle Higgins. They had a tiger by the tail. Stack speculated early, "It is very difficult to convict a wealthy person in the state of North Carolina." *United Press International Photo*

Looking apprehensive at the prospect of gridiron rough-and-tumble, Albert Walker (back row, center) was hardly 18 when Libby was singing on Broadway — for perhaps $10,000 a week, by today's standards. *United Press International Photo*

The crowd that began to gather at Wentworth Court House to see Libby's surrender included the village cripple squatting on the sidewalk to the left of the front door. *United Press International Photo*

Libby, heavily veiled and half hidden, holds tight to her father on her right and is supported on her left by a rumpled doctor from Reidsville, well propped with stethoscope in pocket; Polikoff wanted no city slicker doctor lording it over Wentworth. *United Press International Photo*

Tough, courtroom-wise Bennet Polikoff stands up to make a
statement. Libby sits in widow's black, her father on her left.
Curious local blacks discreetly occupy the balcony; the story had
also circulated that Libby was a mulatto. *Wide World Photos*

This murderous row of photographers (below) could have been assembled
for a double execution at Sing Sing — but were just waiting for Libby to
give birth at the hospital in Philadelphia. *United Press International Photo*

Almost any photo of Libby would be printed after the shooting. This "candid" is so heavily retouched that few of the characters bear any likeness to real people. It's *Revenge with Music* in 1934 — Libby's return to the theater. She is the "puritan maid" at right. *United Press International Photo*

Photographers dogged Libby. The drinking didn't get any less, and the social complications got more. An angry Libby leaves a New York nightclub with one of the attractive women who were so frequently attracted to her. *Culver Pictures, Inc.*

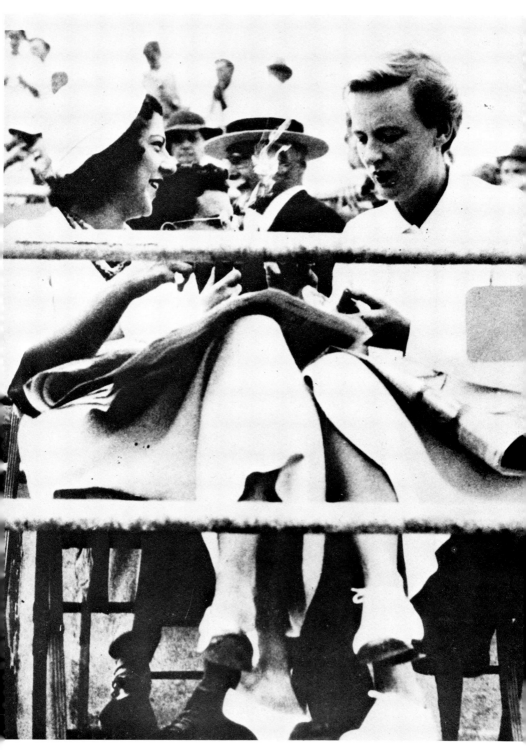

Handsome, wealthy Louisa Jenney, seen with Libby at a steeplechase meet near Baltimore several years after the shooting, had been a clear match for any number of police departments when it came to hiding the singer. *United Press International Photo*

In Depression-battered 1934, Smith's brother, Dick, inherited a one-quarter portion of their father's estate; Dick's share was estimated at $25,000,000! With his second wife, Dick gets ready to launch a 70-foot ocean racing yacht (right) custom-built for him in England. *Wide World Photos*

Dick Reynolds's fortune bought yachts — but a good bit of unhappiness, too. Here, as he gasps for oxygen through a portable respirator in a Savannah courtroom, Wife Number Two divorces him. *Wide World Photos*

Backed by the show's publicity poster and sitting on a chair — the only prop she used on stage — Libby receives the press before the opening of her successful one-woman show on Broadway in 1954. *Wide World Photos*

Perhaps more handsome in her late years than as a pouty revue singer with a bee-stung mouth, Libby continued to perform off and on during the fifties and sixties with composer-pianist Gerald Cook. *Culver Pictures, Inc.*

Searchers bring down Christopher Reynolds's body after his fatal fall on Mount Whitney in 1950. His money was all Libby's now — but much of it she turned over to a memorial foundation that has helped those hurt by the war in Vietnam. *Wide World Photos*

Having been told that her son, Christopher Reynolds, is missing on Mount Whitney, Libby ducks into the cabin of a chartered plane after arriving in California from Paris. Her escort backhands one of the hectoring photographers. *International News Photo*

The critical decisions of suicide-versus-murder revolved around the position and condition of Smith Reynolds's wound, the angle of the bullet's path, and the distance of the gun from his head. John Hinckley, Jr., President Reagan's attempted assassin — in a Polaroid picture he took threatening suicide if actress Jody Foster didn't love him — showed the instinctive angle of a suicide's gun: apparently much different from the situation in the death of Reynolds. (See sketches in last chapter.) *Wide World Photos*

natural. When I asked Ab and Blanche what I did, I thought then I could remember. But finally I said to them, "There is no good telling me any more about it, when I don't remember it.' They were all natural things for me to do, though I don't remember doing them that night."

Higgins then tried to use the party as a wedge; he still thought *that* would be a hard occasion to black out. The singing. The swimming in the chilly lake. "You don't remember being at the party at all?"

She insisted she remembered nothing. Then she volunteered something quite difficult to say, but something she obviously wanted on the record. Otherwise, it certainly would have been better covered the Friday before — with no reporters present:

Mr. Higgins . . . there was another thing that worried Smith terribly, that he told me. It was on Monday night, after we had gone to bed, and it happened on Sunday too. . . . Well, he tried to have physical contact with me and he couldn't, and that worried him so much, and I tried to comfort him and told him that was all right, that it didn't make any difference to me, and he said, "No, I have read in books and doctors' statistics say that women get irritable and can't do without that, and I want you to go out and have an affair with another man." And I said, "I never would touch another man except you." Then he said, "I will have to do something to break up our marriage if you won't do that," and I said, "I couldn't ever in my life, no matter what happened to you, Smith, ever touch anyone else, and I won't." Then he said, "I will have to do something to break up and ruin our marriage," and I said, "That is a very little part of our love. The rest of our love is so big and so great that it doesn't make any difference."

If Smith was impotent . . . and if she was pregnant, as she had suggested to Higgins she might be, whose baby was she carrying?

"There were other times, Mr. Higgins, when he had said, 'You have got to leave me, because I am not making you happy; I'm changing your life.' I said, 'You're *not* changing my life; it's progress; and I will never leave you — never, never leave you unless I thought I was a failure and not making you happy.' "

Smith, she said, seemed to have a complex about happiness. He told her, "I have never had any happiness in my life, Libby — and you are a roaring success. . . . And what kills me is that I don't think I am making you happy, asking you to give up all your friends . . . insisting that we come down here and live . . . and still you say you are perfectly happy and you act it and seem it — but I don't think you are."

"If it would make you happy," she had answered him, "I would leave you if I am in your way." But he had protested that *he* wanted to be the one who would make the gesture; *he* would leave. "Libby," he told her, almost in tears, "the only way for me to make you happy is to get out of your life and you'll forget."

She seemed about to cry. Higgins, in command till then, realized that he would probably lose charge if he got a sobbing, emotional woman on his hands. He shifted his ground, probing with several seemingly abrupt and pointless questions about Libby's sleeping habits and apparel. Losing her emotion and the catch in her throat rather speedily, she volunteered that she often slept in the nude. The gentlemanly jurors squirmed again. It was perhaps an intriguing vision — a long way from the modest cotton camisoles of their own bedrooms. Perhaps Libby felt nude sleeping explained the paper chase of clothing she had left. Higgins did not; he wanted to know about the various pieces of clothing she had left in Walker's room. Libby answered guilessly; her sleeping costumes — or the lack of them — where and when she slept seemed childlike whims of the moment. She answered Higgins fliply that at Reynolda you did things "if you felt like it." She seemed pleased with the explanation.

Higgins switched back to Smith's fascination with suicide. Libby was quite positive: "I knew he had those ideas of suicide before he met me . . . and there are two little things he wrote when he was very young, if you want to see them. I asked once if he had ever wanted to commit suicide before, and he said yes — he had wanted to all his life. And now he had found happiness, and he was afraid it wouldn't last. . . ."

Libby handed Higgins several scraps of paper. He read them to the inquest — and into the record — with some embarrassment. The first paper was headed:

LAST WILL

I will my car to Ab, if he finishes it. My horse to Nancy. My money to Dick. My reputation to my sister Virginia. My good looks to Mary (she needs it).

P.S. You think I am tite, but I'm not.
P.S. Hope you don't feel hurt about this will.

The second note had been written on the back of a statement from Finchley, Clothes & Haberdashery, to Z. S. Reynolds, Woodberry Forest School, Virginia, dated June 1927. The scribble was hurried and childish:

My girl has turned me down. Good-bye forever. Give my love to Mary, Virginia, Nancy, Dick, etc. Good-bye, cruel world — Smith

If the man had not been shot dead, it might have brought smiles.

By her rambling, often painfully personal testimony, Libby had succeeded in controlling the end of the session and in ending it on what seemed like a cheap attempt at a joke; Smith's schoolboy "will" and his "suicide note" had been forced into the record — though they obviously didn't belong there. After the picture of the brooding, troubled young man she had first painted, the appearance of the two ridiculous notes seemed to mock the seriousness of the hearing.

Higgins appeared particularly put out that the notes had been brought forward.

Libby looked drained and exhausted — but also rather satisfied with her performance.

18

Killed by a Person or Persons Unknown

SLOWLY, PATIENTLY, McMichael and Higgins combed through the remaining guests at the birthday party, hoping in their testimony for some glimpse beyond the murky curtain of Libby's blackout. They all came through as considerably reluctant witnesses.

James Shepherd, the last to leave the party, reported bringing Babe Vaught back from their late-night ride "perfectly sober." Shepherd also testified that in his opinion all those who had remained at the house were also sober — with the possible exception of Walker, who Shepherd thought "probably felt what he had had during the evening." It was a typical Carolina morning-after: "I was okay. But boy, was *he* drunk!"

Charles Norfleet, with whom Jim Shepherd had gone to spend the night, would only admit to seeing "something that *looked* like liquor" served at the party, along with some beer and "a tub of home brew." His description of the evening sounded like a continual drifting of people in and out of the woods and off in the cars.

The other partygoers were of little more help in clearing up the inconsistencies. That left Walker. Though in custody, Walker was not handcuffed when he was brought in by the deputies, but he seemed for the first time to have the look of a prisoner.

McMichael couldn't quite figure him out. Walker tried to present himself again only as an attentive and concerned friend of both Smith and Libby. Even according to the testimony of the sophisticated twenty-six-year-old actress, both she and her moody, introspective playboy husband had turned surprisingly often for aid or support or advice to the callow, inexperienced Walker. Yet he seemed to have so little to recommend him in either role.

First, McMichael needed to know more about the period when Mrs. Reynolds was presumably "lost" in the woods. Was Walker sure about that?

"You didn't know, though, Mr. Walker, but that she might have come to the house?"

Walker said he had checked with Smith on that, and Libby wasn't with Smith either.

"Did you ask Smith where she was?"

"No. As I said, there were guests around, I didn't know whether it might be embarrassing to him or not."

"But you hadn't seen anything embarrassing, so why should he be embarrassed?"

"Mrs. Reynolds was tight, Mr. McMichael. I didn't know whether she had passed out or something. Another thing, when I called Smith back I intended to straighten things out about me and Mrs. Reynolds. But he said something about it first."

"Where did Smith say she was?"

"He said, 'I don't know where she is; probably running around in the woods tight or something.' "

All of Walker's protestations that Mrs. Reynolds was not a heavy drinker were going for little credence when Walker turned around and testified that Smith talked as if she were pretty regular about it.

Then McMichael turned to the incident in Libby's room at the hospital. It was strange conduct, and the nurses had been very vivid about it. Maybe Walker could explain?

"When you were in Mrs. Reynolds's room, did you order all the nurses to leave?"

"Mrs. Reynolds said she wanted to talk to me."

"And you told her not to talk?"

"I don't know whether I used those words or not."

"Did *you* tell Mrs. Reynolds she shouldn't say anything? Or that she should not talk?"

Walker protested that he could not remember the exact words.

McMichael's voice turned hard, threatening: "Do you swear that you didn't use the words, 'don't talk'?" McMichael's attack was a surprise. Everything else had been conducted at such a moderate key. Several of the jurymen sat up sharply.

Walker sat up too. "No, sir. I won't *swear* to that."

"If you did use the words 'don't talk,' what did you mean?"

"She was telling everybody, repeating that Smith would often hold a gun to his head, and I didn't see any use for everybody in the hospital to be hearing this story."

"This is the reason you asked the nurse to leave?"

"Yes, sir."

Under repeated questioning, Walker was again vague and conflicting about the incident in Libby's room. He pleaded a fainting spell and said he could remember very little about it.

"What did you tell them at the hospital you had to come back over to Reynolda for?"

"I just wanted to get the bottles and glasses cleaned up. I thought Smith had shot himself. And I didn't think anything different until this inquest."

"You didn't have any bottles in your own room, did you, Mr. Walker?"

"No, sir."

"Why did you tell Mr. Lasater you wanted to get here before the police searched your room?"

McMichael was getting heated up.

And Walker was getting feisty.

"I don't remember, Mr. McMichael. Whatever I told him was an excuse to go back and clean up the glasses and things in the house."

"You didn't know where the pistol was?"

"No, sir."

"Did you ask Mrs. Reynolds where the pistol was?"

"No, sir."

"And you still insist that you never saw a pistol on the sleeping porch?"

Walker insisted he had not. McMichael attacked him on that point from several directions. Walker stood firm. He had never seen any pistol. Actually, if Walker had missed it when he first rushed into the room, that would have been understandable; there was Smith with a hole in the back of his skull and blood oozing out. . . . Then if Fulcher had found a pistol on *his* first calm search of the room, no more would have been thought about it. But when nothing was found by Fulcher or the others until the search at daylight — the suspicion had to land on Walker.

"Mr. Walker, after you had returned to Reynolda from the hospital to change your clothes, did Mr. Barnes ask you or tell you that it was strange they couldn't find the pistol?"

"I think so."

"Did you tell him the pistol was up in the room?"

"Yes, sir. I think so."

"Why did you tell him it was up in the room?"

"I meant purely by my answer that I hadn't moved the gun."

"Why didn't you tell him you didn't know whether or not the pistol was there? And why did you tell him it was up there in the room?"

"I don't know, sir. I just don't know."

If Walker was naive, he was also very firm.

He ignored his contradictions. The prosecutors knew instinctively he would make a poor witness. Hard for a jury to evaluate. Hard to tell honest confusion from artful evasion.

McMichael was almost finished. But he wanted to impress the jurymen with Walker's evasiveness about a couple of more questions.

"Did you make a statement that whatever happened, there was some secret about this matter you intended to take to your grave?"

"Yes, sir. But I don't know why in the world I made that statement."

"Was there any secret?"

"No, sir."

"No reason on earth why you should make such a statement as that?"

"No, sir."

McMichael couldn't keep the disbelief out of his voice. "Did you make a statement to the sheriff's deputy when you were under arrest down there that you didn't care a damn what happened to you?"

Walker stammered on that one. "Well . . . yes, sir."

"Why?"

"By that I meant I was confident in my mind that it was a case of suicide — and I didn't want to see Mrs. Reynolds get in any trouble. As for myself, I knew that I would be all right." Southern code of honor.

McMichael, knowing a bit about Southern chivalry himself, certainly didn't want Walker to have any exclusive use of it. "Or did you mean that if there was anything wrong about the situation you would rather take *all* the blame for it yourself — though you stayed locked up down in that hotel room — than to have Mrs. Reynolds blamed for it?"

Walker flared back: "No, sir. I did *not* mean that. I was too good a friend of Mr. Reynolds not to see justice done. I merely made the remark, feeling confident in my mind that it was a case of suicide — that I wouldn't want to see Mrs. Reynolds get in any trouble about it."

By noon Monday, the brief inquest was over.

After a short deliberation, the coroner's jurymen returned their verdict to coroner Dalton. They rejected suicide. In their opinion, Smith Reynolds had been killed as a result of a bullet fired by "a person or persons unknown." It was terminology that legally *excluded* the unknown person from being Smith Reynolds.

19

False Clues, Confusion, and Crackpots

IF THE INQUEST had begun with a mystery, it had ended with a bigger one. The jury was going against the neat closing-the-case suicide verdict the Reynoldses seemed to want. But it was also saying that it saw no reason to hold Libby Holman Reynolds and Albert Walker as material witnesses or suspects.

The decision had one clear effect. Sheriff Scott saw it as his authorization to continue his investigation to determine the unknown person. With their decision, the jury was acknowledging for the first time officially that a murder might have occurred.

In New York, the *Times* reported the verdict as rendered, but at the same time underscored the suspicion Libby had been under:

The New York Times.

Copyright, 1932, by The New York Times Company.

* * * * +   NEW YORK, TUESDAY, JULY 12, 1932.

Coroner's Jury Holds Tobacco
Heir Died at Hands of "Party
or Parties Unknown."

MRS. REYNOLDS ON STAND

**OPEN VERDICT GIVEN
IN REYNOLDS DEATH;
WIDOW IS RELEASED**

Former Libby Holman Declares
That Husband Several Times
Had Threatened Suicide.

HIS CHUM ALSO IS FREED

In Winston-Salem the *Journal* headlined the story in its biggest type to date — and also pointed to murder:

REYNOLDS KILLER UNKNOWN

With the *Journal's* rather dogged support of the suicide theory now abandoned, it prepared to do quite a significant about-face in its coverage.

At Reynolda, lawyer Alfred Holman knew he had some breathing time — but probably not much. His daughter was wan, despondent, and seemed in poor shape to travel. But he was determined to get her out of town fast. Shortly before 3 P.M. on Tuesday, July 12, the day following the end of the inquest, one of the big black Reynolds family cars was let out through the heavy chain across the main gate at Reynolda and headed for the wonderfully rococo Norfolk and Western railroad station in Winston-Salem. Inside were Libby, Mr. and Mrs. Holman, and Libby's sister, Mrs. Myron Kahn. Libby sat in the center of the back seat between her mother and sister, clad in a black dress and — incredibly for that July day — a fur neckpiece which she could pull up to hide her face partially.

There were only a couple of photographers at the Reynolda gate. They loafed around the asphalt apron where the private drive came in off the highway, lounging on the parched grass or squatting on their haunches just outside the chain across the drive. In spite of frequent cleanups by estate employees, the debris of their profession was all about, discarded film boxes, wadded-up copy paper, old paper coffee cups and sandwich bags, crumpled cigarette packages, cigar ends. Some of their number had been on duty there for almost a week. And their presence could also be counted on to attract a few gawkers, waiting for something to happen. But the watch was small that afternoon. Word had leaked out where the car was headed, and if there was a story that day, it would center around the railroad station and the exodus of the principals from the fatal houseparty weekend. Actress Blanche Yurka and Smith Reynolds's mathematics tutor, Raymond Kramer, had left by train for New York about an hour before. Both had been hunted by reporters at train time, Kramer had marched aboard the New York train, stoutly denying that he was Kramer at all. Blanche Yurka had slipped aboard without being detected, but reporters had ferreted out the location of her drawing room and started a marathon rapping on its locked door.

"I don't want to see anyone," a voice finally responded from inside.

After some fifteen minutes of persistence, the door was cracked open.

"I'm Miss Yurka's maid," said the voice through the slight opening. "She'll be in later." It was *not* one of Blanche Yurka's most convincing performances.

By the time Libby's car arrived at the station, there were some fifteen or twenty reporters and photographers covering the entrance and the trackside. Libby seemed more composed. The fur neckpiece was down — the combined result of heat, resignation, and curiosity. And while Alfred Holman arranged for the baggage to be taken to the train, Libby watched with apparent interest from the back seat of the car. The photographers were kept at a distance by police so there was no exchange.

When the luggage was aboard, Holman tried decoying the press, running to board one of the day coaches and making his way back to their Pullman. It didn't work. Then Libby and her mother and sister climbed from the car and moved quickly through the circling back-pedaling reporters and photographers. She wouldn't answer questions but she made a half-hearted attempt to hide her face from the cameras. Her sister steered her by one arm, with her mother on the other side.

"It's all right. It's all right," her sister kept saying. "Don't worry, darling. It's all right. It takes courage."

It was a long, glaringly public walk through the near-empty station and out through the trainshed. The conductors at the gate were plodding, slow, and officious while examining the tickets to pass them through. Everyone wanted a role. When the door of the Pullman drawing room finally closed behind them, however, they were far from alone. Half a dozen reporters had also booked space on the same train and would ride it all the way to Cincinnati in hopes of getting a glimpse or a statement.

Albert Walker didn't have any distant sanctuary to retreat to. He was holed up at his parents' home on Country Club Road, severely shaken by the whole steamrolling performance.

Back at the courthouse, a handful of newsmen waited for a regular grand jury session to break up; they were sure there would be an announcement of how that panel planned to pursue the Reynolds case.

They were due for a disappointment. The grand jury finally emerged sweating, wilted, and impatient. The foreman said they had heard *no* evidence in the death of Smith Reynolds!

The succeeding grand jury would not meet until July 25. And while it was made clear that the way was still open for the case to be considered by that succeeding grand jury, there seemed to be no official legal opinion that it would be.

With the cast of characters now scattering, and with several members of the Reynolds family and the family advisers pressing to turn off the publicity, sheriff Scott was left with a substantial dilemma. As an elected officer of Forsyth County, he was aware of the need to respond to the needs of his constituency, both to the mass of the voters and, more importantly, to the wills of the powerful few in the community who could put men into office. Scott could not hear a single voice from those powerful men calling for a pursuit of the investigation . . . and there were several forceful whispers that perhaps he should retire gracefully from the field.

He had some practical excuses to do just that. To out-of-town reporters who had complained about the slowness of the investigation, Scott pointed out that he had only eight deputies for the investigation and for everything else his department was supposed to cover in all of Forsyth County. When something as big as the Reynolds case blew up, he had to put everyone on the big case, ignore the rest of the county, and hope for the best. Also, sheriff Scott's investigators were very short of co-operating witnesses who might help them.

City editors around the eastern seaboard and wire-service chiefs faced with the rather large expenses of keeping their top crime reporters in Winston-Salem issued a more or less general recall. Most of the newsmen left Thursday night via the Southern Railway for Washington, Baltimore, Philadelphia, and New York. The remainder left Friday morning for western points. By Friday night, July 15, nine days after the shooting, only the Winston-Salem reporters, plus a handful of stringers from other North Carolina newspapers, still worried the case.

Officially, Carlisle Higgins also seemed to be bowing out. He announced on Friday that with the delivery of the inquest verdict, he had completed his part as directing officer in the preliminary investigation. Whereupon McMichael, who had pursued the inquest testimony most aggressively, told a reporter he was "dismayed!" at his boss.

This seemed to leave sheriff Scott only McMichael for support. With everyone else seeming to be walking away, should he still pursue the case? Then a second ally emerged: the *Winston-Salem Journal*. The paper pointed out that Scott was virtually a "lone wolf" in the case. But if he chose to proceed — and the paper seemed cautiously urging him to do so — then they pointed to several alternatives. He could undertake to place the evidence before the Grand Jury himself — regardless of the county solicitor's reluctance to do so. Or if he did not wish to do that, the paper's editorial page advised him *he could request the governor of North Carolina to assign a Superior Court judge to sit in Winston-Salem as a special committing magistrate, to conduct a full probe* and be responsible directly to the governor!

This was certainly a significant alarm going off. By suggesting that a special officer might be needed to investigate the case, the *Journal* seemed to be saying that the credibility of the investigation by the "regular officer" charged with it was in jeopardy. It was a rather extreme proposal. But also Higgins's reluctance to pursue the case was, in the words of one experienced prosecutor, "quite inappropriate."

Then the paper noted that one more useful supporter was coming on the scene; the *Journal* had heard that Smith's older brother, Dick Reynolds, was on the way — and that when he arrived he would very likely push for "a full investigation."

> Winston-Salem citizens have generally manifested keen interest in the coming of the elder Reynolds, marked by the belief he will offer to assist authorities in every way possible to settle definitely whether his brother met death by his own hand or otherwise.

Reacting to the blast from the *Raleigh Times* that the whole investigation should be pushed under the rug, the *Winston-Salem Journal* strongly urged seeing the investigation one step further. Its reasons were dramatic and possibly libelous ones, slapping at coroner Dalton:

Suppose a coroner should have reason to conceal a murder? Such a question is no reflection, of course, on any particular coroner. But the records show that other public officials have been corrupt. Such corruption is by no means confined to New York and Chicago, either, although these two centers of population seem to be headquarters for such betrayals of public trust at present. . . .

Because the first testimony by the most important of the witnesses was taken in secret session, very few of the truly critical details had in fact appeared. The public, by and large, remained baffled by the cryptic references . . . to concealment . . . to betrayals of trust . . . to corrupt coroners.

Though the *Journal* had given a few words of support, the main impetus for a thorough investigation was being left to two men, neither of whom was very well qualified to push it through: to Scott, short of training, short on professional help, and clearly running into some high-powered resistance against his continuing . . . and to young Dick Reynolds, who had more of a reputation for accomplishing the bizarre and the unexpected rich-boy's trick, than for the somber task the *Winston-Salem Journal* seemed to have assigned to him.

Dick Reynolds's earlier press had not been all that good. Because he was a rich man's oldest son, almost everything he did had been a tempting target for some criticism. Dick Reynolds had been in some abortive but spectacular business and real estate adventures. And in 1927 he had caused something of a two-week sensation on the front pages of the nation's newspapers by "disappearing." At first, the family feared kidnapping. But he was found twelve days later outside a St. Louis chop-suey joint . . . and after heavy but polite police questioning, he insisted that he had simply "needed a vacation." In 1929, he had popped up in the papers again, sentenced in England to five months in jail for manslaughter after a motorcyclist was killed in an accident in which he was involved.

Now the wire service bulletins daily chattered into the *Journal*'s teleprinters from the west coast of Africa and from South America, tracing Dick Reynolds's hurried return to Winston-Salem. Keeping pace with the bulletins from abroad came the rumors from home. And each one gave rise to more questions and confusion. Raymond Kramer, the mathematics tutor, interviewed by New York reporters on arriving home, said that Smith had several times expressed a fear of kidnapping. Kramer indicated that he thought this fear was what had gone through Smith's mind again on the night of his death when the mysterious car had been sighted on the grounds of the estate. Maybe his death had something to do with a kidnapping attempt, Kramer speculated. A rumor was also circulating in Winston-Salem just then about a man in another mysterious car who had stopped at several points near the estate asking directions for "a back way" into Reynolda. New leads to be checked out. But Scott's tiny department was having trouble enough trying to check out everything that had existed before.

Libby broke silence in Cincinnati to say that she had asked that Smith's uncle, W. N. Reynolds, be appointed executor rather than she. Libby had thirty days after Smith's death to apply for a letter of consent to act as executor; she was declining. She said she would never again return to Reynolda except to visit her husband's grave. She said now she realized early in the marriage that Smith intended to take his own life. Then she got on record with Cincinnati reporters the dramatic incident on the liner returning home from the Orient, when Smith had appeared with pistol in hand, saying he was going to kill himself. The reporters scribbled delightedly as she told them of the tearful scene in which she finally grabbed the hand that held the gun, directed it toward her breast and announced to Smith that if he was going to kill himself, he would have to kill her too. But she became annoyed and ended the

THE RALEIGH TIMES

TWELVE PAGES   RALEIGH, N. C., THURSDAY, JULY 14, 1932.   MARKET EDITION

Sheriff Adds To Evidence In Reynolds Case

interview when one of the reporters asked why — if the danger signal had made such an awful impression on her at the time — she had said no more about it to anyone. Why hadn't she tried to get Smith some help? Why hadn't she wondered about what might come next?

In Winston, Scott told reporters how the whole complicated and technical business about the trajectory of the bullet, the position of Smith Reynolds when it was fired, and the position of bloodstains in the room continued to trouble him. He announced that a section of what appeared to be a bullet-nicked doorjamb to the sleeping-porch room would be taken down to his office "for study." It was a move that made a lot of people curious. Just what did Scott know? What was he after?

In additon to the other demands on the harassed sheriff, the screwball letters and calls were beginning to roll in. Some could obviously be ignored. But a few seemed at first to hold promise. Billy Shaw Howell, the raffish Charlotte radio salesman who had been at the party, had something on his mind; now, a week and a half after the shooting, he wanted to come forward to say that the mysterious stranger asking directions for "a back way" to Reynolda might have been him. Scott was understandably angry that Howell had waited so long to come forward. Checking up on that useless "clue" had taken valuable time in the investigation.

A couple of private investigators with no distinctive credentials called to say they would be glad to take over the whole investigation if all expenses were paid. And an astrologer, who claimed to have solved much more difficult cases, informed Scott — and all the papers that would listen — that he had gone into a trance to see if he couldn't straighten things out, whereupon he had conjured up a mysterious black car with New York or New Jersey plates, had seen it drive up to Reynolda, had seen a man alight, shoot Smith Reynolds, and depart. The Lindbergh kidnapping case, then heavily in the news, was not getting all the nuts; the second-stringers and minor leaguers were happily spilling over to torment Scott and the Reynolds family.

Still, he never knew when a *good* lead might come. There was a brief flurry of excitement in the Forsyth County sheriff's office when an authoritative call was received from a Captain Gene Maisie of the New York City Police Department saying that he had personal knowledge of a plot the previous year by a group of New York gangsters "to come to Winston-Salem and put Smith Reynolds on the spot." Scott had not been in the office when the call came and the caller would say no more to subordinates. But when the sheriff tried to get "Captain Maisie" at the New York number he had left, there turned out to be no such number — nor had the New York City Police Department ever heard of Captain Maisie.

But the sheriff was determined to continue. "From the evidence that has come into my hands, I am of the opinion still that Smith did *not* shoot himself. This is still a legally unsolved mystery." He was like a patient old schoolteacher lecturing his class of reporters on why he wouldn't let go: "The coroner's jury failed to find that Smith Reynolds killed himself," Scott told them, "but did say in their verdict that he met his death at the hands of a party or parties unknown. It therefore becomes my duty by virtue of the office I hold to ascertain if possible the party or parties who caused his death." He hoped to have something significant soon. On Monday, July 25, almost three weeks after the fatal party, the next grand jury was to meet in the Forsyth County Courthouse.

The courthouse skeptics were betting that Scott wouldn't get the case before a new grand jury either. The Forsyth courthouse dominated the square on which it sat. Half a dozen main Winston-Salem streets led into the square. North and south, impressive steps led up to the first floor, where the preliminaries of the court were conducted. Several ample courtrooms occupied the second floor. The sheriff's department was on the first floor. The jail occupied the basement. Reporters exchanging rumors on the graceful steps of the building, after talking with Scott, could survey a good bit of downtown Winston-Salem from their vantage point — except across the corner to the northeast, where the view was blocked by a towering office building that gave the impression that it was going to topple down on the courthouse, the judge, the juries, the investigators if anyone did anything wrong. That tower, symbolically enough, was headquarters of the R. J. Reynolds Tobacco Company. And to a lot of powerful men comfortably housed inside of it, Forsyth sheriff Transou Scott was doing far too many things wrong.

Out at Reynolda, the curious in their cars still cruised up and down Reynolda Road outside the estate, trying to peer through the thick shrubbery and the tall trees around the house. And while they could glimpse something of the west wing of the house from time to time through the thinning, sun-parched foliage when they slowed down, the honking of cars behind them and the rough commands of the patrolmen would promptly push them ahead again. Occasionally someone could be seen dimly moving on one of the porches. The heat pressed down like a heavy hand. But there wouldn't be any more cool barbecues down by the lake.

20

"This Is a Frame-up"

LIKE ANY GOOD LAWYER preparing for a trial, Alfred Holman got ready for that possibility by not only working through the details of all he wanted to present in favor of his "client," but also by trying to drag up before himself all the damaging questions he thought his opposition might throw at him.

At that point, Holman was having to act in a strange, dual role of both father and counselor. At the quasijudicial inquest, no lawyer was allowed for Libby. She had appeared as a witness only. No charge had ever been leveled against her. As soon as she was released from her "material witness" status, her lawyer father had been smart enough to spirit her far from further questioning. And yet as Holman read sheriff Scott's almost daily declarations that the case was still unsolved and that it was his duty to solve it, Holman knew there was probably a good chance North Carolina authorities would be after his daughter again soon. The innuendo of suspicion was continually returning to Walker and to Libby.

Speculation and the manufactured rumors were some of the things worrying Holman. Actually, a good Winston-Salem reporter shouldn't have had to "manufacture" much of anything; there were so many legitimate leads that needed running down, all a man had to do was dig a little. But what was strangely absent was the sort of sound investigative reporting that laid down in logical order the unanswered questions and tried to find an answer for them. Some of the questions that a good reporter familiar with the case might have laid out to Scott or McMichael, or Higgins before the second grand jury went into session on July 25 were these:

1. Did Smith Reynolds's fatal wound show that the gun had been against the head when it was fired, as Reynolds himself might have done . . . or was it held some distance away, as an attacker might have held it? Dr. Hanes's testimony on that was unclear.

2. Was it possible for Smith to shoot himself at the angle in which the bullet passed through his head?

3. Were there fingerprints on the gun? And was it definitely Smith's gun?

4. If the gun that shot Smith was Smith's, what had happened to Walker's German Luger, kept in his bedside table?

5. Who besides Walker had access to the sleeping porch during the period when the gun that shot Smith was missing?

6. How could Walker and Libby explain the time that had elapsed between when Fulcher had heard what was probably the fatal shot and when Walker and Libby left for the hospital?

7. Was there any possible medical explanation for Libby's convenient blackout?

8. How authentic were the claims of Libby that Smith had said several times that (a) he feared for his life and (b) that he might even take his own life? If they were authentic, why was no attempt made to guard him from the first eventuality or dissuade him from the second?

9. If Smith had become impotent, as Libby stated at the inquest, was it Smith's baby she was carrying?

As Alfred Holman played out his role of devil's advocate in his own daughter's case, he probably asked himself all the same questions and more. And then tried to wonder how the answers might backfire against Libby. But rather than defensively waiting for some of the backfires, Holman decided to fire off an offensive salvo himself, to put the State of North Carolina on its guard.

On Sunday, July 24, the day before the new Forsyth County grand jury was scheduled to meet, Holman had drafted a lengthy telegram to the Forsyth County district attorney's office and simultaneously released a copy of it to the Cincinnati papers. It said in part:

IF THE STATE OF NORTH CAROLINA THROUGH SUCH FUNCTION-
ARIES IGNORES THE OBVIOUS PROOF OF REYNOLDS' SELF-DESTRUC-
TION, SEEKING NOW TO OVERCOME IT BY GARBLED HUMAN TESTI-
MONY, WHICH WAS DICTATED BY THE STATE COUNSEL BEFORE THE
CORONER'S JURY WITH NO RIGHT ACCORDED TO COUNSEL FOR THE
INVOLVED PARTIES TO CROSS-EXAMINE DESPITE WHICH THAT JURY
BY ITS VERDICT STILL PRIMARILY HELD THAT IT WAS SELF-DESTRUC-
TION, THOUGH CONFUSED BY EX-PARTE EVIDENCE WHICH NECES-
SARILY PROMPTED THE VERDICT THAT WAS RENDERED, THEN THE
GREAT STATE IS GUILTY OF AN INJUSTICE EQUALED ONLY BY THAT
OF ANCIENT TIMES AND THE BARBAROUS MIDDLE AGES.

It was not as much bombast as it might seem at this distance. North
Carolina was old, sensitive, proud — and its history for justice gave it
some reason for that pride. It did not care to be related to the "Middle
Ages" in any way. Regardless of what the law said about the rules of a
coroner's jury — and Holman sure knew the law — he was planting the
idea in the papers that McMichael and Higgins were stacking the cards
against his daughter — "dictating" all that "garbled human testimony."
The reference to "ancient times" and "the Middle Ages" was so odd, it
clearly made most readers stop to think. And for many of them, the
issue of Libby being "a Jewess" fitted Holman's complaint. Holman
meant for them to think about the age-old persecutions of Jews. The
twentieth-century South didn't have such a good reputation on that
score. Particularly some states. And proud North Carolina winced at
being lumped with them. Holman had struck a nerve.

Holman promised to produce Libby at any time North Carolina authorities had a reasonable need for her presence. But in the interim,
Holman told reporters, Libby had gone into seclusion to escape the
"morbidly curious . . . and to recover her sanity and health . . . overcome by grief over the loss of a loved one and by the horrors to which
she had been subjected in an inquisition equaled only to those of the
Middle Ages." North Carolinians winced again at his coupling of their
state with the Middle Ages.

Holman's telegram from Cincinnati hit the papers on July 25, as the
new grand jury arrived to be sworn in by Judge Stack, who cryptically
warned the new jurors (without mentioning any particular case) of "the

difficulty of convicting wealthy people" in the State of North Carolina. Just who did he have in mind? Walker, son of a land-rich estate speculator?

Neither sheriff Scott nor Higgins would comment. Higgins also emphasized that the grand jury had quite a bit of old business to accomplish before it could take up "anything new."

But by Wednesday, August 3, with the old business apparently out of the way, Scott was called before that body for two and a half hours. Then word leaked out from the grand jury room that Stewart Warnken, who had been the first man to arrive at Reynolda after Fulcher gave the alarm, had urgently been requested to supply the grand jury with a detailed drawing of the sleeping porch and the adjoining bedroom and its bathroom. Warnken was on the way down. The grand jury was finally *listening.* Before the session was over, the grand jury had heard testimony from Warnken, Wharton, and Barnes — all three of whom had been called to Reynolda that night — and from Fulcher and Dr. Hanes.

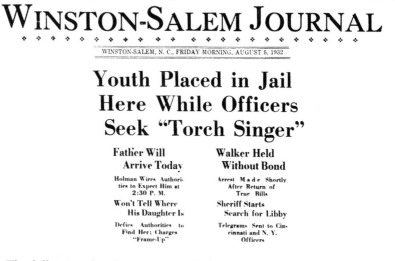

WINSTON-SALEM JOURNAL

❖ ❖

WINSTON-SALEM, N. C., FRIDAY MORNING, AUGUST 5, 1932

Youth Placed in Jail Here While Officers Seek "Torch Singer"

Father Will Arrive Today

Holman Wires Authorities to Expect Him at 2:30 P. M.

Won't Tell Where His Daughter Is

Defies Authorities to Find Her; Charges "Frame-Up"

Walker Held Without Bond

Arrest Made Shortly After Return of True Bills

Sheriff Starts Search for Libby

Telegrams Sent to Cincinnati and N. Y. Officers

The following day the secrecy ended. At 3:50 P.M. before Judge Stack, a grand jury indictment was entered, which stated that "on or about the 6th day of July 1932 Elilzabeth Holman and Albert Walker with force of arms ... did unlawfully, willfully, feloniously, premeditatedly of their malice or forethought wound and murder Z. Smith Reynolds." The defendants were to be arrested and *held without bail* for the next term of the criminal court, which would convene on October 3, unless the governor requested an earlier date! Shortly after four on that sultry afternoon, to the echo of a thunderstorm that was clearing away to the east, warrants were issued to bring in Libby and Walker for first-degree murder.

One hour and twenty-five minutes later Albert Walker was taken into custody at the family home on Country Club Road. But he had had enough warning to get in touch with a lawyer, Bailey B. Liipfert. Liipfert had clout. He also occupied the not-easily-ignored office of chairman of the Forsyth County Democratic executive committee. Liipfert was with Walker when the officers arrived, and he accompanied Walker to the Forsyth County jail. Scott had sent telegrams to the police of New York City and Cincinnati, citing the particulars of the indictment and the warrant calling for the arrest of Libby Holman.

But first they'd have to find her. Reporters reached Alfred Holman at Libby's sister's home in Wyoming, Ohio, a Cincinnati suburb. Libby, he said, was not going to be available for arrest. "Libby Holman told the truth at the investigation in Winston-Salem. She can prove every word she said. I am still my daughter's attorney. This in itself proclaims her innocence of any crime. The first thing a person guilty of such a heinous crime would have done would have been to engage prominent attorneys. She made no move at any time to do such a thing. She had no need to. Another point which proclaims her innocence is that she asked a member of the Reynolds family to act as executor of the estate. This is a frame-up and a terrible injustice to an innocent young woman."

Then Holman booked a Pullman to Winston-Salem to fight in person.

The word that had leaked out to Holman, warning him that his daughter would be indicted and would be arrested, had also leaked other details elsewhere. Several reporters had discovered that the earlier grand jury, after hearing the evidence of the July 11 coroner's inquest at Reynolda, had prepared a "sealed presentment" of first-degree murder way back at that point! (This was, of course, directly contrary to what the grand jury spokesman had said at the time: "No evidence about the Reynolds case was examined.") The presentment had been held in secret by the clerk of the superior court until the July 25 grand jury was sworn in. The buck had been passed as long as possible. Now the Forsyth County authorities had the most celebrated murder case in county history to deal with.*

* The "sealed presentment" was another confusing procedure in the case. And once again, because of the general disappearance of records, it is not clear what this presentment recorded. A former New York prosecutor could only speculate on it in terms of what its use would be in his city: "The North Carolina version remains a mystery to me. Indictments and other charges such as presentments (in New York, the latter are not formal charges, but rather the jury's determination that the facts presented require official corrective action of one sort or another) may be sealed in order to protect a strategic or security advantage. In the Reynolds case, none of this seemed to be applicable. People were not about to flee, witnesses were not about to be silenced or intimidated — or at least it does not appear to be so. The notion of one grand jury's sealed presentment being passed to a second grand jury is unknown to me. I believe that a sealed presentment or a sealed indictment may be activated by simply going back to the jury who voted and asking them to unseal their findings." Yet it was the second grand jury that heard full evidence and brought in an indictment. Whatever the sealed presentment said, however, it obviously made the point that some outrageous problems had been found, and they should be looked into. It had been a forceful statement when a lot of people preferred to look the other way.

21

"You Think My Daughter
Didn't Shoot Him . . ."

ALFRED HOLMAN'S TRAIN from Cincinnati pulled into Winston-Salem
early on the afternoon of Friday, August 5. It was almost a month since
the fatal shooting. Immediately after checking into his hotel, Holman
headed for the Forsyth County Courthouse. Holman looked haggard
and gaunt as he told reporters gathered on the courthouse steps that he
felt every one of his sixty-five years that day. He said the case was af-
fecting his health and the health of everyone in the family. Libby, for
the record, was "unavailable" as much to guard her health as anything
else. What Libby needed now, Holman said, was an accomplished
criminal lawyer. Then he went off to find that man.

As an outsider, Holman needed the best local knowledge he could
get. He went directly to the one lawyer who one day might have to ask
to have Libby sent to her execution — Carlisle Higgins.

It was a strange interview. After the brief formalities of meeting
again, Holman pulled a crumpled list of names from the pocket of his
coat. The names were those of various North Carolina criminal lawyers.
He wanted Higgins's advice on them. Holman was not concerned about
Higgins's surprise; he was fighting for his daughter's life, and a little
advice out of the Carolina "old boys' network" might be critical. Holman was entitled to advice from the most "educated" people he could
find. And "old boy" Higgins was it.

"What do you think of Kollipop?" Holman had then asked. Higgins
quickly decided Holman could only be referring to Bennet Polikoff, a

bright young lawyer who had handled several assignments for Higgins. Higgins could certainly state these facts about Polikoff. They were, after all, points of record.

"That answers my question," said Holman. He left.

It turned out that Polikoff was already pushing for the case. Polikoff was married to a Cleveland girl. Her family knew the Holmans. They had recommended Polikoff. He had volunteered to help.

After leaving Higgins, Holman had gone to Polikoff's office, a short distance away. He was soon back at Higgins's office.

"Polikoff says he needs Graves [William Graves, an accomplished Winston-Salem criminal lawyer]. What do you think of him?" asked Holman.

Higgins thought pretty highly of Graves, as a matter of fact. "When I was stumping six counties to get this job," he told Holman, "he was my campaign manager. And a damn good one." Though he couldn't say it, Higgins considered Graves the best criminal lawyer in Winston-Salem. Now Higgins was likely to be facing his old friend across the court.

Then Holman came up with a complete surprise; it was utterly improper. In fact, it came perilously close to being a bribe. Was it Holman's idea . . . or Polikoff's? Both of them knew better. But Holman was prepared to take any risk for his daughter.

"Mr. Higgins," Holman said, "I think *you* think my daughter didn't shoot him. Lots of others think otherwise. Would you resign and take the case?"

Since Holman was himself an experienced lawyer, he would have known exactly what was involved with his proposal. Had Higgins accepted, aside from the legal and ethical questions it would have raised, the decision would certainly have meant the end of Higgins's career as an elected official. But the fee prospects were obvious; when the case was over, some really big money might be paid to the man who could prevent the painful indignity of Smith Reynolds's widow being convicted of murder.

Higgins's refusal was polite. He said he must stick by his duties as chief prosecuting officer of Forsyth County. Holman shrugged off Higgins's refusal. He went directly to the office of William Graves. The two men were closeted for more than an hour. When Holman emerged a short time later and headed back to the courthouse, it was in the company of Graves, the brash, confident Bennet Polikoff, and a cluster of reporters.

They made an interesting team. Graves was obviously the old, gray fox, Polikoff the young lion. What made Polikoff's entry into the case even more interesting was the fact that he and McMichael, sometime partners, could probably predict each other's tactics.

On the short walk to court, Graves and Polikoff had made it clear to the reporters circling in full bay around them that Holman was not necessarily trying to defy North Carolina law in refusing to produce Libby Holman Reynolds. He was simply trying to protect his ill and fragile daughter. Then the three entered the big courtroom on the second floor and sat patiently waiting for a chance to discuss the question of bond with Judge Stack.

It was a futile wait. Judge Stack finished the day's proceedings without making himself available to the three men. He did, however, sign a petition presented by Albert Walker's lawyer on a writ of habeas corpus that called for a hearing to see if Walker was eligible for bail. Walker now sat in the jail a floor below. He was clearly shaken by everything that had happened so suddenly. But he was also calmed a bit by having his meals sent in from a hotel down the street, and his lawyer had assured Walker he wouldn't be in jail for long.

As Graves and Polikoff left the court, they said they were encouraged; if any bail was granted for Walker — which seemed likely — it was probable that Libby would be eligible for bail, provided that they could assure the court she wasn't going to disappear again once she was out on it. Holman also had a last word for reporters; he implied that officials in Cincinnati were not really pressing the search for his daughter in response to sheriff Scott's telegram; the implication was that Cincinnati officials also felt Libby was clearly innocent. "If I had any thought whatsoever that she had anything to do with the slaying of this boy," Holman said, "I would, with tears in my eyes, be the first to ask that she be punished."

Sheriff Scott had widened his hunt for Libby in the meantime. When Ohio deputies had gone to the home of Libby's sister, they had learned that Libby had left in the company of an old friend, Louisa Jenney from

Montchanin, Delaware, who had driven hurriedly to Ohio just before Libby disappeared. Scott then asked authorities in Newcastle County, Delaware, to check out the Jenney home in Montchanin.

A man there who identified himself as the chauffeur would say only that Mrs. Jenney was not home and Miss Holman was not there "now." The ladies were on the run. Louisa Jenney was rumored to be sheltering Libby on her yacht. Louisa could bring it off. She was a niece of Pierre du Pont and married to John King Jenney, a major Du Pont executive. But Scott was ready to send a deputy and, in deference to decorum, his female secretary to bring Libby in when she was found.

"Bringing Libby in" was a prerequisite to anything else that might happen, because McMichael assured reporters that there was no possibility of bond for Libby *unless she appeared in court personally for the arguments in regard to bond.* If McMichael was certain of the legalities of that aspect of the proceedings, Higgins was vague on another point: the stiffness of the bond — or the question of whether there would even *be* a bond. He indicated that might depend on the severity of the charge the state would try to prove against Walker and Libby. Higgins said he wasn't at all sure now whether he was going for first-degree murder . . . or for a "lesser charge" . . . since he "wasn't sufficiently acquainted with the evidence." For a case that had been the major topic of conversation along most of the eastern seaboard for the past thirty days, this had to be a surprising statement by the prosecutor who was going to have to try the case!

On Saturday Judge Stack was finally prepared to hear the arguments. The court was a wide, shallow room. Attorneys and the spectators looked to the east at the judge — and into a blinding morning sun, with George Washington and Andrew Jackson, a native son of North Carolina, surveying the assembly from the wall behind Stack.

Dapper Bailey Liipfert began his arguments for Walker. He was pressing the state to admit that in light of the "meager evidence," Walker should be considered *no more* than "an accessory after the fact." An accessory was clearly bailable status and would call for relatively low bail. In addition, Liipfert argued that while Walker's father was considered a wealthy man, his holdings were largely in real estate and he was cash-poor. The bail should be low. The implication then charmingly went that since they were all Carolina gentlemen, there was no reason to believe that Walker had any intention of fleeing the scene — regardless of the severity of the charge or the modestness of the bail. Judge Stack looked to Higgins for the state's reaction.

Higgins took his time, uncoiling leisurely. They might all be Carolina gentlemen together, but he was also a vote-getter and an officeholder. And careful. He could be vulnerable some November-to-come on charges of favoritism to the rich. There was a whispered conversation with Scott over the wooden rail separating spectators from court officials. Higgins had a problem; if he asked for no bail or the very large amount that a first-degree indictment could call for (rather than the lower amount that would be sufficient for "an accessory after the fact"), he might have to give some indication of the evidence the state held to support such a severe indictment. That was not desirable. He turned toward the bench and announced to Judge Stack that as far as *"this* defendant" [Walker] was concerned, the state considered the offense to be bailable. His elaboration was a slap at Libby, implying that while he considered Carolina gentleman Walker a good risk to turn up later for trial, he might not be so sure of the out-of-state lady. Then he cautioned Libby's attorneys that regardless of any assumptions they might choose to make, the state's acquiescence to Walker's bail was no precedent for the way in which the state might choose to approach the case of Mrs. Reynolds. The distinction was clear to North Carolinians. Higgins promised, however, that if she would give herself up, the state would look with favor on a resolution already made by the North Carolina Bar Association calling for a special trial term of the court to meet on September 5, less than a month away. This would at least bring the issue to a head sooner.

Judge Stack nodded and ruled. Albert Walker could be freed on a $25,000 bond signed by his father. Holman could now hope that if his daughter turned herself in, she could likely be kept out of jail for some bail — even a higher one. But she also seemed to be moving up to prime suspect. Walker was fading. The principals waited respectfully as Stack tucked up his robes like a dowager and stomped to his chambers — then they moved to the traditional forum of the steps outside and the waiting reporters.

"What about Sam Leibowitz?" was one of the first shouted queries. The controversial New York criminal lawyer, who had made a national reputation in his courageous defense of the "Scottsboro Boys" in an ominous antiblack, anti-Semitic Alabama rape case, had flown to North Carolina and had been met at the airport by one of Polikoff's employees. Leibowitz wasn't talking. Finally, under repeated prodding, Polikoff said the New York attorney was having no part in the case, although he had been asked by several of Libby's Broadway friends to "look the situation over" on his way to Atlanta to see his client Al Capone in the federal penitentiary. In spite of Leibowitz's fame and reputation, his representation of Mr. Al Capone was not a highly desirable association for Libby at that point. Holman glared at Polikoff.

"Where's Mrs. Reynolds?" the shouts came now. "Is she coming in?" "We heard she's in Cuba." "Or Mexico!"

Holman held up his hands for quiet. "We are making every effort to get her in shape to give herself up. That's all, gentlemen."

Somewhere in hiding Libby heard each bulletin in turn and waited for the telephone call from her father that would tell her what she should do next.

22

"Let's See What This Libby Woman Looks Like"

THE LITTLE TOWN of Wentworth, North Carolina, lies in pleasantly roll-ing country about thirty miles northeast of Winston-Salem. It is the county seat of Rockingham County and is proud of its tradition. Driv-ing up to Wentworth from Winston, you move through progressively richer looking country — from the slightly rolling, occasionally pine-studded terrain around the tobacco city, north through productive farmland that follows the easy contour of the ground.

Most of the land is under cultivation. But along the shoulders of the road and in the occasional cuts through hills that intrude, you see the bright rust-buff of raw North Carolina clay. It looks as if it would make great bricks — but would hardly grow a peanut. And yet the prosperity of the farms on either side of the highway belies this. The farms are not big, showy spreads such as you might pass in Iowa or Ohio, taking off almost as far as the eye can see. But they are neat, tight places, with every inch under cultivation. Tidy brick or frame houses sit along the road, with a couple of outbuildings behind, well repaired but usually not recently painted. Worn farm machinery, looking well-loved and in good repair, stands in the rear yards. And there are swings hung from the trees in the front.

The look of the farm layouts seems to say that their owners are quiet, respectable, churchgoing people and knowledgeable farmers. The names are a strange combination of the short, sharp, monosyllabic names emblematic of this part of the South — Cates, Chick, Huff, Gow,

Cobb, Mabe — and those others that roll off the tongue with memories of the British Isles — MacFarland, McLaren, Campbell, Simms, Saunders, Collins, Darby, Fitzgerald.

On a stout wooden post by most of the front driveways is the round galvanized tube that accepts the *Winston-Salem Journal*, delivered suitably early every morning for these early risers by an old man and a boy out of Wentworth in a Chevrolet flivver. It is easy to imagine the disapproval of such quiet, productive country people as they read each morning in the summer of 1932 of the antics of the Holmans and the Reynoldses and the Walkers down in Winston: "All-night parties. Midnight swimming. All that likker. And the women, Mother, probably wearing God-knows what . . . or God knows *nothing.*"

As you approach Wentworth, off to the northwest you can see the Blue Ridge Mountains rising smokily and invitingly on the skyline. You are nearing the Virginia line, and the best farming country will give out soon in favor of rough hill terrain. Wentworth comes at you around the corner of a road with something of a surprise. By the time you have braked and slowed, you are almost in front of the Rockingham County Courthouse, an impressive but somewhat severe and architecturally nondescript red brick building with white stone trim. In another twenty years its time for appreciation — and preservation — will come. It sits slightly skewed to the highway and only twenty feet or so off to the east of the road. It was clearly built when an older road went by — and to dominate its site on top of a slight rise.

Unlike the courthouse and courthouse squares in so many Southern towns, it does not attempt a Grecian look. It is pure North Carolina, circa 1880 — and proud of it. No statue of a Confederate soldier guards the front lawn — or what is left of a lawn after the deputies' cars are parked. North Carolinians are strangely modest about their Civil War distinctions. One out of four soldiers killed at Gettysburg was from a North Carolina regiment. And several bloody fights in that terrible war took place within a couple of hundred miles of Wentworth. But almost universally through the state, the clashes of the war and North Carolina's contributions to it are underplayed. It is as if there had been a slightly sad event within a family that had turned out not quite to fulfill the grand design planned for it; nothing you are ashamed of, mind you — but nothing to dwell on for too long, either; just gather yourself together and move on to the next thing.

In early August of 1932, the judge and prosecutors responsible for "riding circuit" — and so for affairs in Rockingham County as part of their circuit — were holding sessions in Wentworth. Judge Stack sat in the court. The cases were the routine ones you might expect in that county and in that time. A large number of them had to do with non-compliance to the novel North Carolina alcohol control regulations. But the biggest story on the morning of August 8, 1932 — in spite of the fact that there had been some attempt to keep it hushed up in Winston — was that Libby Holman Reynolds was going to be turning herself in sometime that day in this small market town.

In the course of any year in Wentworth, there are not many events that assume the dimensions of "news stories." Maybe two first-class fires a year that would take down a good-sized tobacco barn; once they started in the old unpainted barns, usually far from any firefighting equipment and well dried out by years of use, they could be fires of a spirit that even a big-city fire buff would admire. Then every five or six years there might be a cutting or a shooting that resulted in death; but often it was the death of somebody "who got what was coming to him." God's justice. Then there were the fights, largely fierce, but also largely brief family or interfamily affairs with lots of salubrious making up after they were over. And finally there was the eternal moonshining; that was never much of a surprise because everybody in the county, including the sheriff, usually knew who was doing it from the beginning.

The last legitimate theater in Rockingham County had been seen sometime around the turn of the century when a touring company on a misdirected cultural missionary tour through North Carolina hit Wentworth. And very few people could recall ever seeing "an actress" — much less one accused of doing in her husband.

As a matter of fact, nobody could be absolutely *sure* Libby would really come. But certainly hope of her arrival was a most appealing rumor and a welcome change from the weekly routine. Alfred Holman had been down in Winston-Salem for several days, conferring with lawyers Graves and Polikoff. Polikoff had made it known that he had a prisoner habeas corpus petition ready for a hearing if Libby were arrested elsewhere before she could turn herself in. This would force the state to produce Libby in court and would force a hearing on whether or not it was lawful to hold her without bail. Since Polikoff's habeas corpus request could legally be heard before *any* judge in North Carolina, there was some reason to believe that if Libby turned herself in, she should do it far from Wentworth. A hearing might go more rapidly elsewhere, with less chance of miscarrying or turning into a show.

On the day before — Sunday, August 7 — Holman had appeared to answer questions in front of the Robert E. Lee Hotel in Winston after a long conference with lawyers Polikoff and Graves. He seemed to reporters more rested and affable than he had been when he had arrived on the Friday afternoon train. He said he thought it reasonable that his daughter might appear "in the state" sometime early in the week. She had nothing to hide; it was simply that he did not want her, in her pregnant condition, to suffer confinement in a North Carolina jail.

Monday morning was hot and close almost the minute the cooling early morning fog burned off the tobacco fields around Wentworth. And on the roads leading into town the old sedans and the pickup trucks were bouncing along with everyone dressed as they might have been for Saturday afternoon when rural North Carolina came to market.

Because of the layout of the town and the diminutive size of it, there was really only a single place where people could congregate — the triangular strip of ground in front of the courthouse. By 9 A.M. that triangle was densely crowded, and the flivvers and pickups were parked on the shoulders of each side of the high, crowned road for a hundred yards north and south of the courthouse. The sun beat down fiercely. But the crowd didn't seem to mind. The people were strangely silent. And strangely immobile. The ladies clustered together in the limited shade offered by the high-peaked front of the courthouse and talked quietly in little knots of well-starched and fresh-pressed fabric. Many of them wore straw bonnets that were reminiscent of an earlier day and left the faces of the wearers in a pleasant shade; it caused a man coming up with eyes squinting in the bright sun to move his head in close and stare hard, as if to see who he was talking to. The sizes and shapes and external appearances of a great many of the ladies was much the same — as if they were members of some well-matched chorus out of a WPA Writers Project folk drama about the Middle South. The men, in matching uniform of their own — well-washed khaki trousers or scrubbed overalls, tieless white shirts buttoned at the neck — stood in their own groups, some distance away and rather gallantly exposed to the rapidly strengthening sun. They moved about more than the ladies and the conversation was a bit more boisterous, frequently broken by a husky laugh, a bit of backslapping and handshaking, a shifting of a straw hat farther back on the head, a heaving up of a heavy belt over a widening paunch, a gold pocket watch coming out to be snapped open ceremoniously, examined authoritatively, then closed with decision. But generally it was a quiet crowd, though not quite as relaxed as a Saturday-afternoon-market crowd, in spite of its dress. For there was an expectancy about it, a waiting for the announcement, for the arrival of importance.

Those large, heavy-lidded gold railroad watches snapped open and shut on 10 A.M., 11 A.M., 12 noon. The sun grew increasingly hot. The crowd began to thin a bit. In that part of North Carolina in the lean days of the summer of 1932, a man could not afford to stand in town *all* Monday morning waiting for something to happen. By noon perhaps a third of the men had decided the holiday was over, had abandoned their points of observation on the courthouse triangle, had herded up their women and children, had cranked up their sunbaked flivvers and headed back for their farms. The day had not been totally lost, however. There had been some good visiting.

Two rumors, both correct — but both impossible to confirm — caused the remainder to wait a bit longer just when the heat and the whining children and the conscience pangs of Southern Baptist morality about not working on Monday morning were getting the best of them. Sometime shortly after eleven o'clock the word was passed that Libby had checked into "The Hotel" in Reidsville, about ten miles away — at five o'clock that morning! That meant she had been traveling from some wonderful, mysterious hideaway all that night!

Now five o'clock was not such an outrageous hour for the fresh-starched ladies who made up the waiting crowd. Five o'clock was when they were usually getting up — often thirty minutes or an hour before their men. Rake out the stove fire, and start coffee and bacon and some cereal or grits. But they weren't, my God, *traveling* at that hour from God-knows-where and after God-knows-what-sort-of-all-night extravagance! Those ladies decided they might just stay and see what this "Libby woman" was like. The curiosity was not all disapproving. Some of it was simply curious. Envious. Secretly sympathetic: "If *I* could just get out of these hills and stay up all night dancing, that would be *all right* with me!"

The second rumor came in about noon when the meager shade of the few trees and the few tin-roofed sheds and storefront canopies were providing only the barest, cramped shelter for lunch and the unwrapping of a cold sandwich made sometime near five o'clock that morning and the washing it down with a NeHi or a Dr Pepper. With some lunch, the buzz of the flies seemed a little less annoying and the whirr of the overhead fans in the grocery stores seemed a little more cooling. The word then spread that a lawyer in Winston had called the court clerk in Winston who had called the court clerk in Wentworth to say that Libby was definitely coming in to give herself up sometime between two and three o'clock.

The wise heads in the crowd — the ones who "knew Tom, who knows the clerk down there, and we'll find out" — went off to find out; they returned and said "it looks to be true." So those who could settled down a bit to digest the heavy meat sandwiches and the pickles and the hardboiled eggs and the cold pie and rest a bit without having to be on too much of a guard until, say, quarter to two.

If Libby mourned her talents as a dramatic actress, she must have known instinctively the value of an entrance. Her audience, when she arrived at Wentworth, was in high anticipation. It was not all that different from Broadway.

23

"She Skipped like a College Girl"

SHORTLY BEFORE 3 P.M. a small convoy came over a gentle rise into baking-hot Wentworth. There were three cars. Two contained reporters who had been camped outside the hotel in Reidsville since shortly after Libby's 5 A.M. arrival. The third, a black limousine in the lead, contained Libby, Alfred Holman, Dr. M. P. Cummings, a respected Reidsville physician, and Graves and Polikoff.

The expected thing would have been for them to drive up in front of the courthouse, get out quickly, and hustle Libby inside — though not because any of those good country people were so bereft of manners as to push and crowd and clutch for a Libby Holman souvenir; this wasn't New York or some grabby, uncivilized place; all Wentworth wanted to do was to *stare.* But regardless of Wentworth's civility, that particular arrival ceremony called for something more dramatically stage-managed by Polikoff.

The automobile convoy rolled sedately up the easy hill where the Reidsville road enters Wentworth from the north. The big, black limousine had Virginia plates and was clearly the most elegant thing in Wentworth that shimmering, hot afternoon. And it was in commanding contrast to the dusty sedans and coupes and pickups parked along the shoulders of the road leading to the courthouse. The limousine was freshly washed and shined and looked to be almost funereal — honestly enough, since it had been rented from a Newport News undertaker. At the top of the hill the limousine pulled to a stop, ignoring the open space in the road in front of the courthouse where the crowd had drawn back and a rented laundry truck sat parked, with a cluster of newsreel cameramen kneeling inside the railings around the roof of it. Instead, the car had halted in front of the home of Mrs. Harold Reid — about seventy-five yards opposite the Rockingham County jail — easily the grandest house in Wentworth.

There was no movement in the car for a moment or two. The country people stood back respectfully — but staring hard. There was no rushing forward. No shouts of "There she is!" No sudden surge to touch. The two cars carrying the reporters had been slowed somewhat by the people in the road and were fifty yards behind. Then the back and front doors of the limousine opened almost simultaneously. Polikoff and Holman got out quickly. Then from the rear there emerged a surprisingly small figure in loose, flowing black that contrasted sharply in the bright sunlight with the white suits of the men and the bright red-orange glare of the clay at the edge of the road. Graves and Dr. Cummings bustled out behind her. Quickly and almost as if a swirl of papers were being blown along a lawn by the wind, the group from the limousine moved all-as-a-unit to the open doorway of Mrs. Reid's house. The door closed.

Little more than two minutes could have elapsed from the time the car had been spotted along the Reidsville road until the time all its occupants had disappeared into the dark interior of the house.

It had been a carefully scripted performance. And if only a few in the patient crowd had actually caught a glimpse of the heavily veiled figure of the actress, there seemed to be no great welling up of disappointment. The people still stood back quietly around the black limousine.

There was a respect for Mrs. Reid's hard-baked, browning lawn; no one trampled it. In about five minutes, the raw figure of L. M. Sheffield, the sheriff of Rockingham County, emerged from the courthouse. With some dignity because of the importance of his mission, he made his way through the knots of people along the road and up across the lawn to Mrs. Reid's front door. It was opened before he had a chance to knock. And he too disappeared into the cool gloom of the front hall.

By prearrangement, sheriff Sheffield had come to serve a capias, placing Libby Holman under arrest; it was the figuratively much-handled legal paper with which sheriff Scott's telegram had armed half a dozen sheriffs and police chiefs in Cincinnati; Wyoming, Ohio; Wilmington, Delaware; New York City, and at various other points — as he tried to trace Libby in her flight from arrest.

Inside, in an awkward ceremony before the slight, drained figure of Libby, Polikoff acknowledged the capias and indicated his client. Then Polikoff and Graves followed Sheffield back out into the bright sunlight and back across the respectfully well lined route to the courthouse entrance.

The three men were talking casually in low tones along the way. Part of the ritual was to pretend there was no other soul there, that they were strolling casually through a deserted town in the lonely heat of a fierce North Carolina summer afternoon. Certainly that's the way they did it in New York. No more than a glance was given to the photographers, whose cameras clicked as they backed away ahead of the trio . . . or to the curious eyes on either side. Everyone was playing his part correctly.

Once inside, Polikoff and Graves followed the sheriff up the heavily varnished stairs into the impressive courtroom that ran across the front of the building on the second floor. At the high bench, flanked by the flags of the United States and the State of North Carolina and backed by that traditional portrait of George Washington by Gilbert Stuart, sat Judge Stack. Polikoff was called. He stood and began his statement, reading his writ of habeas corpus, which called for the court to produce the "prisoner" it now held in the harsh confines of Mrs. Reid's parlor.

Judge Stack interrupted. The court could hardly produce the prisoner when the prisoner so clearly was not in the court's physical possession. Would Mr. Polikoff be so good as to produce the prisoner so that the court might in turn "produce" her if that was called for? There was a delay while Libby was sent for.

Now, holding tight to her father on one side and Dr. Cummings on the other, she started across the ground to the courthouse. She was so heavily veiled that even in the bright sunlight her face could hardly be seen. If there had been only a few murmurs and some open staring when Polikoff, Graves, and sheriff Sheffield had walked the distance, now there was a total and embarrassed silence. Even some averted eyes by the flustered countrywomen. Here was what they had all come to see. Yet suddenly many seemed obviously uneasy about viewing it.

It was a procession seemingly in slow motion. Once Libby had passed, the crowd flowed cautiously into the road behind her. Only the reporters and photographers circled around ahead of the three as they walked, snapping pictures and asking their same old questions to which there were no right answers. Twice Holman responded sharply that his daughter had no statement to make. The singer gave no indication of hearing or seeing any of it.

In the courtroom, Libby took a seat indicated for her in the front row, between her father and the doctor. The heavy veil still covered her face. Judge Stack nodded stiffly in her direction as she entered and was seated; again she did not appear to notice. Nor did she seem to pay any attention as the argument droned on and there was the slow sonorous reading of the charge against her. The language was stilted, formal, archaic. How did it relate to the wild events of that night?

> The jurors of the State upon their oath do present, that Libby Holman Reynolds and Albert Walker, late of Forsyth County, on the 6th day of July, A.D. 1932, with force and arms, at and in the aforesaid County, did unlawfully, willfully, feloniously, deliberately, premeditatedly, and of malice aforethought, kill and murder Smith Reynolds contrary to the form of the statute in such case made and provided, and against the peace and dignity of the State.

What did all that formality have to do with the bourbon, the barbecue, the laughter, the hugs, the romantic warm night . . . the sharp cannonlike shot . . . and Smith's bleeding body?

With Walker already out on bail, Polikoff was arguing the precedent of that action and the good character of his client that warranted her bail also. If there was some evidence, Polikoff argued, that she was a greater risk of fleeing or a greater suspect than Walker, then perhaps the state should reveal something of that now to justify jailing her.

Carlisle Higgins got slowly to his feet for the first time. Polikoff half turned from facing the judge to see how Higgins would answer. Higgins's soft drawl was hardly audible past the fifth or sixth rows of the court. The state, Higgins said matter-of-factly, was at that time of the opinion it might not possess evidence to support a charge of premeditated murder. . . .

Judge Stack — who had been looking down at some papers on his desk during the reading of the charge and Polikoff's recital of the reasons why his client should be entitled to bail — looked up quickly. Polikoff exchanged a surprised glance with Graves, who was seated behind him. Even Libby straightened slightly from the position in which she had been slumped with her head on her father's shoulder.

What did Higgins mean? The state had gone before the Forsyth County Grand Jury only a short time before and presented evidence asking for a first-degree indictment of Libby and Walker. On the basis of that evidence and that request, the grand jury had brought in its murder indictment. Was the State now saying, "It was all a mistake" . . . that the necessary evidence had not been there?

"The state has no objection," Higgins continued, "to a reasonable bond. Neither does the state waive the right to go after a first-degree murder conviction if the evidence to support it is found later." Higgins sat down.

Though surprised — Polikoff was not ready to be taken in by some trick. Either the state was reluctant to give the defense any hint of what the evidence might be, or perhaps the state's case really *was* weaker than had been indicated. But Polikoff's first job that sultry afternoon was to make certain his client did not have to spend any time in a grubby North Carolina jail. He quickly began to lay the groundwork for low bail.

Regardless of Libby's personal deprivation because of the loss of a loved husband, Mr. Reynolds's death had been costly to his client. More costly than anyone would ever know. Regardless of her earnings as an entertainer in any given year, Polikoff assured the court that his client's personal estate was now not much more than $10,000. Her fame might dictate a high bail — but her financial situation should dictate a low one. In addition, Polikoff pointed out, everything about his client indicated that regardless of the severity of the charge, she would be available to answer when the court required it; she was an educated woman and an honors graduate of the University of Cincinnati; she came from a cultured family; she had a "tradition of responsibility." Disregarding all that, Polikoff continued, there was simply the practical matter that there was nowhere for Libby to go to escape recognition, notoriety, and attention: ". . . for her, there is no escape, even if she desired to get away. Where could Libby Holman go without being recognized? She could not take six steps in the streets of a city as small as Reidsville without at least a dozen persons following her."

Polikoff may have exaggerated. While Libby might have had a hard time taking the six steps in New York, Washington, Philadelphia, or Chicago . . . in Reidsville, she could have taken her six steps in absolute anonymity.

The afternoon was hot, and Judge Stack was not in the mood for sparring . . . or declamation. "I'll fix it the same as the other one. Will that be satisfactory?"

Graves rose to his feet in answer. "We're prepared to post $25,000."

Judge Stack nodded. From the back of the room, at Polikoff's beckoning, a somewhat flushed agent of the Hartford Accident and Indemnity Company approached the bench. He would post the $25,000 bond. Judge Stack nodded again. The agent hurriedly filled in the form the court clerk proffered, forgetting to fill in the name "Reynolds" after writing "Libby Holman" on the form. He was called back to add the last name. The judge glared.

The Hartford man, H. C. Horton, then sat down with a sigh of relief; he had been prepared to go to $50,000. William E. Church, clerk of the Forsyth County superior court, had been brought by Alfred Holman to Wentworth so there would be no question of that court's acceptance of the bail. The papers changed hands. Everything duly examined and attested to. The proceedings were over. There was a brief recess while most of the crowd filed out. Then Judge Stack resumed his circuit-riding court for another hour, meting out justice to dreary alcohol regulations violators. The flies buzzed occasionally. The fans whirred erratically, as if any moment they *were* going to gain momentum and do something useful about cooling the courtroom after all.

Libby Holman Reynolds had left sedately on the arm of her father and her doctor. The black sedan had been waiting out front. Alfred Holman handed Libby inside, still heavily veiled. Then he had spoken briefly to reporters: *"Res ipsa loquitur."* The blank looks abounded. He came down from his triumph: *"Res ipsa loquitur* means 'The thing speaks for itself.' " His daughter was now free on bail — and to gain that was the reason he had not wanted her to come back earlier as an arrested fugitive. His daughter had accommodations at the Belvedere Hotel in Reidsville. She was going back there. She would certainly spend that night there. She needed rest. She had no special plans for leaving Reidsville. She might spend several nights there. She had no statement to make, other than to say she wished to be left alone in order that she might recover her health. "Now," her father had said, ducking into the car, "you must let us go." This time, no reporters' cars followed the limousine. There was a certain finality to it. Libby had been charged, bailed. And the state had shown a sudden surprising reluctance to press for a first-degree murder indictment. It was a puzzling turn of events. And one critic of the legal issues of the case felt that, viewed against Higgins's tough stand toward Libby at Walker's hearing, his statements at Wentworth were "like the statements of a man whose objectivity was very much impaired, leading to a number of conclusions obviously damaging to the interests of the people of North Carolina."

THE RALEIGH TIMES

| FOURTEEN PAGES | RALEIGH, N. C., TUESDAY, AUGUST 9, 1932 | MARKET EDITION |

Libby Holman Disappears After Securing Bond; Flees From Reidsville In Night

The night of Monday, August 8, was hot and still in Reidsville. It was rather quiet, even for a town that was often regarded by its younger citizens as "rather quiet" on a rip-roaring Saturday. Reidsville was a solid, marketing town. It looks today much as it did in 1932, offering a certain simple grace. In the second-floor-front "suite" of the Belvedere Hotel occupied by Libby and her father, the overhead fans turned slowly in their cycle, but they hardly stirred the air. Outside the summer dusk came late. Inside, Libby, her father, her brother, Polikoff, and Graves were finishing an unimaginative fried chicken dinner sent up from the hotel dining room, a place not universally known throughout the Piedmont for its fine food.

Down in the Belvedere lobby a couple of reporters from Winston-Salem and Raleigh were on watch, although Alfred Holman had said Libby would not be leaving until Tuesday at the earliest. It was a dull assignment. About eleven o'clock when the all-night clerk arrived at the front desk, the reporters left a couple of numbers for him to call if anything happened, gave him a couple of dollars for his trouble . . . and left for supper and to try to find something to drink.

Shortly after 2 A.M., when the night man was partially dozing and the last lonely traveling salesman had left the lobby for the loneliness of his room, a petite, dark-haired creature in a white dress came rapidly down the stairs, crossed the lobby, and entered a car that had swung quietly into place in front of the hotel.

The night clerk sat up sharply, ready to bawl out some hooker trying to slip away from an upstairs room. Then he realized he was witnessing the departure of the most notable guest the Belvedere had had in the last dozen years. Gone was Libby Reynolds's black veil and the heavy mourning ensemble. "She had a beret cocked over one eye and she skipped across the lobby like a college girl," the night man reported to the furious reporters when he finally had the presence of mind to get them on the phone.

They had bet their couple of dollars on a chance for some bootleg booze and a few hours' sleep before resuming their watch. Now they had lost both — and their quarry.

Reidsville enjoyed part of its growth in north central North Carolina because it had become a road and rail junction. The feed and tobacco warehouses, pale red-brick or weathered corrugated iron sheds, with little character and no cheer other than the "Clabber Girl" and "Bull Durham" and "Yellow Bowl Snuff" posters that decorated their sides, lined the rail tracks that snaked into the town from five directions. Freight was king. But every railroad that valued its public relations also knew enough to rattle through a few first-class passenger trains every twenty-four hours so the big shippers could come and go from Reidsville in comfort.

So there were several escape routes that Libby could have taken to get out of town by train or car. And when the reporters arrived at the hotel, sorted out the story, and made plans to follow, it was too late to do anything but try to guess which route she had taken. Polikoff and Graves, when contacted in Winston-Salem, feigned ignorance and pretended indifference.

"She is, after all, covered by her bond," Polikoff pointed out to the newsmen. "When she is required to turn up, she will. In the interim she needs to rest. This has taken a lot out of her — physically and every other way."

Nobody was sure just where Libby had *come from* when she appeared in Wentworth to turn herself in. Which made it hard to narrow the field as to where she might be *heading back*. One rumor had it that she had been flown down by private seaplane from up the Chesapeake to someplace on the Virginia south shore and had then come on by car. She could be heading back the same way. Or there were two or three railway stations within a couple of hours' drive of Reidsville where she could have escaped from a car into the privacy of a Pullman drawing room on a New York-bound train making an early morning stop. It wasn't as difficult as it would have been if she were still ducking the authorities. She only had to watch out for the reporters now.

24

Flight of a Grieving Wife

FROM THE BEGINNING, North Carolina editors had been on the rack as to just how they were going to cover the story. Many papers had jumped gratefully at the opportunity to set the whole thing decently aside as a suicide when the first reports had alluded to this and the first "family spokesman" had gently headed everyone in that direction. But then one suspicion after another came along to make it difficult to accept that verdict; *the damn case just wouldn't go away.* Everytime it was settling comfortably into the back pages, some new development drove it back onto page one.

With Libby and Walker now out on bail, some papers — and their readers — were still pondering editorially just how strong the evidence before the grand jury had really been.

The prestigious *Charlotte News* seemed to resent the fact that the grand jury had even passed the case on to the court, if, as Higgins had said, the state might not possess the evidence. "No person," wrote the *News* editorial writer, "should be indicted for a crime unless there is reasonable cause to presuppose conviction."

The *Winston-Salem Journal* countered with a stand that the grand jury indictment should simply represent that there had been sufficient evidence presented before the grand jury to justify a trial in open court to find out just what had happened. If the *Charlotte News*'s opinion of justice held true, said the *Journal*, then every American who went into court indicted would go in presupposed guilty.

Now with the North Carolina papers fighting among themselves, with Libby Holman safely out of the state on bail, and with Albert Walker all but forgotten, the legal antagonists began to maneuver.

Every trial lawyer anticipates the time when he has to stand in a courtroom and select a jury that will give his client "a good trial." "A good trial" is not necessarily a fair trial. A good trial to the defense lawyer means having a jury that will sit through the evidence, listen to it all, and then bring in a verdict for acquittal without performing in any unexpected way that sets up the mechanics for a retrial. To the prosecutor, the quality of a jury should be just the same — but the final verdict should be the opposite.

The prosecution and the defense would be selecting from local citizens who had been inundated with newspaper, magazine, and radio publicity about what was termed "the biggest case of the decade." These people would be asked to swear that they had not been prejudiced by what had gone before and that they had no preconceived notion about what their judgment in the case might be.

It was an impossible request to make of them — and an impossible oath for them to take — if it all were taken literally: "Mr. John Doe: just because Mrs. Reynolds has been indicted for first-degree murder by the grand jury, just because she was in the room when Smith was shot, just because she claims she can't remember anything about the period before or after the shooting — that does not precondition you to suspect her, does it?" The juror is supposed to answer, "Not at all" — *if* he wants to serve.

The best hope on either side is to get a box full of jurors who may indeed have a good bit of public knowledge about the case, yet who will try to judge it fairly on the evidence presented.

Often in advance of a trial, it is a useful technique for the defense lawyers and the prosecution to leak to court reporters some of what they will try to prove. The leaking can be done in the guise of pretrial interviews, speculations, statements of points that are "self-evident." And now both sides maneuvered in this pretrial sparring. Most of it would be conducted in the Winston-Salem papers for the benefit of those prospective jurors. But it would also spin out as tantalizing news to titillate hundreds of thousands around the country who had followed the story daily with a hunger for sensation and an eye for the philanderings of the very, very rich.

The defense forces started to try to create subtly the picture of their clients as injured parties, hungering for a trial to clear their names. Further, Liipfert's strategy dictated that Walker and Libby should be split apart as far as possible in the public mind. If nothing else, it gave the *illusion* of some difference in the severity of the charges against the two. The rumors linking them romantically were too dangerous for the lawyers to permit them to be tried in the same proceedings, which seemed to be what the prosecution was aiming for. Walker would be depicted by his lawyer as a bewildered, faithful young friend and admirer of Smith's, who had thrown himself with sophomoric enthusiasm into a good evening of partying — with the tragic results. That Walker could be romantically interested in his best friend's wife was patently absurd.

The tactic of Walker's lawyer would be a success. As time went on, Walker sank into the background. The case in the state's mind, and so in the public mind, became more and more a solitary case against Libby.

Libby was to be painted by her defense lawyer as a grieving wife. Famous, talented, beautiful, obviously attractive to many men — but genuinely attached in an almost motherly way to this rich young husband whom she was subtly encouraging and coaching toward his own distinctions in the air.

As far as the alcoholic birthday party was concerned, it was difficult for the defense attorneys to know how badly that could hurt them. Since those attending the party were so mum about what had taken place as to be unbelievable, the way was open to the prosecution to spread almost any story they desired about what *might* have gone on there that night.

Some of the rumors were so indelicate that they could not be dealt with openly by either of the antagonists. Yet the public already wallowed in speculation: that Libby's pregnancy was not by Smith; that he had been infuriated to find out that she was a Jew in his WASP stronghold: that Libby was just after his money and had no intention of living at Reynolda as his wife. . . .

Scott and McMichael did their share in keeping the rumors flowing to the press, though neither man alluded to specific evidence that had been presented to the grand jury to secure the first-degree murder indictment. And though McMichael's superior had been the man to say in Wentworth that he was not sure the state had evidence to go for a first-degree conviction, McMichael indicated to reporters several times that he had *much* more evidence in hand than he had revealed to the grand jury. He hinted that it was "sensational stuff."

The crackpots got into action again. Defense lawyer Graves told reporters that he had received an intriguing letter in a woman's handwriting, postmarked Charleston, South Carolina, and signed "An Eye Witness." The woman said she had been at the Reynolda birthday party, had seen Smith put the gun to his head three times before pulling the trigger and killing himself. "Libby was too drunk to know what was going on," the letterwriter said. Graves did not present the communication as a crackpot note, however. It aided his attempt to prove that Libby had not killed Smith — even at the cost of branding her a drunk. Would he try to get the letterwriter as a witness? He wouldn't elaborate. But, said reporters, it should be easy enough to determine whether or not the note was authentic? There had been only so many women at the party?

Graves would only say that Libby was impatient for a trial, that she wanted "vindication as soon as possible," unless the trial came at a time when it might endanger the baby. And she was still well hidden.

The most oft-repeated rumor was that she had returned to Oakington, the palatial estate on the western shore of the Chesapeake Bay below Wilmington where she was presumed to have spent some time before her hurried trip to Wentworth. The Oakington country certainly had the right image: the haunt of rich Washingtonians and Marylanders; historic Revolutionary and Federal houses refurbished into great estates by old money and new; yachts anchored out front; fox hunting in the back.

Prying newspaper reporters discovered that Benjamin Ray, chief of police of Aberdeen, Maryland, in whose province Oakington fell, had gotten a request from Joseph Pussey, estate supervisor at Oakington, to provide some guards for the drives of the estate, starting the day following the Wentworth proceedings. Chief Ray said he would assume that Libby would be coming there.

The gracious Oakington estate had been the property of the late Commodore Leonard Richards, U.S.N. Its proprietor at that point was his son, Leonard Richards, Jr., a vice president of the Atlas Powder Company of Wilmington, a DuPont subsidiary. It had been searched once — by the sheriff of Hartford County, Maryland, immediately prior to Libby's surrender at Wentworth — when he was pressured into a visit there by Transou Scott's dog-eared order for her arrest. The sheriff found only that his quarry had obviously heard he was coming. A housekeeper admitted that Libby had been in the house for the last three weeks under the care of a physician, and she had left with "the doctor" shortly before the sheriff arrived. A couple of other servants were not so well coached. A garrulous old gardener said the "ailing" Libby had been playing tennis with two lady friends several days before and had finally left Oakington the day before the Wentworth hearing, by speedboat. The sheriff also discovered an extensive wardrobe belonging to Libby in the house. It certainly *did* look as if she planned to return.

"This is all news to me," Leonard Richards manfully blustered to assembled reporters who descended on his Wilmington office. "I did not know Mrs. Reynolds was there. In fact, I didn't know anyone was there." Then a talkative — or cooperative — private guard at Oakington told reporters at the main gate that he thought they were up the wrong trail now, regardless of the fact that Libby had been there before. Personally, he had had a telegram from her asking him to meet her in Stamford, Connecticut. Off they roared on another chase. It was a beautifully planted decoy.

On the Thursday following the Monday hearing at Wentworth, with at least one small portion of the press trying to find out where and why Libby was going to Stamford, Connecticut, the story was circulated that a woman living across the little bay from Oakington had just seen Libby departing from Oakington by speedboat with two men and two women, heading for the John J. Raskob estate at Centreville, Maryland — on the eastern Maryland shore almost directly across from Annapolis. The wealthy, powerful Raskob was a former national Democratic Party chairman. One of the men in the boat was reported to be Raskob's elder son. If the story had no real basis of fact, at least it continued to place Libby in the right sort of company. Then the trail ran cold.

On August 11, William E. Church, clerk of the superior court in Winston-Salem, announced that Libby had "forfeited all rights as administratrix of the estate of Smith Reynolds" by failing to request this right. Her claim would have been fought by the state under any circumstances, he said: she was not a resident of the state, and she was under indictment for first-degree murder.

At the capital in Raleigh, the state bar association had been pushing for a term of court to begin early in September, instead of its scheduled start in October, so a trial could be held a month earlier. But as August wore along, it became clear that there would be no September trial. The prosecution was making repeated protest about the lack of time to prepare its case. In addition, there was obviously increased behind-the-scenes friction that often left Higgins, McMichael, and Scott publicly challenging each other.

Scott would drop his laconic hints about clues to be run down. McMichael would suggest sensational evidence would soon be revealed. Higgins would question whether the prosecution had any case that it could take to court for first-degree murder.

On the defense side, Graves and Polikoff continued to insist that their client wanted her day in court as soon as possible to clear her name. The two lawyers feared a trap by Higgins, but they knew the delaying tactics and the prosecution's seeming indecision was a help to them.

As for Ab Walker, now it was almost as if he had never been a part of the indictment. His lawyer, Bailey Liipfert, made no noises, no public statements, no legal motions. No member of the Reynolds family consented to see Walker or even speak of him. And he had made no attempt to contact Libby after he left her at Reynolda shortly before the inquest.

Now the concern of a number of people turned toward the return of Smith's brother, Dick Reynolds.

On August 10, word was received that Dick had landed in Trinidad from a Munson liner that had brought him up the coast from Pernambuco. On the twenty-first he arrived in Miami. Two days later he reached Winston-Salem.

He arrived to supervise a grim task.

At midnight, August 23, the body of Smith Reynolds was exhumed from its grave in Salem Cemetery to undergo a secret autopsy under the eye of coroner Dalton.

25

Death "at Close Range"

NO FORMAL LEGAL DOCUMENT could ever adequately describe the syste-
mized, cold, methodical, scientific, horrifying, necessary procedure that
was going on in the brightly lighted Winston-Salem operating room in
the early morning hours of August 24, 1932. But it should have been
done about nine weeks earlier. The cold methodology performed on
the waxen, artfully embalmed, but somehow still-human form of Smith
Reynolds was being done, as the legal paper stated,

> . . . in order to determine the course of the bullet which caused his death,
> and which of two wounds was the one of entrance and which was the
> wound of exit of the bullet, and also to determine whether the gunshot
> would have occurred with the muzzle of the pistol in contact with or very
> near the head, or whether the same was fired with the weapon at some
> distance therefrom, and also the course and angle of the bullet through
> the brain. The undersigned are advised that such post-mortems will dis-
> close these facts which are material as bearing upon the guilt or innocence
> of the persons accused.

The request of the autopsy had been dated August 18, a week and a
half after the hearing at Wentworth, North Carolina, when Libby
turned herself in. The autopsy request had been approved by Judge
Stack August 20, two days after submission and the day before young
Dick Reynolds arrived in Miami from South America. *It was almost as if
the State of North Carolina were considering for the first time* that an autopsy

might be useful in getting to the bottom of this complex, sensitive case. But only when an angry Dick Reynolds was arriving to force it.

Performing the autopsy for coroner Dalton were four Winston-Salem surgeons, all prominent, three of whom had attended Smith at the hospital. It would not have been unreasonable for each of those three to have formed a strong point of view already, particularly about the correctness of their earlier postmortem at the hospital, right after Smith died. But no one raised the question of whether they should disqualify themselves.

Dr. W. M. Johnson had worked on Smith at Baptist Hospital and had attended Libby on her return from the hospital to Reynolda after the shooting and during her incommunicado period of mysterious blackout. Here was a man who enjoyed the title of physician to the Reynolds family, who had been with Libby almost exclusively from the period shortly after Smith's death until the arrival of Mr. and Mrs. Holman from Cincinnati. What he might have witnessed with his patient — whether she was delirious, suffering from loss of memory, or was rational — might have been of great interest to both the prosecution and the defense in the case. At least he might have been able to explain Libby's blackout. It is interesting to speculate on the ethics of the thing and on what Dr. Johnson might, or should, have been called to testify in court. Was all that he had seen and heard in Libby's room privy information between doctor and patient? Or was he treating only the physical well-being of his patient . . . and was any information she might have given out consciously or unconsciously about the shooting something he could be required to reveal under questioning in court?

The second doctor was Fred M. Hanes, the distinguished Winston-Salem surgeon who had testified at the inquest. He had been among the first to see the wound, before too much major medical attention could have disfigured its contour in an effort to save the young man's life. In addition to appearing at the inquest, Hanes had also testified before the grand jury. What Dr. Hanes said was a confidential matter in grand jury files — files that have been carefully misplaced with so much of the rest of the information about the case. But presumably what he said added substantially to the weight of evidence that convinced the second grand jury to bring in a murder indictment.

The two other doctors at the autopsy were A. D. Valk, who had also been in the operating room at Baptist Hospital, and T. C. Redfern. The autopsy would take about two hours.

The embalming job had been a good one and the coffin had been tight, so the effect of decomposition had not been far advanced. But there was the strong odor of an embalmed body, which none of the doctors, except the coroner, had handled since medical school. None of them had the meticulous training and specialized experience of a forensic pathologist.

It was not to be a full autopsy with Smith's whole body emptied out, pared, slivered, weighed, tested. Whatever else Smith might have been suffering from at the time of his death was secondary. The medical search now was to center as exhaustively as possible on the head wound. Before peeling back the scalp, the doctors examined carefully the supposed entrance wound, high in the brow above the right eye. But they were at some disadvantage. The lump that Dr. Hanes had described around the wound when he saw Smith at the hospital had been painstakingly removed by the embalmer, to prepare the face for the casket. And any trace of powder burn around the wound — if one had been there earlier — had been scrubbed or tinted away by the embalmer's cosmetics. Wrestling the awkward body onto its side, the doctors then examined the presumed exit wound behind the left ear. This, necessarily, had been less tampered with during the embalming, but the hole was small and neat. It did not seem to reflect the exit of a bullet that had been so battered in its passage through the skull that, according to investigators, it flew apart in several fragments when it emerged.

The skin across the top of the skull was peeled back. A circle of skull was taken out so that the doctors could examine the brain. The path of the bullet could normally be followed by the damaged tissue, but now there was no clear clue to its direction. Parts of the brain had already been removed by probing at Baptist Hospital. The whole horrible process was hardly a fraction of the use a thorough autopsy might have been nine weeks earlier. It was like examining the mechanism of a clock whose works had been rattled about haphazardly — and then left in some disorder, simply to fill the cavity. When the doctors finished their earlier examination, it never occurred to them that Smith's body would ever be examined again.

Before dawn, the medically battered body of Smith Reynolds was back in its resting place in Salem Cemetery. Perhaps only a dozen people in the city knew the autopsy had taken place. But one of those dozen was Dick Reynolds, and that morning, a few hours after the autopsy, he had talked to reporters for the first time. By then he was aware of the autopsy findings.

He said he was convinced Smith had not committed suicide.

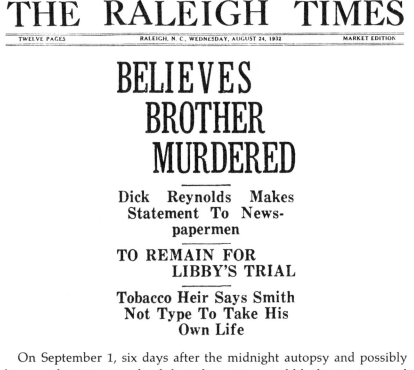

THE RALEIGH TIMES

TWELVE PAGES   RALEIGH, N. C., WEDNESDAY, AUGUST 24, 1932   MARKET EDITION

BELIEVES BROTHER MURDERED

Dick Reynolds Makes Statement To Newspapermen

TO REMAIN FOR LIBBY'S TRIAL

Tobacco Heir Says Smith Not Type To Take His Own Life

On September 1, six days after the midnight autopsy and possibly because the state was afraid the information would leak out piecemeal elsewhere and in garbled and damaging fashion, the prosecutor reported that an exhumation and autopsy had taken place a week before.

The reporters and most of their readers were just as confused when the announcement was over as they had been before. It is perhaps no wonder.

The finding of the autopsy, said Carlisle Higgins, "confirmed the testimony of Dr. Hanes given at the inquest." Though the three doctors from the first autopsy had apparently rubber-stamped their earlier findings, their participation raised the question that their objectivity might be totally impaired by having done the earlier examination. A clear conflict of interest. When the evidence was finally offered in court, a good defense lawyer could point damaging suspicion at that autopsy report. At this point, however, only the prosecutor could ask for new doctors. And he seemed to accept it all.

Higgins said that the bullet had been fired "at close range," had entered the right temple, and after ranging downward through the head, it had emerged behind the left ear. "Close range" was a surprisingly legally imprecise term. From across the room? From hand-to-hand distance? From contact? Higgins's office would not elaborate.

"Close range," the autopsy report phrase, might — in the mind of the man who said it — mean anything from six inches to three feet from the skull. Dr. Hanes had said as much. *What it did not seem to mean was that the barrel of the gun had been placed in contact with the head.*

But even the vague "close range" terminology argued strongly against suicide. It was too hard, too illogical to shoot *yourself* at close range in the temple. A suicide would jam the gun against his head. And that would be the end of it. No niceties. No tricks. No deceptions.

The tragic aim of many suicides is to make those who are left behind feel sorry: "I killed myself. And I bet they will all feel bad now that they weren't nicer to me." The last thing many suicides want is to mask the fact that the death was self-inflicted.

And so, the vague, unexplained press release of the second autopsy did not contradict much of what most people already believed: that Smith had probably been murdered.

Exactly one month after Dick Reynolds made his statement about the shooting of his brother, Libby broke her long silence.

She did it in what would have been a peculiar way for most people — but in a manner that was uniquely available to her as a Broadway figure. She told her story through a nationally syndicated columnist, Ward Moorehouse. It was first published in the *New York Sun* on September 24, 1932.

Because it *was* her first statement, because she undoubtedly gave the interview only on the condition that she could approve Moorehouse's final story (and because Polikoff was too smart a lawyer to let her do anything that would be injurious to her cause), the Moorehouse column should be regarded as a biased "position paper." Although at several points later in her life she started to write her own story and even to collaborate with others, she would always reach that point in her life that concerned the incident at Reynolda — and either freeze, unable to go any farther . . . or her lawyers would get wind of the project and scotch it. Since *the Moorehouse story is the only public statement she ever made about the case*, it is probably worth printing here, virtually in its entirety:

Libby Holman Tells Story of Her Tragedy and Plans for the Future with Her Baby

Smith Reynold's Widow Breaks Silence for First Time since July 6

Describes the Tragic Night

Wants More Than Acquittal, She Says Nothing Short of Complete Apology

By Ward Moorehouse

"It's the knowing that I'm going to give birth to the child of the man I love that affords me my only gleam of happiness, that gives me any desire to live at all. The fact that within four months I will have a child — *his* child — makes me strong enough to fight for a complete and absolute vindication. God in Heaven knows that I did not kill Smith Reynolds."

So said the dark-haired, husky-voiced Libby Holman Reynolds, who, as a Broadway blues singer, skyrocketed from obscurity and $35 a week to $2,500 a week and Broadway stardom, who married the twenty-year-old Zachary Smith Reynolds, heir to the R. J. Reynolds tobacco millions, and who in November will stand trial before a North Carolina jury on a charge of murdering her husband. . . .

I have just returned from an Eastern shore of Maryland estate where she is making her home until the time of the trial. For three hours, in calm, dispassionate tones, she talked to me about the "Reynolds case," of her life with her young aviator-husband, and of happenings at Winston-Salem and elsewhere on and after the fateful evening of July 5.

(Moorehouse was openly sympathetic. He had scored something of a beat by getting Libby to give him the interview — even if he knew his column was being used by Libby for a one-way press conference. To distract, he first waxed irate about the actress being subjected to "common-criminal procedure" — fingerprinting, mug shots, interrogation. Then he lectured the reporters who trailed her "as if they were so many wolves." He told of her surrender at Wentworth. Then her flight.)

As the guest of a friend at a remote estate, she has found placidity and an approximation of peace. Clad in a dark blue frock with pin point dots and knitting small pink garments as she sat relaxed in a big arm chair, the deep-throated Ohio singer spoke unhesitatingly of the tragedy at that grim homestead called Reynolda. . . .

"I didn't shoot Smith," said Libby, "God in Heaven knows that. The Reynolds family knows it in their hearts. I loved Smith as I never loved anyone before or ever will again. The fullest and richest hours of my life were spent with that dear boy. I loved him tenderly and dearly and completely and to him I meant everything, everything. He was utterly dependent upon me. When I realized that he was gone, that he was dead, that after that visit to the cemetery I was never, never to see him again, I didn't want to live. My life was over. To learn that I, his wife, was actually suspected of murdering him stunned and horrified me, but it didn't matter. The fact that he was dead had caused nothing to matter until" — there she paused and went on quietly — "until I knew positively that I was to have a child. With that knowledge, with that gleam of happiness, I had something to live for, something to fight for. And now, I want to go through with the trial. . . . I don't only want acquittal. I want a complete apology."

She went on slowly: "I've got to be cheerful for that's the only way. But it's the waiting that's hard. If the trial were tonight, right now, it would be easier. I'd just stand up and tell the truth. If they didn't believe me they'd just have to go ahead and hang me. . . ."

She paused, put down her knitting and gazed out upon the emerald, rolling countryside. "It was after the funeral, after the cemetery, that people began swarming into my room. I was told that the coroner wanted to ask me some questions. It didn't matter. I didn't know what it was all about. I didn't care. Smith, my darling Smith, was gone, lost to me forever, and I didn't want to live without him. It was when the questioning began that I realized with horror that I was being suspected of killing my husband. Then I said to myself, 'In God's name, how can things like this happen to people? . . . The terrible irony of it. I, his wife, and Ab Walker, his best friend, suspected of doing away with him, of shooting him through the head.' Ab Walker worshiped Smith. He was utterly devoted to him. If Smith had said, 'Ab, go shoot yourself,' Ab would have done it." . . .

The widow of the youngest member of the Reynolds clan was talking of Smith's passion for revolvers. "He was never without a pistol," she said. "He often said to me: 'Well, if anything happens, there's always the little Mauser.' Many, many times I'd see him holding the pistol to his head. More times than I can remember, he threatened suicide. It seemed to be forever on his mind. He threatened to kill himself if I didn't marry him. He threatened it in New York and in North Carolina. He often slept with his pistol on the table at the right of the bed, and many times he'd get up in the middle of the night and tell me he was hearing footsteps. He had the delusion that he might be kidnapped and held for ransom. . . .

"Smith was morbid, and because of his morbidity and because of his strange delusions, I'd often sit up with him until 6 o'clock in the morning, arguing and pleading. He once wanted to give up aviation because, he said, a man couldn't do but one thing at a time and he wanted to devote all his time, all his thoughts to me. He seemed to be getting more and more dependent on me. He had some strange delusion that I was going to leave him. He'd often disappear for hours at night and come back weeping with joy because I had not fled. . . .

"It will be hard to convince most people that I married Smith Reynolds because I loved him. There were times when I pleaded with him to get himself disinherited. I told him that we could get along and he knew it. During my married life I paid my own way. I saw nothing of any Reynolds money. Why, I had much more money than Smith had — much more. I paid my own bills, paid for my clothes. I made a lot of money on stage." She shrugged her shoulders. "Well, I guess it's a good thing. This trial will take every penny I can scrape up. I'll have a child to support and I'll go back on the stage. That's the only thing I know how to do. . . .

"If I had been in the State of North Carolina the day of that indictment they'd have jammed me into a patrol wagon. . . . The whole thing has been a terrible prostitution of justice, and the one person who could defend me, Smith Reynolds, is gone. . . . If Smith had really known that I was going to have a child the whole terrible thing might never have happened. . . . My baby will be named Smith, of course. Boy or girl, that's the name."

Where would this girl of tragedy like to be when the child is born? "I don't know," she said. "Not Cincinnati — not the South. Maybe in France. I felt like a man without a country." She paused and repeated the thought — half to herself: ". . . a man without a country. But tell Broadway I'm not weakening; that it's my fight and I'm game. I can take it."

She was standing in the doorway as I rode away, Libby Holman Reynolds, the coed from the cornbelt who came to Broadway with a B.A. degree and a husky voice; who received $35 a week for singing the melodious "Hogan's Alley" in "Merry-Go-Round" one season, and who got $2,500 a week for singing "Moanin' Low" in the next. Libby Holman Reynolds, 26 years old, a creature of triumph and tragedy, who, within the next four months will be called upon to experience a murder trial and motherhood. . . .

The column was the sort of preconditioning of the public that a defense attorney always hoped for. But rarely got. You couldn't buy that sort of publicity.

Or could you?

26

"The Most Massive Clam-up
I Ever Encountered"

IN THE LATE SUMMER and early fall of 1932, after two months of nearly continuous front-page attention, there began a phase of the story which one investigating officer called "the most massive clam-up and know-nothing I have ever encountered." Another, a deputy who was one of the first officers to reach Reynolda after the shooting and who worked extensively on the case during the summer and fall before the "clam-up" and subsequent events ended the investigation, said that "the case died from a sudden, massive disinterest," to which a former sheriff of Winston-Salem's Forsyth County then added: "And I know where all that disinterest came from." The inference of Reynolds pressure is clear.

However, climate for creating "massive disinterest" in the Reynolds case did not have to be developed as a heavy-handed and obvious maneuver. Much of it could have come about without the Reynolds family's having to give any public indication that shutting down the story was something they would look on with a good bit of favor. The assumption of what they *might* favor could be easily made from their earlier statements about the case. And once it had been made, there were a number of public servants and private participants who would find it easy to justify their own actions on the Reynoldses' behalf by rationalizing that theirs was clearly the best course of conduct.

Americans in the last few years have become all too familiar with a bureaucratic atmosphere, like that behind Watergate, that creates a climate in which it seems justifiable to follow any course of action and break all manner of rules when trying to anticipate the direction of a superior. Certain specific directives need never be given. But when hints were necessary to direct the action of a few men at the top, those hints were all too evident. So "the massive disinterest" began to settle in around the edges . . . and some thoughtful attention came from the top.

Carlisle Higgins had been exposed to some of that attention — in a roundabout way. Early in the investigation, William N. Reynolds, who was the family member closest to the children, had called Higgins aside and informed him that, regardless of state progress in the investigation, "the family would make available to him any amount of money he wanted to investigate this thing!" It had sounded then to Higgins like the efforts of a grieving family to get all the questions answered, with the killer — if there was one — brought to trial. And Higgins was certainly running shorthanded, while the pressure to turn up new evidence was mounting rapidly. Nevertheless, the offer was a somewhat unusual one. Regardless of whom the investigator officially reported to, in effect the family was getting its own private investigator into an official role in the case.

However, the hard-pressed Higgins accepted and hired a former FBI agent who was recommended by the family. Higgins could assume the agent was reporting to Will Reynolds, too. That meant a private citizen had an open conduit to privileged official state information — and potentially could result in a charge of obstruction of the ordinary process of justice and interference with the state. But the man was fast, competent, and thorough, and his work was useful. Higgins needed him.

Higgins was also disturbed by the sideshow aspects of the case: "Reporters were running all over, badgering everybody. And certain people who had little part in the case could get their opinions spread all over the front pages just by answering any damn-fool question."

With his early conspiracy case coming closer to trial and with the Holman-Reynolds investigation developing new sensations and new false leads almost daily, Higgins had to shut himself up in the Carolina Hotel each night and turn off the phone in order to get some peace.

Even that didn't always work. One evening after a wearing day he had locked himself in and fallen into bed immediately — only to be wakened about 9:15 by an insistent knocking on his hotel room door. It was the bellhop; there was a lady downstairs in "a car 'bout as long as a Greyhound" who wanted to see him. Exhausted, he sent word he'd rather see her in the morning — and fell off to sleep again. Again the knocking and the message that the lady would wait all night if necessary. It was Mary Reynolds Babcock; she just wanted to tell Higgins that she knew her brother "always had a gun" and had talked on several occasions about killing himself. She was prepared to testify to that. It was essentially not very useful information at that stage — but it had served the purpose of jangling Higgins wide awake, and seemed to be another clear message from the Reynolds family: "the man committed suicide."

Higgins had been in an unenviable position since the beginning. Any way it ended, his investigation would result in a black mark on a powerful and influential family. And all paths to the ending would give Smith's name, Libby, and the family months of intense publicity with a potential for the worst sort of exposure, in a decade famous for its delight in sensational journalism. A judgment of suicide would carry all the stigma of our society and the endless speculation of "why did he do it?" Establishing that Smith had been murdered by unknown persons opened up even more juicy speculation and invited rumor-mongering about sinister and illicit dealings Smith might have had: philandering? gambling? smuggling? bootlegging? All were suggested. Charging that he had been shot by Libby and/or Walker meant the hot light of a trial. And even if the accused were acquitted at a trial, the damage was done. The publicity could only be slightly more terrible if Libby and Walker were finally convicted.

As county solicitor and an elected official, Higgins had to be both an effective officer of the court . . . and an accomplished politician and vote-getter, if he were to maintain continuity and strength in his office. Regardless of any pressure that might be coming from the Reynolds family, his close association in the Reynolds case with several of his sometime political allies had the potential now for embarrassing him. With one opponent in the anticipated trial being Graves, his old campaign manager, and another being Liipfert, his superior in the state Democratic party organization, the lineup across the attorney's table already promised intriguing possibilities for charges of conflict of interest later, if things developed oddly.

On October 9, 1932, the giant Guaranty Trust Company of New York filed Smith Reynolds's will for probate in the New York surrogate court. It was a surrogate judge's dream. These legal worthies collect fees on the estates that pass under their jurisdiction — much in the manner the old English feudal lords and sheriffs who were given rights to collect a share of the value of all the wines that passed through a port, all the wool shipped out of a county. So filing in New York immediately made some surrogate judge in North Carolina furious. Guaranty Trust stated that the will had been signed on August 21, 1931, and that there was "no known codicil reversing it." August 21 was five days before Smith landed his amphibian alongside the *Berengaria* and demanded to be taken aboard for the voyage to England. At that point, he had already planned to divorce Anne and was deeply involved with Libby.

Under the terms of the will Smith's share of the inheritance from his father would basically be divided among his two sisters and his brother. But some supplemental provisions were noted: three $50,000 bequests were made under the 1931 will. One went to Anne Cannon Reynolds. The second was to little Anne. The third $50,000 went to Albert Walker.

The niggardly bequest to Anne and little Anne would improve substantially by an additional $500,000 to each of them if they would give up all rights to Smith's estate whenever it came up for settlement. (And Smith's lawyers had written into the will wording that Anne specifically promised then that she would not contest any later will on the grounds that she had no right to sign away the rights of her daughter.) Anne had agreed to these provisions at the time. And to make it less appealing to her to change her mind at some later point after Smith had died, the will filed in New York (with its $50,000 bequests for Anne and little Anne) stated they would also lose the two $50,000 gifts if Anne had a change of heart at that point and decided to contest the will after Smith's death.

To Anne, in 1931 with a divorce in the wings, agreeing to the $500,-000 final settlements for herself and her daughter would have seemed like a practical solution. And little more than one of principle. Smith's cash at that point was limited to his $50,000-a-year allowance. By agreeing to the stipulations for the various grants, and by agreeing to a divorce (and that she would be the one to file for it) Anne, Sr., and little

Anne secured a $1,100,000 commitment from the Reynoldses at a point when Smith was still almost ten years away from his inheritance. So in 1931, Anne had gone moodily off to Nevada to her divorce ranch with at least that security legally in hand on Smith's death.

The Reynolds lawyers figured that the settlement with Anne had cleared the way for any child by Smith from a *future* marriage to participate in the distribution of R. J. Sr.'s fortune, in the event of Smith's death before he reached twenty-eight; R. J. Sr.'s will superseded anything Smith would write, and R. J. Sr. had specified that if Smith's death occurred, Smith's share would go to Smith's children.

R. J. Reynolds, Sr., was quite obviously content to provide for his grandchildren. But the old tobacco baron had clearly set things up so that no ambitious fortune hunter could get at it. They could only enjoy its benefits through their Reynolds spouses.

But one thing R. J., Sr., hadn't figured on was the sort of situation which now existed. If it was ruled that his son had committed suicide, he would have thoughtlessly deprived any lawful wife of the support she was entitled to when the estate was distributed. Lawyers speculated that Libby could make a decent case for herself as a participant in R. J. Sr.'s estate distribution to the late Smith Reynolds, since she was clearly Smith's lawful wife. And — had he survived to receive his inheritance — she would have enjoyed the wifely benefits of it. If it could be proved that Smith killed himself, he had willfully deprived her of these benefits. Further, there was the case of the child she carried, a child she claimed was Smith's.

Even though Libby was still in hiding when Guaranty Trust filed the will for probate in early October, she began to get a great deal of impromptu help from lawyers who were only too eager to voice their opinions to the newspapers, perhaps for their own vanity, perhaps in the hopes that they might get in on this wonderful mother lode, too. A. C. Blumenthal, a New York theatrical figure and sometimes acquaintance of Libby's, had already volunteered the services of his $100,000-a-year lawyer, Jimmy Walker, former mayor of New York City. Blumenthal thought Walker might be of "some help to the defense." In a North Carolina courtroom, the dapper, wisecracking former mayor would have been a decidedly questionable asset to any defense (but where Jimmy Walker *could have been valuable* might be unraveling the behind-the-scenes politics of one of his New York surrogate courts). However, Bennet Polikoff already had an inside track on that assignment — provided he could keep Libby out of a North Carolina jail, a North Carolina court, and off North Carolina's death row.

A prominent New York estate attorney, interviewed by a reporter outside Manhattan's Surrogate Court chambers, considered that Smith's lawyers were very astute to have filed the will for probate in New York. Under New York State law, a surviving wife would have a right to take an "intestacy share" of the estate, regardless of the will provisions. And the same attorney speculated that the right of her child, by the dead husband, to share in the estate might even be argued to be similarly "absolute." These provisions might apply even if the other beneficiaries named in the estate had to give up some of their share by will in order to make up the totals for the two intestate shares, the New York attorney speculated.

The two states involved picked up the avaricious spirit of the thing and began to bicker. New York claimed the will was drawn in New York and was valid in New York. Therefore it must be probated there. The majesty of carrying out New York estate law was surely sweetened by the fact that the state intended to pick up about $1,900,000 in estate taxes if the will went through the New York probate court. But A. J. Maxwell, the North Carolina revenue commissioner, fought it as an attempt to circumvent the spirit and letter of North Carolina law: "I think the will was executed and probated in New York simply for the reason that a minor could not make a legal will in North Carolina, and Mr. Reynolds was a minor. Whether he was a resident of North Carolina or New York *is* a question of fact. And in my opinion, facts will sustain his residence in North Carolina."

The amount of Smith's eventual inheritance was estimated at somewhere between $15,000,000 and $20,000,000. And for most of the country in that Depression fall, it was the sort of money that could not really be imagined.

27

A Little Not-So-Subtle Pressure

OCTOBER IS A particularly beautiful time of the year in western North Carolina and in Winston-Salem. Sitting as it does on the rolling edge of the North Carolina highlands, Winston-Salem begins to get its fall colors early. The October nights are becoming cool and there are the first of the early-morning heavy dews of fall. The days sparkle and the afternoons can be warm, but still with the hint of November in the late afternoon light. Natives regard it as "perfect football weather," an important commodity in a state whose population seems to divide its Saturday afternoons into either hunting or filling the stadiums at Chapel Hill, Wake Forest, Duke, or North Carolina State.

But old Chapel Hill fan Carlisle Higgins was finding it hard to take the time to make the eighty-mile trip to the University of North Carolina stadium on Saturday afternoons that October because the Reynolds case just wouldn't seem to stay neatly tied up waiting for the trial to unravel it. His room at Winston-Salem's Carolina Hotel was no sanctuary, even with the telephone cut off. There was often a reporter in wait for him in the lobby with "just one question." Then there were the crackpots. And after them, there was the problem he was having with the several people who had some authority to investigate the situation — or thought they did. Most notably McMichael.

He had finally forbidden McMichael to hold any more press sessions unless he, Higgins, was there. And McMichael took this directive sulkily. Keeping Scott on short leash was a different matter. The results of Scott's findings were legally the property of the county solicitor to use as he saw fit. But Higgins couldn't tell Scott how or what to investigate . . . or, more important, when to stop hunting and when to stop talking. It seemed to Higgins, heavily distracted with trying to prepare his conspiracy case for court with one hand and juggle the tricky Reynolds matter with the other, that either McMichael or Scott was releasing something new to the papers every time he turned around.

As far as the family went, Higgins felt reasonably well covered there — except for young Dick Reynolds, something of a renegade. Higgins was in regular touch with Uncle Will Reynolds, the family spokesman. And Higgins was aware that the ex-FBI man, whom Will had paid to join Higgins in the investigation, was certainly reporting directly to Will. With luck, Higgins was getting everything that Will Reynolds was. But he couldn't be sure.

In early October, Uncle Will had taken another step that quite enraged Higgins. At Will's direction, B. B. Womble of the prestigious Winston-Salem law firm of Manley, Hendren & Womble had assembled his own press conference, to make public a letter Will Reynolds had ordered delivered to Carlisle Higgins's office. To make his firm's position clear to the reporters, Womble revealed that for the last two months Manley, Hendren & Womble had been retained at the family's request to investigate the case and advise the family on whether or not the family should support the state in prosecuting Libby and Walker. But, Womble said, after two months of investigation, the firm had been "unable to uncover evidence which in our opinion would justify us in advising the family to join in the prosecution." He said the letter from Will Reynolds, which he then handed to reporters, reflected the family's reaction to the law firm's advice. Womble's phrase "join in the prosecution" was an odd one — as if they would even share the cross-examination duties and all the rest.

The letter was a strange combination of accusation and reluctance to accuse; it acknowledged the unlikelihood of Smith's committing suicide and the strange aspects of the case; and it ended with a rather imperious set of suggestions on how the Reynolds family advised the state to proceed:

Mr. Higgins:

Ever since the death of my nephew, Smith Reynolds, I have been very much interested in and have given very careful and thoughtful attention to everything that I could learn about that tragic occurrence.

Knowing Smith as I did and realizing the many fine traits of character that he had, I am convinced that his attitude toward life was such that he would never have intentionally killed himself. Nothing that I have been able to learn about the case has been sufficient to change my mind in that respect.

On the other hand, it is equally true, in my opinion and in that of Smith's brother and sisters, that the evidence fails to prove conclusively that Smith was murdered.

I realize that the matter of handling these indictments is officially in your hands as the representative of the State and that no individual has or ought to have anything to do with the question of whether or not the cases are prosecuted or are dropped. But there has been a great deal of comment and speculation as to what the attitude of Smith's family is towards these cases.

With that fact in mind, I am taking the liberty of writing you this letter by way of disclosing that attitude and of saying to you that if in the discharge of your further official duties with respect to these cases you come to the conclusion that it is right and fair and in the public interest that the cases be dropped, then that action on your part will certainly have no criticism from me or from the other members of Smith's family.

In fact, I think that under the circumstances, all of us would be quite happy if it should be your decision to drop the cases. Distressed as we all are over Smith's unfortunate death, none of us could find any pleasure in a prosecution that was not fully sustained by the circumstances of his death.

I am taking the liberty of sending a copy of this letter to Judge Stack for his information.

W. N. Reynolds

No one could say that the wishes of the family were not clear. In the Reynoldses' company town, that was damn near an ultimatum!

As it turned out, practically every radio listener in North Carolina "read the letter" before Higgins did. When he was finally reached by reporters at his home in West Jefferson, he parried as diplomatically as he could; he hadn't even received the damn thing! "I will consider the letter carefully — *coming from the source it does*" — Higgins supplied the emphasis — "but I shall make up my own mind, regardless of who wants this or that done. This is my responsibility, and I intend to follow it." He was clearly annoyed, with a right to be.*

When reached for comment, Bennet Polikoff said he was not surprised at Will Reynolds's letter — perhaps because the leaks the defense had been making about what would come out at a trial had probably helped trigger the letter. As for his client, he said she might prefer a trial so she could finally clear her name. He would have to consult with Mrs. Reynolds and with his co-counsel, William Graves, who was busy in New York, before he could say anything more.

What Graves was busy at was lining up defense witnesses. He had just completed an arrangement with Dr. Charles Norris, chief medical examiner of the City of New York, to testify at the trial. Norris was the right man for the defense. His credentials were excellent, his training and practice were forensic medicine — and though he admitted he was not too familiar with the case, he volunteered to reporters that from what knowledge he had, the death of Smith "looked like suicide."

As each October week went by with no trial date announced, the big blocks of hotel reservations for the visiting press were moved ahead. The temporary telephone and telegraph wires for their use sprayed out a half-dozen windows of the Forsyth County Courthouse to raw, new poles set in the lawn. The curio hawkers, recruited by the same people

---

* If the role of the Reynolds family in attempting to influence the case was not illegal in any way — it was certainly highly unusual. A former assistant district attorney in New York tried to look at it as if the interference had been in a case of his: "It is not for the family of the victim of any crime to avoid trial. In this respect the People of the State and the interests of the community and society in general take precedence over both the victim and the victim's relatives. Once a crime had been committed, the complainant is, in reality, the State. Accordingly, the Reynolds family's public requests to avoid trial were gratuitous in that they did not have legal standing to do so. In the last analysis, their standing in society and in the real world of power overcame their lack of legal status. I know of no way whereby the family of a victim of a homicide can successfully 'refuse to press charges.'

"The Reynolds family had a perfect legal right to voice their desire, however, with respect to the trial or to the avoidance of one. As private individuals their right of free speech took precedence over any consideration of the prosecution and the interests of the State in general. The judge could not have gagged them, nor could I believe that such a gag rule imposed on a private citizen would have been customary or legal. The victims of a crime could verbalize their opinions as often as they chose (provided, of course, they did not incite to riot or create some other illegal situation as a corollary to their invocation of their free speech rights — the old adage, you cannot shout 'fire' in a crowded theatre)."

who handled pompons and banners at football games, had their supply dumps stocked: glossy photos of Libby and Smith; Libby on stage in a revealing gown in her prostitute role for *The Little Show*; Libby being strangled on a bed by Clifton Webb in the "Moanin' Low" skit, with a bottle of gin beside her; oversized picture postcards of Reynolda, plus a crude floor plan of the second story sketched on the back, the "murder bedroom" and bed drawn in, with Smith's body sprawled on it and all the appealing legends: "Bloodstains," "Pistol," "Path of murder bullet." There was even a composite picture — made by pasting photographs of Smith's and Libby's heads onto the bodies of some posed actors — purporting to show the two and a number of bathing-suited figures cavorting with bottles and glasses in a wooded background; it was labeled "The wild party before the fatal shooting!"

Dick Reynolds was the one family member who seemed unwilling to have the family representatives speak on his behalf. Since his return from the coast of Africa, Dick had been an aggressive and outspoken believer that his brother would never have committed suicide. He had prompted the midnight autopsy. He had urged on Scott and McMichael. He had conferred repeatedly with the FBI sleuth brought in to help solicitor Higgins. He refused to talk to Walker, whom he knew well enough. He was privately bitter at Libby, whom he had known before Smith had. Yet on October 19, the same day that Polikoff spoke publicly demanding a speedy trial for his client, Dick called reporters to the richly paneled study at Reynolda. And after going through a rambling review of how he saw the case, he announced that he too would go along with a family decision not to press for a trial. But his final sentences were not too convincing: "I am still convinced he did not commit suicide. But it might have been an accident — I guess." He refused to answer any more questions and left the room, instructing the uniformed guards who had been on the grounds since his return to see the reporters off the property. Their departure was rude, hurried, and ended with some scuffling at the gate.

28

"I Request a Nol-Pros"

THE FORSYTH COUNTY COURTHOUSE in Winston-Salem where the Holman-Walker trial was to be held is somewhat different from the stereotyped columned and porticoed courthouses of Southern books, movies — and particularly of actuality. It follows the solidly imposing tradition of modern civic buildings, rather than the highly creative flights of some postbellum architects, bent on designing "something memorable."

Of the several courtrooms available to the prosecutors, the largest — the spacious room running along the east side of the second floor, where some of the earlier sparring had taken place — was reserved for the trial. It would seat about four hundred people. By the end of summer 1932, Forsyth County authorities already had press requests to fill up almost half these seats — with more requests coming in daily; the trial promised to bring a modest three or four weeks of boom to Winston-Salem hotels and restaurants. With the press would come all the camp followers of such an event — those who had some small roles on- or offstage, plus the curious and the morbid. The presiding judge was to be Judge Stack.

Those familiar with the testimony at the inquest were aware of the substantial murky areas where the prosecution had to discover or deduce from the answers of the defendants themselves just what had happened, though it was always questionable if the defendants would

be put on the stand. There were the several rather critical inconsistencies of time and place and action that had cropped up in their testimony
at the inquest. If certain of these could be resolved, the court would at
least know *when* Smith was shot and perhaps who might have been in
the room when it happened: Walker still maintained he had not been
there. Libby had first sent out from her bedroom the story that she had
"run to" Smith — and then that she had already been in the room. On
all other points, she stuck with the story that she was in her mysterious
blackout from the night before the party until twenty-four hours after
it.*

In their last stories before the trial was to begin, the better reporters
concentrated on a scene-setting tight examination of the facts. These
were meant as a sort of "score card" for serious followers of the trial.

---

* Could Libby's blackout have been medically real?

A leading New York psychiatrist with a generous amount of experience in cases of
mental shock, talked of such cases to aid in the research for this book: "It's always dangerous to make judgments without seeing the person. But you can probably safely speculate that one of five things might have happened to cause a 'blackout,' as Mrs. Reynolds
called it — four of them medically understandable.

"First, it could have been hysterical shock resulting in retrograde amnesia. The trauma
of the event, the sight of her husband shot — by himself, by her, by Walker — could
have been enough to put her into this shock, wiping out the memory of a considerable
period both before and after the event. And when she recovered, she might not even
have been aware of the blackout, if someone had not told her.

"Second, it could have been toxic amnesia brought on by the trauma of the event and
accentuated by alcohol and/or drugs. The wiped-out period before and after could just
as well occur in this situation, too.

"Or third, it could have been an amnesia caused by a series of psychotic episodes, with
the trauma of the event triggering the blackout after a series of those severe happenings.

"Fourth, it could have been what is called by the rather flowery name of *folie à deux* —
the madness of two. If you are emotionally involved with someone who is unstable, you
may — in a moment of extreme stress — momentarily become the other person, particularly after some threat from that other person. If Smith had threatened Libby over and
over with the gun over a period of time . . . then had come out on the porch that night
with a gun and more threats, she could have momentarily become *him* . . . threatened
him, got possession of the gun, and shot him. Actresses are also often emotionally capable of higher uses of the 'disassociative mechanism' — in other words, assuming the role
of another — than other people. That's part of what makes them good actresses. So 'becoming Smith' under all that pressure was even easier. Further, if she were a bisexual . . .
she was potentially more aggressive, and perhaps more capable of violence, than the average woman.

"And fifth, it could have all been — as you suggest — just a fine job of acting.

"Today in such a case, it might be possible to get a court order to put such a person
into hypnosis or administer the so-called 'truth drugs' to find out if she could remember
more about the lost day before and after the shooting. I doubt that would have been
either legally or medically possible then."

The things they were looking for answers to were fairly basic to the case. A thorough summary would have covered these points.

1. The doctors who had treated Smith at the hospital were all well-trained men with highly respected medical reputations in the community. But none of them had any real experience with gunshot wounds, and none was anything like a trained forensic pathologist, as a bit city medical examiner must be. They had been called quickly to try to save Smith's life. And they apparently did all that was possible. But then they were pressed into the less familiar role of trying to perform some of the functions of medical examiners. This was where they were unqualified for this intensely specialized job, and this was where unskilled opinions raised questions, rather than settled them.

2. Dr. Hanes had testified that the entrance wound was "probably" the one in the upper right temple at the hair line — with the exit wound being below and behind the left ear. But when questioned about the odd downward path the bullet would have to take to follow this course, he admitted he really wasn't too sure of his probabilities, and in effect at this point he disqualified himself as an expert witness: "I am just giving you an opinion, such as you would have yourself."

3. Dr. Hanes had testified that around the wound on the right temple were slight evidences which were attributed to powder burns. "Not marked, very slight, just on the edge of the wound, a blackening of the edge of the wound which it seemed possible to us at the time were powder burns." But then he admitted that the doctors could find no trace of scorched or burned hair anywhere around the wound; scorching and burning was what you would expect to find if the end of the pistol barrel had been placed directly against the temple, as a suicide would have done, with the muzzle flash burning out all around it.

4. Though Dr. Hanes suggested that the slight powder burns at the temple had come because the muzzle of the pistol must have been resting "almost, if not quite, on the skin itself," *he also conceded that similar slight burning could again occur if the pistol had been held as far as three feet away from the head* — where a suicide could never have held it. So the exact position of the gun continued in doubt.

5. Dr. Hanes and his colleagues at Baptist Hospital could find no powder burns on the tissue *inside* the skull. Powder marks there would also have been a strong indication that the pistol had been directly against the temple when fired. A second element of proof of suicide missing.

6. If you concede Smith had been shot from the front, it would have

been extremely difficult for Smith to hold a pistol conventionally and shoot himself *downward* through the upper right temple. It would have taken another person holding the gun.

7. Then there were the questions about the amateurish mishandling of the gun when it was finally found at the house, eliminating any possibility of recovering a useful fingerprint from it — if any prints in fact existed on a gun obviously left there to be discovered.

8. Though the gun found and presented at the inquest was assumed to belong to Smith, no attempt was ever made to determine whether the bullet that killed Smith actually came from that gun. Nor was there an attempt to determine when the gun had been most recently fired.

9. Walker claimed he owned a German Luger and kept it in his room next door. Walker's gun was missing after the shooting. Could Smith have been shot with Walker's gun, which might have been the reason for doing away with it? That no attempt was ever made to find out what happened to Walker's gun — in the long list of questionable omissions in the investigation — is among the most glaring malfeasances of all.

10. Both Walker's and Smith's guns were said to be automatics. But then there was Libby's statement, made several times — even publicly in the lawyer-approved Moorehouse interview — that the gun she saw Smith holding was "a revolver," an odd specific for her to make. Walker had also said in his first statements to reporters that he had found Smith on the sleeping porch "with a revolver nearby." No attempt was made to resolve the contradictions.

Finally, there was the critical timing. From the inquest testimony presented, it was established that the fatal shot probably came about fifteen minutes before Blanche Yurka caused the discovery of the shooting.

12:30   Mrs. Reynolds, observed by Fulcher, weaves from the woods into the kitchen garden, behind the house, soon to be followed by Walker. Fulcher leads the two of them toward the house, where Smith is watching them come in. Fulcher leaves, believing they are all retiring.

12:45   Fulcher hears what he thinks is a shot, goes out to the side of the house where the sleeping porch is, to investigate. Listens for a few minutes. Hears nothing else.

12:55   Fulcher, seeing nothing out-of-the-way, starts off down to the lake on his one o'clock rounds.

1:00   Baptist Hospital receives the call to send an ambulance to Reynolda House.

1:10   Walker's car arrives at the hospital with the fatally wounded Smith — passing the outgoing ambulance along the way.

If you accept that Fulcher noted correctly the time of the shot — and as a watchman and a deputized member of the sheriff's office, that's the sort of observation he was supposed to make correctly — then at least fifteen minutes passed between the shot and the call for the ambulance. A reasonable question would be: what were Libby and Walker doing during this long period?

Libby's pregnancy argued for an early trial. It was openly understood that by the beginning of September she would be about four-to-five months pregnant, with a baby due in January or February. Neither side could be sure what the effect of a pleasantly rounded Libby Holman Reynolds on the witness stand would be on twelve jurors. The prosecution could speculate that it might result in a wave of sympathy that would cancel out damaging testimony. The defense could concern itself with the fact that Libby's girth would be a constant reminder of the ugly rumor that was going around that the baby was not Smith's — but Walker's, or that of some unnamed Broadway playboy. Libby's remark at the coroner's inquest that Smith was distressed because he was not capable of making love had leaked out and circulated widely.

The North Carolina Bar Association had stated an early trial was most desirable, and a number of politicians and state officials were grimacing under the barrage of publicity as the pretrial speculation dragged on. Between the shooting in early July, the indictment from the grand jury on August 4, and the surrender of Libby Holman at Wentworth Courthouse on August 8, there had been long dry periods of no hard news. Yet, with an open case of such wide interest, editors all around the country, and particularly up and down the eastern seaboard, felt a need to print *something.*

Reporters soared on flights of late-evening newsroom fantasy to examine any number of dragged-in-by-the-tail topics: "The Role of the Business Barons in North Carolina Law," "R. J. Reynolds and His Feudal Fiefdom — the Whole Darn State!" or "Jazz and Booze Run Wild among Tarheel Young" or "What Happens When Youth Takes Over the South's Enlightened State." North Carolina leaders knew the trial would bring two or three more weeks of its own lurid stories. But when it ended, they hoped another tempting whipping boy would pop up somewhere, to set the press off on a new chase.

So, amid the last-hour statements of total confidence that "justice will be done" by the prosecution, and sonorous claims of "the innocence of my client" by the defenses, a trial seemed welcome to all.

One of the most difficult parts would come first: the selection of a jury that was presumably unbiased, objective, uninfluenced by the rolling barrage of publicity that had issued from the newspapers, radio, and newsreels since the shooting occurred.

In certain ways, the search for such a jury in Winston was totally unrealistic. Nor would a change of venue, moving the trial to another part of the state, have accomplished much. Neither side thought there was much of a chance of picking a jury "a man could have success with" from the highbrows in the three central North Carolina communities that made up "The Triangle": Raleigh, home of North Carolina State University; Durham, site of Duke; and Chapel Hill, a pleasant little town which only existed to serve the University of North Carolina, the oldest state university in the nation. Then how about the rural eastern countries? That was "colonial" North Carolina, which prided itself on a certain independence — and orneriness. The livelihood of many of the citizens of rural eastern North Carolina was tied up with sending leaf tobacco west to the Reynoldses' factories in Winston. Most of those hard-pressed farmers soaked up every word of what was happening "over west," with some feeling of escape each night from the blistering heat of their fields and worries about their leaf. There was a certain amount of chuckling over them hell-raisers in Winston. Some could even feel it was just a family affair where the handsome profligate son had been sowing a few wild oats, and he got caught. Hell, it wasn't their son. But then, life was tough and violent on the sandy farms in the eastern pine woods, too.

So it was rise or fall with Winston, where at least half of the community, directly or indirectly, lived better or lived worse as the fortunes of the Reynoldses and their tobacco company rose and fell. For a lot of prospective jurors, this was something of a family affair, too.

Summonses for the first panel of veniremen were to go out to some three hundred voters. The jury panel was drawn to be a reasonable cross-section of Forsyth County. But as is usual in the case of jury service, by the time the people with the influence, with the arrogance, and with the civic disdain got through with their wheeling and dealing, most of the group that finally would report would be more representative of Winston's lower middle class: small merchants, factory workers, laboring men, a few farmers from the fringes of the county, some old retired types. By law, no women, no blacks.

The choosing of twelve good men and true was certainly not easy. Nobody in Forsyth County could honestly say he had "no opinion" about the case. Nor had jury selection reached the precision it has reached today, with psychiatrists, psychologists, computer programmers, and behavioral scientists sitting in consultation with defense lawyers. Polikoff, Graves, and Liipfert and their two small staffs had only their instincts to help them.

What the prosecution must attempt to establish was that Smith could not have killed himself. And since Libby and Walker were the only two people either with or near him, one of them must have held and fired the gun. Then they had made a bungling, amazing attempt to extricate themselves. Bungling, because they did so many things that were quickly transparent. Amazing, because to a certain extent they seemed to have been successful.

If the prosecution did not handle itself well in all this, all the defense had to establish was that the burden of proof was on the prosecution.

On a chilly overcast afternoon on the fourteenth of October, with the first heat of the season clanking and banging and hissing through the courthouse radiators, Carlisle Higgins asked reporters to meet in his office. The men present were all local reporters, though several of them were stringers from other North Carolina newspapers or for the national wire services. The big boys had all gone home. They filed in, hoping at last for the announcement of the trial date. Higgins knew them all well enough, and he exchanged banter with them as they settled around the room extracting paper and pencils.

"Gentlemen, in the next twenty-four hours I will decide whether or not to drop the case against Mrs. Reynolds and Mr. Walker."

He let it sink in for a moment. There were some nervous glances around the room. One or two of the reporters felt sure they had missed something earlier, some indication that Higgins was considering the move so definitely. The whole town had been getting ready for a first-class murder trial!

"I'm considering two alternatives. One is a nol-pros with leave. That means, in effect, that I could return the defendants to their status before the indictments. But I could still restore the case to the court docket at any time by obtaining a report of the indictment from the grand jury. There is *no* double jeopardy here. These people will not have been tried."*

The reporters scribbled frantically.

"Or I could ask for a simple continuance — which means I just postpone any activity. But the indictment would still legally stand.

"That's really all I'm going to say right now. Now I suspect you boys had better get over to see Mr. Polikoff. He'll probably have something to give you."

Polikoff's office was only a few blocks away. He wasn't there when they all first charged in. But when Polikoff, at an appointment across town, was told what the reporters were there for, he hurried back.

Polikoff arrived striding rapidly. And he was the one with the first questions. What exactly had Higgins said? He heard one reporter's version, then checked around the circle of men to make sure there was no disagreement. It was hard for him to hide his delight.

"Well, my client really *has* been pressing for a fair and speedy trial so that she can clear herself completely. But naturally, no one looks forward to the emotional and financial expense of a trial. And considering all that, I suppose a nol-pros stance on the part of the state would be acceptable to her. I would have to consult."

As soon as they left, his first reaction was to call Libby, a step he

---

* A New York trial lawyer commented on Higgins's chances of getting Walker and Libby Holman back on trial after making this decision: "In New York State we do not have a procedure similar to *nol pros.* I must, therefore, give my view by analogizing the North Carolina procedure with a New York application that calls for the dismissal of the indictment. I think that it is more than a semantic difference, however. I do not understand Mr. Higgins when he speaks of restoring the case and going forward with a trial in the event that new evidence is uncovered. Although it is, strictly speaking, not double jeopardy in the classic sense of the constitutional admonition, it is highly doubtful that a second indictment charging the *same* crime would issue following an earlier dismissal of an indictment charging the *same* crime."

could not take from his office, since he had taken the precaution of not letting any of the staff know where she was. Then he wondered if Higgins was setting up some sort of legal trap. It would be cruel to give Libby hope — and then have it snatched away. He tried Higgins's office, and the prosecutor came on the phone immediately.

"I figured you'd call, Bennet." Higgins confirmed his conversation with the reporters and volunteered that he had requested a hearing before Judge Stack the following day. If it was granted, he was sure Judge Stack's clerk would be in touch with Polikoff. Would that be convenient?

Polikoff acknowledged as urbanely as possible that he thought he could appear if necessary. Then he hurried home to call Libby and Mr. Holman.

The courtroom in which Judge Stack received them the next day showed all the preparations for the big trial. There was new white paint on the walls, covering the faded green and cream "county issue" paint. New venetian blinds hung at the high windows behind the judge's bench, replacing the old window shades which occasionally had a habit — when billowed out by a breeze — of suddenly rolling up in the middle of a hearing with a rattle and bang that scared hell out of everybody. A new set of state and national flags bracketed the judge's desk. And several rows of spectator seats had been removed from one section so that three long tables could be moved in for reporters. There was already an air of excitement and tension about the room. Ab Walker slipped in last.

The hearing had come up so quickly that only a few reporters other than the local men had been able to get to Winston-Salem in time. The spectator seats were mostly empty. It all went as rapidly as if it had been rehearsed, conducted in the sotto voce tones that were scarcely louder than a judge-lawyer conference at the bench. Clearly, no one was playing it for effect. There was virtually no one in the room to play to. Higgins spoke first.

"It is my duty to determine what course the state shall pursue. Like any other question of human judgment, there may be an error of judgment if I proceed to trial without sufficient evidence; any discovery of additional evidence thereafter would be of no avail. But if I pursue the course I have decided upon in this case, if there should be additional evidence available hereafter, the state could still proceed to trial. So, in determining the course that I should pursue, I have decided that if I make a mistake, it will be the one that leaves a way open for its correction.

"If the defendants are not guilty, the least the state can do now is to stop the prosecution. If they are guilty, then the door should not be closed to prosecution should sufficient evidence to justify it be available at any time hereafter." He looked briefly at the defense table for some reaction from Polikoff or Liipfert. They sat stonefaced.

"It will be recalled," Higgins continued, "that practically all of the evidence which is now available was presented to the coroner's jury who heard the testimony. Also presented were all of the witnesses who attended the party, likewise the evidence of all persons who were in the house at the time of the killing, as well as the evidence of the physicians who made the postmortem. All this was heard by the coroner's jury. And that evidence was found insufficient to justify a charge against any person. As for the grand jury who preferred such a charge, I have no criticism to make of their actions, for I know it was honest and sincere. Yet the grand jury did not have the benefit of the evidence at the party, or from those in the house at the time of the shooting. Your Honor, after a careful investigation of this case in which the defendants are under indictment for murder, I am thoroughly satisfied that we do not have sufficient evidence to justify the state going to trial.

"For these reasons," Higgins concluded, "I request that a nol-pros be entered in this case." He sat down abruptly.

The judge looked to Polikoff and then to Liipfert to see if either desired to speak. Neither man rose to his feet. Stack nodded and addressed the court:

"It is the duty of the solicitor to protect the innocent as well as to prosecute the guilty. It is my custom to abide by the solicitor's wishes."

At that point, Judge Stack delivered himself of a rather unjudicial opinion for the benefit of those present. He said that all he knew of the case was what he had gleaned from the newspapers, and if all the evidence the prosecution had was what had been summed up there, then it did not strike him that it would secure a conviction. "Mr. Clerk," he directed, "let the defendants be discharged and their bonds released." He rose and left the court. There was a moment of decorum while he disappeared — and then a rush by the reporters to the phones.

The handful of spectators sat stunned. "He took a hell of a risk preempting the jury's right to decide the thing," another experienced prosecutor said after reviewing the record. "There were too many questions unanswered. It should have gone to a jury."

29

Persecution? Racial Prejudice? Undue Influence?

POLIKOFF WAS DELIGHTED. He spoke to reporters on the steps outside the court. "The action," he said, was "the most complete exoneration possible under the laws of the State of North Carolina. The decision by the solicitor was the only logical solution of the case." He applauded the state for avoiding the trial.

And then he dropped an interesting teaser: "Of course, we knew all the time that exoneration would be the result in the case. The solicitor had only the evidence in the possession of the state to consider. He did *not* have the benefit of evidence in possession of the defense counsel."

William Hendren of the family law firm had been seated at Higgins's side for the brief proceedings. Did he agree with the state's decision? Had he pushed for it? Hadn't the family entered the case to make sure there really would be a vigorous prosecution, to see justice done in Smith Reynolds's memory? Hendren glared at the reporter who asked the question; it had been delivered with some sarcasm.

"Speaking as one of the counsel for the family, I assure you we agree with the state's decision."

"But do you agree with the solicitor that there's not enough evidence to go to trial with?" The reporter was insistent.

"I have no other statement to make." Hendren shouldered the reporter aside and started across the street to the Reynolds building, *"I'm not* the person to answer that question." You could get the impression that he did not agree at all.

W. N. Reynolds, Smith's uncle, had waited for Hendren outside the courtroom. Reporters knew he had been active in urging the investigation, had supplied the money for Higgins to employ the ex-FBI investigator, had been prepared to bring the Womble law firm in on the side of the state. "Uncle Will" was also close-mouthed. All he would say was "It meets with the approval of the family." Then he escaped too.

Walker hurried out, would say nothing. His father was waiting at the curb to drive him away.

The reporters were mystified. For weeks they had been telling each other that Higgins would finally get some answers. He was known as a hard man in court. The betting was heavy that Libby and Walker would be convicted — though probably not for first-degree.

Now suddenly they were both walking away free! One of the men remembered Stack's earlier piece of wisdom to the grand jury: "It is hard to convict a wealthy person in the State of North Carolina." It was hard even to bring one to trial!

The *Winston-Salem Journal* of November 16 was fairly successful in editing out the tone of puzzlement from its news story of the court session. But its editorial page writer allowed some of the paper's wonder and questioning to show through:

> Perhaps the State has followed the right course. But if this is so, it is all the more pity that a nation has been entertained by sensational stories, digging deep into the inner lives of every principal in the Reynolds tragedy. It is all the more pity that officers handling the investigation have been laid open to the charge of persecution, and the community to charges of racial prejudice.
>
> All of this could have been avoided, perhaps, had officials conducted an immediate and thorough investigation after the tragedy, without recourse to secrecy.
>
> On the other hand, the verdict might have been the same, but suspicion would not have been built up in the public mind to the extent it was by reason of the procedure followed.
>
> Doubtless Higgins will receive some criticism at this stage for taking a nol pros in the case. There may be some suggestion that the State Attorney was influenced by the decision of the Reynolds family in the matter. But the Solicitor apparently probed the case and weighed it well. He saw, we presume, what many of the laity were able to see from the head-

lines — that while mysterious circumstances revolved about the case, there was little tangible evidence with which to convince a jury.

Persecution? Racial prejudice? Secret hearings? Undue influence? Though the *Winston-Salem Journal* was now retiring from the field, it had nevertheless sounded a few interesting buzzwords. If the court was a place to get some questions answered, none had been. Now the speculation could do nothing but continue; had a deal to drop charges been made?

And if so, who now owed what to whom?

30

The Multi-Million-Dollar Sweepstakes

THOSE WHO EXPECTED some gala victory celebration from Libby's camp when the news was announced that the charges against her had been dropped were disappointed — though several newspaper columns suggested that a party had been planned (one even giving the menu). A party would have been in character perhaps for the image that had been built of her in the newspapers. But Polikoff had been calling the shots for some time, and he was not going to let her make a mistake like that. *She stayed under cover.*

With Polikoff and Graves not talking and with Libby still in hiding, one reporter tracked down Walter Batchelor, Libby's New York manager, who had been at Reynolda just before the shooting. Was it true that Libby already had had plans to go back on Broadway before the charges were dropped? And what about stories that she was flooded with offers now that she was free? Batchelor dismissed the rumors. "Exploitation!" Miss Holman was not rushing back on stage in some "sideshow" to titillate the gawkers. She was a star! For the time, Batchelor said she would stay in seclusion, resting and recovering her nerves and emotions — at least until her baby was born. In the meantime, he would look over some of the more "substantial" opportunities for her that had been pending those several months. A number of them were quite interesting.

The tabloids had quickly christened Libby's unborn child "the $20,-000,000 baby." The label would stick regardless of statements from several reliable sources, who kept insisting that the final money to be settled on the child was nowhere near that. Then, of course, there was always the speculation about how much Libby might go after for herself.

The lawyers had already tasted blood. Rumor was out that Polikoff and Graves had put in a $1,000,000 bill for their services. Obviously, there was nothing Alfred Holman could drop on the market that would raise a sum like that for his daughter's defense. And Libby had already stated that her net worth at that point was "less than $10,000." One way or another it looked like it was going to have to be Reynolds money that would pay a bill like that. After all, Libby *was* a Reynolds — and the money had been spent keeping the Reynolds name out of trial.

As for how she was going to get something for herself, Polikoff soon dispelled all the speculation. Early in December, he announced that negotiations had been started for a financial agreement between Libby and the family. The main objective was support for the baby. Polikoff carefully referred repeatedly to "negotiating an agreement." That seemed to imply some prior consent "to agree" on the part of the family. Perhaps now it was just a question of "how much."

A few days later, the Guaranty Trust Company of New York, temporary administrator of the will, began to grapple with the question of Libby's right under the recently liberalized New York intestate law, in which a wife was guaranteed a share in her late husband's estate, regardless of what his will might say.

Considering the New York provisions, the absence of Libby from the will did not bother Polikoff. He would base his arguments on the fact that the will had been drawn while Smith was still legally married to Anne Cannon. Smith could not prudently have made provisions for Libby at that point. Yet it was clear, Polikoff said, that in light of the deep love that Libby had testified existed between them, "Smith would have intended to provide handsomely for her, had he been given time to do so."

At that point, less than two weeks before Christmas, Libby came out of seclusion. She announced that she had taken a house in the countryside west of Wilmington, Delaware, to await the birth of her child. She would be near her friend Louisa Jenney, who had sheltered her at various times during her hiding out from the authorities. And her mother would be living with her. The plea went out to press for privacy. There was really nothing more to say at that point.

Early in January, Libby paid a visit to her obstetrician in Philadelphia. With Libby's permission, he announced the baby would be born in late February or early March. Tentative reservations had been made at the University of Pennsylvania Hospital. Needless to say, thousands of newspaper readers stopped to count back nine months on their fingers, coming up with June as the month of conception. At that time Libby would have been safely installed at Reynolda. The finger counters settled in to suffer the wait.

They suffered practically no time at all. Shortly after sunup on January 10, Libby checked into the hospital "for observation." At 6:48 P.M. a son was born. The hospital announced that he weighed three and one-half pounds, but was perfectly healthy for a premature baby. He was immediately put into an incubator, with the speculation that he might have to stay in the hospital for as long as three months. The mother was also doing nicely.

Nicely enough to make a few telephone calls. Two days later Arnold J. Brock of the New York firm of Goldsmith, Jackson, and Brock announced they had been retained *a month before the charges were dropped against Libby,* to represent her and her child. His opinion, said Brock, was that she and the boy were entitled to Smith's *entire estate.* Brock told reporters that he would attack Smith's will on several points: Polikoff had already acknowledged that as "a friend," she had no legal status when the will was written. But Smith surely meant to provide for her. In any event, it was drawn before he reached the legal age of twenty-one under North Carolina law — and R. J. Sr.'s trust fund operated under North Carolina law. Therefore the will was invalid. Since Smith had died legally intestate — without a will — intestacy rules would apply. And thus Libby was entitled to one-third of the whole for herself and the remaining two-thirds for her child.

It was getting interesting. And would get more so. In Baltimore, the Safe Deposit & Trust Company of Baltimore, holder of the $60,000,000 estate of R. J., Sr., confirmed that Smith's share might be a good bit less than the $20,000,000 figure which everyone had grown so fond of. Then the Safe Deposit & Trust spokesman threw in an interesting qualifier: the money could only go to children of Smith who were "living" at the time of his death. Was a child born within six months after the father's death deemed to be "living" at the time of the father's death? Someone scrambled around and found a legal precedent wherein a baby born ten months after the father's death was ruled living at the time of the father's death. Under that precedent, Libby's baby clearly qualified — assuming no one would successfully contend he wasn't Smith's child.

Brock had scared the Reynolds family with the intentions of his client. She was not going to settle for a handout. The rumor was that Libby was smoldering because of the family snubs and the fact that when the Womble firm joined the state in the investigation of the shooting, the Reynoldses were in effect making a public statement that they contemplated helping to prosecute her for first-degree murder. In general, they had badly underestimated her stubborn pride.

On January 13, 1933, the day after Brock had announced Libby's claim on the whole estate, Alfred Holman came up with a compromise.

Well, maybe Libby Holman didn't need it *all.* He had a suggestion that might help all the parties concerned. Because it came at a time when Libby was feeling fairly vindictive, and was in a good position to act so, the fact that she was offering to show some mercy smacked of a deal. Holman proposed that in return for a "modest sum" for Libby and "certain altruistic actions" by the Reynoldses, she might give up her claims.

Interesting. Altruism was not a strongly recorded concern for either the Reynoldses or the Holmans at that point. Holman said a written proposal was on the way to all the interested parties, including Smith's brother and sisters: R. J. Reynolds, Jr., Mary Reynolds Babcock, and Nancy Reynolds Bagley. Because of this announcement, the proposal was in reporters' hands long before any Reynolds family member got it; Holman was learning fast how to fight the sort of fight required: get on record first.

At this point — almost as if by prearranged signal — virtually everyone involved went underground. The emergence would not begin until mid-April, three months later, when the telephone calls and letters of deal and counterdeal appeared to result in at least a few of the points of compromise Holman seemed to have in mind. But there were problems.

Anne Cannon Reynolds was gumming things up, for starters. She broke out into the open first. After reading story after story about Smith's big money and Libby's "$20,000,000 baby," she could only have felt that she had signed away too much in August 1931 when she and her child had settled for the $1,100,000 for rights in the estate. On April 21, the Cabarrus Bank of Concord, North Carolina, co-guardian for little Anne, filed a complaint against the child's grandmother, Mrs. Joseph F. Cannon. The stance of "the family bank" in suing Mrs. Cannon was, to the public, an odd and apparently ungrateful one — but it was really nothing more than an interesting legal stratagem by the lawyers to cover the fact that big Anne now wanted to break the agreement for big money she had signed in 1931.

Mrs. Cannon was little Anne's other guardian, and the bank — in the guise of looking after the interests of their ward — was giving suitable legal window dressing to the fiction that the reliable Cannons didn't want to go back on their word, but the Ebenezer Scrooges at the bank were now making them do just that. The bank's complaint was asking the court to "force" Mrs. Cannon to join with the bank in seeking to invalidate the $500,000 settlement little Anne had received for giving up her claim to the estate earlier. Little Anne's mother could now fight for at least half of all of Smith's money.

Fight for? Maybe it wouldn't be necessary. A few days later, the Reynoldses' lawyer, Hendren, who had represented the family at the proceedings to dismiss charges against Libby, promptly acknowledged the strength of Anne's claim by releasing a copy of a response he had written to Anne's lawyers, citing — as if already settled — "an agreement" whereby little Anne and Libby's just-born son would share *equally* a $4,000,000 payment from Smith's estate. All the remainder, estimated at $7,000,000 to $10,000,000, would go to set up a charitable foundation named for Smith. The foundation would work particularly "for orphans of members of fraternal orders and for religious causes." If it was a reaction to Libby's January threat to go after the whole estate — followed by her father's "compromise" suggestion — it seemed to be working.

"Orphans and religious causes"? Wonderful! There was a strange new mist of sanctity rising up around old R. J. Sr.'s name — after all those decades of cussing, brawling, and hard dealings in the auction sheds. R. J., Sr., and his lifelong adversary, Buck Duke, would have hardly recognized the same sweaty "leaf money" they had been fighting over.

Now three of the four camps involved in the case had been heard from. (Camp number 4 was occupied by Albert Walker and would remain totally silent; he had been well warned to stay out of the whole thing. He was, in fact, delighted to find that the papers no longer even bothered to mention him in connection with Smith's death.)

Three weeks later, after the last behind-the-scenes hand of this high-stakes poker had been dealt, it seemed that a compromise had been reached that gave each party a feeling of having won something major. On May 9, 1933, in Salisbury, North Carolina, Judge Wilson Warlick of the superior court signed a judgment authorizing the executors of Smith's estate to pay little Anne $1,500,000 — this to be in addition to the $500,000 "non-contesting money" awarded to her in the settlement papers filed by Smith when he had divorced her mother back in August 1931, plus the $50,000 due her on Smith's death. Another $2,000,000 was to go to Libby's son, $500,000 to Libby, and the rest to the charitable foundation to be organized. It was the judge's understanding that all parties to the proceedings had generally agreed to these terms.

So sure were the Reynoldses that they would get this agreement with their various powers of persuasion that almost thirty days earlier (on April 14, when the Cabarrus Bank & Trust Company was still thrashing around in preparation for filing its complaint against Mrs. Cannon) the three surviving Reynolds children had already decided where the money was going to go. On that date they had "delivered" to W. N. Reynolds a letter that he had written for them:

Dear Uncle Will:

Having heretofore agreed between ourselves upon a common desire to establish, out of the trust funds created by the wills of our father and mother for the benefit of our brother, Smith Reynolds, to which we may now be entitled and of which we may hereafter obtain possession, a trust of charitable, benevolent and eleemosynary purposes in the state of North Carolina, we write to confirm this agreement. . . .

Save for this purpose named, we do not expect to claim or recieve any part of such estates, other than such sum as is necessary to reimburse us for expenses incurred.

The sole reason for our participation in the litigation now pending over this property, distasteful as it will doubtless be, is to do what we can to make effective this plan, thus honoring and perpetuating the memory of our brother, Smith.

We understand Mrs. Smith Reynolds and the mother and grandparents of Anne Cannon Reynolds, 2nd, are in accord with this plan.

> Affectionately,
>
> RICHARD J. REYNOLDS
> MARY REYNOLDS BABCOCK
> NANCY REYNOLDS BAGLEY

Even in the carefully phrased legal language of the letter, the bitterness over the money came through. The family had made it clear who it was who made things happen in the settlement of Smith's affairs. But Libby *had* scared the hell out of them!

It was not until the fall of 1935, more than two years later, that associate Justice Heroit Clarkson of the North Carolina supreme court wrote a decision on behalf of the court that finally ended the fight for the dollars. Clarkson approved all the details of the organization of the foundation. And he recorded that in the court's opinion, the decision to establish a foundation had been the key to the settlement of a dispute that could have dragged on for years. (It was canny old Alfred Holman, a man some of the young Womble lawyers had taken to calling "a country lawyer," who had come up with the foundation idea — when everyone else had his blinders on for a slugging match. At least Holman could read an opponent.) The court called it a "fair, just, and equitable settlement." A report filed by the foundation with the state recorded its start:

> Securities valued as of May 12, 1936, at $7,210,887.51 were placed in the Zachary Smith Reynolds Trust, with the income to be paid to the Foundation. Twenty percent of the income was to be retained and added to the trust, until a total of $50,000,000 should be reached.
>
> Accordingly, the trustees were advised at their meeting on December 2, 1937, that the first income was payable to the Foundation in the amount of $162,241.39. A resolution was adopted selecting for the first project a program for the control of venereal disease in North Carolina and a grant of $100,000 to the State Health Department was approved. With this action, the Foundation became a functioning organization.

Now the money was finally safe from that crazy Jewish blues singer from Cincinnati.

31

The Murder Made Everyone Rich

THE DEATH OF Smith Reynolds launched, in effect, a wonderful multi-million-dollar business that has employed lawyers, accountants, and foundation executives prosperously for all the years since then.

But the foundation in memory of Smith had, by the end of 1982, paid out some $125,000,000 to charitable causes, largely in North Carolina.

Estate taxes initially probably amounted to about $2,000,000. Then there were the handsome cash settlements:

Albert Walker	$50,000
Libby Holman Reynolds	500,000
Anne Cannon Reynolds	500,000
Anne Cannon Reynolds II	2,050,000
Christopher Reynolds	2,000,000
Smith Reynolds Foundation	7,210,900
Smith Reynolds's personal estate	200,200

Smith's brother and sisters contributed substantial additional money to build the foundation. And subsequently the W. N. Reynolds Trust paid a total of almost $39,500,000 into it. It would take a gaggle of financial specialists, trust officers, city, state, and federal tax collectors to estimate the hundreds of thousands of income all this has generated for hangers-on.

Certainly, too, the work and experience of the Smith Reynolds

Foundation gets some credit for inspiring three other Reynoldses to start foundations. These today have assets in the neighborhood of $70,-000,000 and carry out their own good works.

So, without the violent end of the playboy aviator, none of this would have come about. The vast wealth of the four Reynolds children might well have traveled sedately down through each generation, never presenting the outside world with the dilemmas of filling out the countless foundation bequest applications and spending the foundation's $125,-000,000. Poor Smith in death may have accomplished much more good than he ever would have been able to do in life.

But how did each of the principals fare who saw this lively financial fallout begin?

Albert Walker took his $50,000 and sank farther into obscurity. Not long after the indictments were dropped, he moved to the Southwest, labored away dutifully, routinely, and unremarkably, lived without attracting attention, developed a terminal disease, and died there — far away from the recollections of all those in Winston-Salem who remembered. After Libby and Walker passed each other outside the doorway of the inquest room at Reynolda House late one afternoon in July 1932, there is no evidence that he ever saw her, spoke to her, or wrote to her again. And that, too, was rather sad. A few moments of intense relationship may have been the basis for all the trouble.

Blanche Yurka was a figure in the New York theater, and she was honored on her retirement with a surprising and touching demonstration of respect. Her love for the experimental theater included trying some wildly unexpected roles for herself, as well as coaching others. In one of the roles — a singing effort — she is supposed to have inspired the Moss Hart quip: "If I had heard Blanche Yurka sing, I think I would have shot myself first." Shortly after research began on this book, the Forsyth County sheriff's office received a letter from her requesting the return of the blood-smeared black dressing gown that she had worn that night at the hospital. It was found and returned, one of the few relics of the case to survive. Carlisle Higgins indicated that Yurka probably knew much more than she was telling. But she would not be interviewed for the book — unless she were first paid $15,000; presumably that was the value of the information that she had witheld from the authorities. She was in a unique position to know a few things, having been Libby's "nurse" during the sixty hours of her seclusion at Reynolda right after the shooting. One deputy sheriff on the case remembered her as "a tough babe." She still was when interviewed one spring afternoon in her New York apartment. The actress was then in her eighties and was reduced to a "walker" when moving around the room. She was wonderfully convivial, totally in charge of the conversation, but — without the $15,000 changing hands — she was wonderfully uncommunicative of anything that was new.

Transou Scott was defeated for office a few years after the shooting by Ernie Shore, the former big league baseball player, who — though immensely popular in Forsyth County — always thought he had defeated Scott too easily. Shore heard later that he had had some powerful help in the county organization from politicians and businessmen he hardly knew.

After Shore had been in office for some time, however, he became intrigued with the case. He had, after all, been a member of the first grand jury that passed on the "presentment" leading to the indictments. *But when he began to search through sheriff Scott's files, he found to his surprise that only the most minor, trivial references to the Reynolds shooting remained; the files had been thoroughly cleaned out.* When Shore's intentions to open the case again were known, he suddenly was hounded by a series of crank calls, waking him up in the middle of the night, summoning him and his deputies out and around the county to mysterious rendezvous to which no one else ever came. The calls and the criticism and a whole series of minor harassments didn't stop until Shore let it slip out that his interest in reopening the investigation had subsided. Whoever was guilty of the official misconduct of destroying the records was never called on it.

Louisa Jenney, Libby's well-heeled friend from Delaware who had hidden her for so long when she was avoiding the law and the press, was killed a few years ago in the crash of a private plane off the East Coast. With her Du Pont connections, she had made things happen when other of Libby's friends couldn't. A fit antagonist for the Reynoldses.

Bennet Polikoff split the $1,000,000 defense fee with his fellow defense lawyer, Graves, and followed Libby to New York, where he represented her for the rest of her life in her unending wrangles with the

Reynolds trusts, the tax courts, the Orphans Court of Baltimore, and the Baltimore Safe Deposit Company.

Bill Graves used his $500,000 fee for good living.

Earle McMichael, along with sheriff Scott one of the few aggressive investigators in the Reynolds case, settled into private practice in a comfortable suite in the Reynolds building tower. He too prospered well, with some handsome fees always coming when needed from the most unexpected sources. He refused to be interviewed.

Carlisle Higgins went on to a distinguished career in the North Carolina bar, on General Douglas MacArthur's legal staff in Japan, and as a prosecutor at the Tokyo war crimes trials. Before returning to private practice in the 1970s, he served as a justice of the North Carolina supreme court. "He was," said a colleague, "a man who *had* to serve."

Except for former deputy sheriff Guy Scott, who helped his brother Transou investigate the shooting, and former sheriff E. G. Shore, who succeeded Scott, Carlisle Higgins was one of the few survivors who would speak freely on the subject. He said he still felt he did not have evidence enough to go to trial; he believed Smith's death was a suicide. This is where he parted company with a number of others.

In an interview when this book was in preparation, Carlisle Higgins chose to make the following points.

He regretted that he did not make the Reynolds case the highest-priority business of his office the moment he heard of it. But at the time a number of other pressures seemed paramount — and the Reynolds death seemed so clear-cut, a simple case of suicide. So he had delegated much of the early investigation and preparation to associates. The evidence of great friction and divisiveness among Higgins, McMichael, Scott, and Scott's staff of deputies still rankled. "Often I found out things . . . I knew things that McMichael and Scott didn't know," Higgins said. He said he had not asked for the first-degree indictments that came through the grand jury.

"The sheriff got the grand jury indictments solely on the basis of *his* testimony before them. I thought that was a mistake. But I was young. The pressure was on from all the papers. I didn't think the state had a case — but I wanted to find out. I probably didn't stop it as soon as I should have."

Higgins regarded his most reliable witnesses as Miss Yurka and watchman Fulcher. Certainly his most reliable background witness was the loyal family maid, Plummer Walker. And it is essentially on the basis of their testimony, and on the medical testimony of Dr. Hanes, that he made his major decisions.

"Blanche Yurka was not drinking at all when she was at Reynolda. In fact, she rather preened about it. And, as I remember, she didn't go down to the lake. She stayed at the house because she felt a little like an outsider. So I think her observations of the night were among the sharpest of all. She was cold sober, and there weren't too many who could answer to that muster that night. . . . She could probably tell you a lot more about that night than she told us.

"Miss Yurka says they got Smith to the hospital that night in a hell of a rush. Now if Libby had wanted to kill him, would she have gotten him to the hospital that fast . . . ?

"At the hospital, I don't know . . . they all behaved pretty strange. But who would behave normally in a situation like that? As for the incident in Libby's room, I don't put too much stock in it. They had given her a shot to calm her down. Ab must have gone in trying to comfort her, sat on the edge of one of those big hospital beds — and over they went. He wasn't trying to get in bed with her then, for godsakes. . . .

"I put a lot of faith in Dr. Hanes's inquest testimony. . . . There were no powder burns, according to Dr. Hanes, on the skin. But there were powder marks *inside* the skull against the brain. To me, that was conclusive evidence he shot himself. . . . If a man shoots himself, he puts the barrel of the gun *against* his temple, and then the powder burns would be forced inside with the bullet to mark his brain, just where we found them. Someone else wouldn't put the gun directly against the temple . . . probably wouldn't have a chance to. Then there would be burns on the skin. The fact that there weren't, convinced me."

(*Dr. Hanes's testimony would seem to contradict this critical point.*)

"As for the missing gun, I recollect that Dr. Hanes had taken it, and I recollect it was clearly Smith's gun. . . .

"As for Transou Scott, he didn't get within ten miles of Reynolda for almost twelve hours. He didn't have much experience either. His brother, Deputy Guy Scott, was steady and reliable. But Transou . . .

"I was surprised when the indictment came through. I thought Libby and Ab were being railroaded. There had been a case in the South where a young Jewish fellow had been railroaded on a rape and murder charge, and I didn't want to see Libby get railroaded the same way. . . ."

In 1912 in Atlanta a young Jewish factory supervisor named Leo Frank had been arrested, charged with, and convicted of the murder of a non-Jewish girl who worked in the factory. When his death sentence was commuted to life imprisonment, a Ku Klux Klan–organized mob abducted him from a Georgia prison farm and lynched him, after several days of anti-Semitic violence in several cities. For the surprising solution of that murder, see Appendix II.

"As for Libby, I think she was too much for Smith. There was the age difference. And then she was pretty sophisticated. Smith probably knew more about airplanes and engines than anyone of his age in the United States — but that was about all he knew. That long session with her manager in the living room while they were reading the play — it was all going over his head. He knew he was losing her. He sat at her feet and listened. And he just plain got discouraged. Things had always gone pretty much his way before. Both Smith and Dick were spoiled. Smith used to get twenty dollars a day allowance when he was still in grammar school. That would be about seventy-five or a hundred today. His father was too old and his mother was too busy to bring him up right. It was all maids and nurses. . . .

"The papers had a lot to say about me holding the inquest closed. But I hold my inquest open or closed as I please, and I expected the state attorney general to do the same. I was a constitutional officer and not responsible to any judge or anyone else. Those reporters were running all over Reynolda, and I told the coroner to get some guards and close them out. Then we started our hearings. . . .

"The reporters went to the judge for a writ of mandamus on the basis that the inquest was a court and a court must be open. But I pointed out to the judge that one court can't mandamus another. The judge withdrew the writ, but we let the inquest stay open then anyway. That was the only influence on me then to close the inquest—all those reporters running all over the place. . . .

"When young Dick Reynolds got back to Winston, he was naturally suspicious. Transou was telling him one thing. And McMichael another. But I was in contact with the Reynolds family lawyer all the time and that lawyer was sitting next to me when I filed the nol-pros in front of Judge Stack to have the charges dropped. I had kept Mr. Will Reynolds advised all along. I said, 'I don't think we have a case,' and he and his lawyers agreed. Mr. Will told me, 'If you want to go that way, we'll back you.' I don't like to go into court if I don't think I can win. And I didn't think I could win that one.

"Why didn't I drop the charges up at Wentworth? Well, there wasn't any deal up at Wentworth. The reporters had been on me hard, running pictures of the jail cell in Winston with captions that said, 'This is where Higgins wants to put Libby Holman.' Miserable-looking place! Well, I didn't want to put her in jail. But I wanted her to come in. Graves asked me if he brought her in would I promise not to send her to jail, would I waive bail? I said I couldn't promise anything. But when she came in, I told the judge then I didn't believe the state had evidence to go for a first-degree murder conviction. . . .

"Libby was a pretty good girl. I didn't want the little lady to have to go to jail. . . ."

Neither did a lot of other people who had a far bigger stake in the situation than a young prosecutor trying for convictions and also trying to win the next election.

"Regardless of the fact that we had a hell of a time getting anybody who was at the party to answer questions," one of the deputies in the investigation remembers, "we established that it got pretty wild. They were a bunch of young people who needed a drink and who would take more than one. Nude swimming and that kind of thing. Really not too darn surprising how it ended up."

Almost from the beginning, he said, a number of those closest to the case discounted the suicide theory; Libby and Walker were known to have been "pretty thick," and it was established that Libby was not as unaccustomed to pistols as she claimed.

Would a jury have convicted her? Probably. But not for first-degree murder. An all-male Carolina jury in 1933 wouldn't have gone that far with "the little lady."

Forty years later a North Carolina lawyer, Jerry Paul, would raise a fire storm of indignant voices when he said after successfully defending Joan Little, accused of murdering her jailer, that he could assure any verdict anybody wanted if he were given enough money to spend.

Lawyer Paul got the money he needed for the defense. And he won the acquittal — not by some mysterious pressure tactics, but by buying the information and expertise he needed to choose the right jury to win the right verdict. But the result was the same. Money brought it all about. Paul was attacked. No one spoke in indignation against the Reynoldses.

The issues in the murder case against Libby Holman Reynolds and Albert Walker were far different from Joan Little's plight. But it was clearly a case where money and power were applied to bring about "the right verdict." And from the way it was handled from the very beginning, it was apparently regarded by almost everyone involved as a case that was too important to be subject to the same sort of investigation and justice that conventionally dealt with first-degree murder.

That was for "Saturday night specials." What we have been dealing with here was just "a private affair." Among a few well-to-do friends.

32

"Blues, Ballads, and Sin-Songs"

THINGS WERE NEVER quite the same again for Libby Holman. One of the first "truths" she found out was that had she gone through the trial and won acquittal that at least would have brought a certain finality. But simply being free because the charge was dropped for a lack of evidence was quite a different matter. The court spectacle would have been grim and sensational. Embarrassing and degrading testimony would have been widely reported. But had a jury heard it all and still found her innocent, the verdict of innocent would have been remembered, too.

Now people always remembered the unresolved status of it all. She was an indicted murderer, who, through good fortune, influence, or a deal, was walking free.

Free — and with $500,000 of Smith's money in her bank account and another $2,000,000 settled on the little boy who occupied her nursery. So soon after the Depression, it was hard to feel too sorry for Libby Holman on the money count.

For one thing, a great many of the people who had read the stories of the shooting, the investigation, the near-trial, and now the enormous terms of the settlement had long been jobless or were trying to scrape along on niggardly salaries. Franklin D. Roosevelt had come into office on March 4 of 1933, and even though his first financial measures were drastic and controversial, they had not had all the effect he had hoped for. When he took his oath, half the banks in the country had been closed by their own financial failure, and the new President had closed all the rest of them for four long days while he and his aides hammered together a National Emergency Banking Relief Act that would stabilize the financial situation of the whole nation. Those who had to go without cash for only four days were the lucky ones. Some 14 million people were unemployed. Ten thousand dollars a year was a very comfortable income for a businessman, with the average far, far less. And here were the stories of Smith scraping by on a $50,000-a-year allowance, Libby pulling down $2,500 a week on Broadway, Anne Cannon Reynolds scorning a $1 million settlement and still going for half the estate. Perhaps the only thing that put the whole story into any sort of perspective for newspaper readers was that the amounts of money being fought over were so vast that most people couldn't really conceive how vast they were.

For a while Libby made a real effort to stay quietly out of the public eye. In spite of her protestations to columnist Ward Moorehouse when she thought she was facing trial that she would name a boy or girl after her "beloved Smith" — the child was named Christopher. After his shaky, premature start he settled down to be an easy baby. With the staff that Libby maintained, she did not have much to do. She began then the vigorous correspondence that she would keep up for much of the rest of her life. First there were files of letters and wires to answer from friends who had offered support after Smith's death and through the long period leading up to the dismissal of charges. The number of supporters had been rewarding, though certain of them, Libby knew, had fired off a sympathetic letter at one moment (half hoping for an answer that could be dined out on) — then, having written, felt perfectly free to tear her down in gossip for the next few weeks. Libby answered them all, mostly effusively, a few in a more cautious and measured tone. Then there was nothing much more to be done.

Through this strange period of "retired living," a dramatically new and not very pleasing experience for her, she had listened attentively to the show and cabaret offers that came in through her agent. Most were junk. But in the summer of 1933, she saw the chance she felt was worth the risk to get her back on the stage. Arch Selwyn and Harold B. Franklin were planning a new musical for the fall. It had the working title of *Revenge with Music*, and the book, lyrics, and music would be by her old good-luck charmers Howard Dietz and Arthur Schwartz. The offer had not exactly come in over the transom. Libby had been in repeated contact with Dietz and had told him how much she wanted to come back, though frankly she was a little scared. Dietz was somewhat apprehensive, too. The show was properly an operetta based on a classical story by the Spanish writer Pedro Antonio de Alarcón, called *The Three-Cornered Hat* — a long outfield throw from the bright, brittle revues and the slinky, sexy roles that had gained Libby her reputation. But she kept the pressure on Dietz, and he finally agreed to give her the job.

The crack Dietz-Schwartz team promised a good chance of success, as did the rest of the cast. Included were Charles Winninger, famous for his long-run role as Capt'n Andy in *Showboat* — a role he would continue for years on radio — and Ilka Chase, the sophisticated comedienne. Libby worked hard in rehearsals and when the show opened at New York's New Amsterdam Theatre on the evening of November 28, 1933, it had received a surprising amount of favorable out-of-town publicity. The music was good. Two fine songs in particular have survived: "If There Is Someone Lovelier Than You" and "You and the Night and the Music," which Libby sang into a hit.

A certain amount of the advance publicity had to do with Libby's return to Broadway. But she was definitely number two in the billing beneath Winninger, the star. Most of the speculation, however, centered around Dietz and Schwartz's also trying something so different from their previous shows. The two had selected *The Three-Cornered Hat* with some care. It had long been a great Spanish classic, and its setting offered a chance for all the color they felt was so essential to a big Broadway production. Several months of research preceded the writing, with the two men immersing themselves in Spanish literary history and the musical styles of the time. There was little of the trial-and-error, shooting-from-the-hip approach to the writing that had worked so instinctively and successfully for them in putting together the revues.

One opening night, there was an enthusiastic house on hand, and there seemed to be little of the sour-grapes feeling that Dietz and Schwartz had experienced on other opening nights, when they often felt that half the sophisticated audience had come to see them fall on their faces. The applause was warm. But they had learned not to trust a first-night audience. The memories of *The Little Show* and the resounding boredom of its opening-night audience in Asbury Park would never leave them.

Walter Winchell loved the show and spilled over in his column, giving it "five stars." That was rare for him. But a number of the reviews were mixed. And Dietz, for one, felt the show never got moving spontaneously.

Libby was only adequate, and Dietz thought privately he had miscast her in his attempt to help. Something was missing in her delivery, too. The husky, sexy voice was there, but he found she had been taking singing lessons and they seemed to have spoiled her voice. She had lost her ability to project the lyrics so that every word was understood. It was the first time she had sung professionally in more than two and a half years. And it showed. But the applause was always tremendous after "You and the Night and the Music."

Revenge with Music ran for a respectable 158 performances. And when it closed, Libby didn't need old friends Dietz or Schwartz to tell her that the intimate little revues were more her métier. She resolved that her next show would be just that. *Revenge with Music* was to be her last big Broadway musical, except for an appearance in 1938 in *You Never Know*, again with Clifton Webb.

The next year, however, she was the *subject* of the entertainment: Hollywood issued *Reckless*, starring Jean Harlow. It was a thinly veiled account of the Reynolds murder. Later, a best-selling novel, *Written on the Wind*, would do the same. Friends said Libby was furious and railed at Polikoff to take legal action. But he knew that would just bring the whole case up for another press rehash.

In the next few years, there were some carefully selected nightclub engagements and some small concerts — usually for charity causes Libby was interested in. But the big musical offers did not come. Still, Libby moved easily and often with the Broadway and Hollywood crowd. And since she was a gracious hostess with plenty of money, her invitations were frequently tendered and always well accepted.

In 1939, Libby married for the second time. Her new husband was Ralph de Riemer Holmes, a journeyman actor and son of an accomplished character actor, Taylor Holmes, who had significant roles in such controversial film classics as *Nightmare Alley* and *Beware, My Lovely*.

Ralph Holmes was a likable young man — and, like Smith, a good bit younger than Libby: roughly eight years. Shortly after they were married, however, Ralph left Libby and the marriage behind for the war. Following his actor brother, Phillips, he went to Canada to join the Royal Canadian Air Force. Both brothers got their wings in Canada and soon moved to England. After Pearl Harbor, Ralph transferred to the U.S. Army Air Corps, but Phillips stayed with the RCAF. In 1942 Phillips was killed in action and Ralph went into the first of a number of long spells of depression. To distract himself, he threw himself into the war, trying one type of flying after the next: the Air Transport Command, ferrying in bombers and fighters, then into combat with a squadron of Mustang fighters ranging out over France to escort the bombers off to their targets and to provide cover from the German fighters when they came back. He even put in a period as a bombardier in the heavily pounded daylight bombers flying deep inside Germany at a time when trained bomber crews were seriously depleted by losses. It was almost as if he were courting the sort of death that had taken his brother. In the fall of 1944, after having been in the air over Europe for many combat hours since the invasion of Normandy, Holmes was furloughed back to the United States, considered too exhausted to fly further.

By then, Libby maintained a handsome country house near Stamford, Connecticut — handsome enough so that in February of that year she had appeared in Orphans Court in Baltimore to pressure the Baltimore Safe Deposit Company, which managed Christopher's trust, to give her $500,000 from the trust to maintain the Connecticut home in the style her boy required. By then, the marriage to Holmes had soured and it was not to Stamford that he returned, but to a small walk-up on East Sixty-sixth Street in Manhattan. There, on Tuesday night, November 20, the much-decorated and severely depressed Captain Holmes was found dead. He had apparently been dead for several days. When an autopsy was performed, the medical examiner listed the probable cause of death as an overdose of sleeping tablets. Combined with lots of whiskey. Captain Holmes was just thirty.

Libby, who had been in Palm Beach at the time, was hard hit. It really was the second Holmes tragedy that had rocked her; rumor was that she had first been in love with Phillips, but that Ralph had married her when Phillips departed, "just to take care of her for Phillips."

Libby needed to forget the grim memory of Ralph lying dead in the East Sixty-sixth Street walk-up, alone for that week. All around the country there was a demand for theatrical talent to entertain servicemen, and Libby suddenly saw it as a chance to perform and a chance to forget. From the spring of 1945 until the end of the war, she was a tireless traveler and performer for the Hollywood Canteen, the American Theater Wing, and the Armed Forces Entertainment Committee. And on her own she arranged big shows at military and naval hospitals on both coasts. The audiences were appreciative, undemanding, and most of them had not been reading the newspapers when Libby was making headlines back in Winston-Salem. That was an advantage.

Encouraged by the wartime reception, in the fall of 1948 Libby tried to arrange a concert tour along the East Coast. At appearances in Washington and New York in October and November, she got pleasant receptions for a mixed program of folk music and the old 1930s show music. But the thirties songs were out of fashion at that time, and the folk was too new for that audience; it would be another fifteen years before the young college crowd would pick up on it. Several reviewers as much as said that she was "an interesting oddity." And without mentioning the Reynolds affair, they clearly alluded to the fact that many in the audience seemed to be coming to see her out of curiosity. She retreated once again to the luxurious estate in Stamford that she had named "Treetops."

Given that disappointment, there were still surprisingly good years to come after the 1948 concerts. Christopher was in his teens, an appealing boy with a good mind. But the stories of the money and of the death of his father still followed. Libby tried to keep a lot of that from him. But there were others who made sure he heard it.

As his father had responded to the thrill and challenge of aviation, Christopher turned to skiing and mountain climbing. He decided against the stylish Eastern "preps" and opted instead for Vermont's radical Putney and then Colorado Rocky Mountain School, where back-packing, white-water canoeing, rock climbing and downhill ski racing were practically part of the curriculum. He became resourceful, confident. The outdoor situations he could handle. But also in his teens, and in spite of the protection of his money, he began to learn the bitter sting of anti-Semitism. One incident stuck in the mind of a friend from those days. There was a Christmas dinner with some of his mother's friends from the old Du Pont crowd at a beautiful estate near Wilmington. Toward the end of the meal when the chairs were pushed back and the brandy came on, one of the guests told a mildly off-color and derogatory story about Jews. Christopher got up without a word, threw his napkin down, and left the table. *"That's* what's wrong with the world today," he told his friend who followed him. "Bastards like that." The friend tried to calm him down. "Come on, you're embarrassing your mother. He didn't mean any harm." Christopher was near tears: "They never do."

Weekends at Treetops were usually lively, with half a dozen houseguests of varying ages in residence: Christopher's friends and his mother's. Libby continued to be the gracious hostess, and she was doggedly faithful to the old friends who had been faithful to her back in the Reynolda trouble. And now she was drinking less. Ulcers pained.

A visitor from those days remembers that the house was always kept gorgeously, its sunny rooms were always banked with fruit and flowers. Libby loved her flowers and greenhouse, working there and in her gardens for long hours. Even though she loved to party and would occasionally sing — though usually only as one of the group — she was "a very private person." The approach to Treetops was across a small bridge, and she often said she liked to think that she could drive in there and mentally pull the bridge up behind her against the world. Within the house, Libby had her own somewhat-removed suite of rooms, to which she could retire and let the company stay up playing and partying late, if they wished. But she often stayed right with them.

For the most part, the world had stopped bothering her. Her reputation in the Stamford-Greenwich area was more as a hostess who could be persuaded to back a cause, assembling a supporting cast of New York and Hollywood "names" for a benefit, or throwing open her gorgeous house and grounds for a charity party.

Then the bad luck came back again. In August of 1950, Libby was on a vacation trip to Europe. Young Christopher, then seventeen years old and already an excellent skier and mountain climber, was on a climbing trip with a friend, William Wasserman of New York, at Mount Whitney in California. The boys had arrived early Sunday morning by car at a point called Whitney Portal, at the foot of the 14,496-foot peak. They had told the manager of the camp where they had been staying that they had supplies for two days, that they had climbed the Alps, and please don't worry about them. On Thursday, when they still had not returned, the camp manager called the sheriff's office. By dusk Thursday, a search party under the direction of a deputy sheriff had made its way up the west side of the mountain and camped at the summit. There was no trace of Reynolds or Wasserman. On Friday morning with the arrival of light, the search party looked down the sheer east face but could see no sign of the two boys. Twenty expert climbers were brought in to join the search, along with planes and helicopters. Two days later, on Sunday morning, Wasserman's body was discovered near the summit, with Christopher's body found crumpled in a crevasse about 200 feet from the top. Shortly after they were found, a chartered plane arrived at Lone Pine, California, the nearest airfield. When Libby climbed out of it, the only news the deputies had for her was bad.

Even before the body of Christopher had been found, the distasteful rumors about "the money" had begun again. A Winston-Salem lawyer had volunteered that all the money left in Christopher's trust would now go to Libby under New York State law, which said the estate of a minor automatically reverted to the parent or parents surviving. He noted that Christopher's trust had already totaled $6,502,000 six years earlier. His money had traveled like his father's; most of it never had time enough to find its way to him.

And so, seventeen years after all the careful negotiation to keep Reynolds money out of Libby's hands following one tragedy, another tragedy had delivered a large portion of it right to her.

Seclusion at Treetops didn't help after the accident. There was too much of Christopher there. In a few months she was in Europe for several concerts. The international crowd and the American expatriates gathered around and were supportive. After one concert, she was introduced to Alice B. Toklas, and there was an exchange of letters and visits between this unlikely pair through the next several years, with Miss Toklas in her tiny hand thanking Libby for the songs: "You have given me so much pleasure. . . . Your concert — then meeting you."

There was another year of heavy travel, trying to get the memory of Christopher's battered body out of her mind. And then in 1952, she gave an inspired concert in London which brought telegrams of congratulations from stars like Mary Martin and Broadway theatrical powers like Gilbert Miller, along with most of her other old show-business friends. Maybe she *could* come back. She had found the clue to a new style; it was a combination of the old blues, the folk music, and some new country songs that had their background in the old ballads brought over from Elizabethan England. The audience was receptive, though one of Libby's most lasting and loyal friends, from the heart of country-music country, said he always found something incongruous about that husky, sexy voice singing the songs he had always heard in the somewhat nasal country style.

Libby honed her performance, and in the fall of 1954 she felt she was ready to try Broadway again. On October 4, 1954, she opened at Manhattan's Bijou Theatre in an "evening with Libby Holman" that was cautiously limited to one week: it was billed as *Blues, Ballads, and Sin-Songs*. Libby would be the only performer.

Once again, the old fans turned out — and there seemed to be fewer voyeurs among them who had just come to stare at a woman who was suspected of murdering her husband. Among the reviewers was Brooks Atkinson, who had been one of the first to spot Libby's star rising back in the thirties. Atkinson's report probably best tells the story of that successful week.

Atkinson warmed to the folk songs and ballads, but he too found it somewhat hard to reconcile her husky, sophisticated voice with the country music. But he was encouraging: "Miss Holman's voice was never one of the marvels of the world in comparison, for example, to Marian Anderson's. But last night it did have a quality of broken-hearted passion that convinced you she had suffered."

After working her way through a pleasing program of folk and blues and using only a common chair as a prop, Libby swung into "Body and Soul," "Moanin' Low," and "Love for Sale." Atkinson responded as enthusiastically as did the rest of the audience:

> These are works of art that Broadway can understand. In the years since those songs were new, Miss Holman has learned so much about singing that the old vulgarity has gone out of them. She sings them artistically now, which is a pity. But it is comforting to hear that deep, sultry, fluctuating voice again in some practical Broadway music . . . her earnest,

throaty tussle with her blues, ballads, and sin-songs last evening set one playgoer to musing about an occasion twenty-six years ago when Miss Holman did her suffering in the midst of a gutsy show.

Libby played to a good house all week — and again the telegrams poured in: Richard Aldrich, Marc Blitzstein, Ted Lewis, Howard Dietz, Arthur Schwartz, Langston Hughes, Ilka Chase, Jo Mielziner, Sam Rayburn, William Inge . . . and Blanche Yurka, a voice from the past.

Strangely, in spite of the success of the Broadway comeback, Libby did not take her "evening with Libby Holman" very far. Perhaps it was because she knew that outside New York there might be few audiences who would be so receptive. Perhaps she just didn't want to spoil the memory. After all, she now had the satisfaction of knowing she could still do it.

But even with the success of that week on Broadway behind her, there were some career concerns Libby couldn't let alone — and one of these that still nagged her was her thought that she really could have been a great dramatic actress. In 1958 she arranged to get the lead role in an odd dramatic-operatic production called *Yerma*. It was to tour in the West. Then, if successful, it would be brought to New York. She worked hard at her part, and mention in the reviews for her were favorable enough. But the show failed to pull an audience. The whole experience was as disappointing as the Broadway week had been rewarding.

The disappointment sent her back to her folk songs with a new determination. She preferred to call it "earth" music. With her accompanist, Gerald Cook, a suave black pianist who had been working with her since her USO show days, she started on a methodical search of the Library of Congress archives for all the background she could discover on the folk songs she planned to sing. The arrangements Cook then worked out for her, though often sounding almost contemporary, were skillful presentations of the manner in which the songs had been sung originally. Folk was coming into its own, and Libby was suddenly popular with young people, the college crowd. They hadn't heard many of her "old" songs, rarely called for them. And Libby was relieved. She began to refer to the music she had ridden to fame on in the twenties and thirties as "smarty-pants stuff from Tin Pan Alley" and would usually politely duck a request when it came: "I'm sorry, we haven't rehearsed that. I haven't done it in so long." Then she would turn to the bright requests for "Strange Fruit."

The "earth" music, the research in the folk and Americana archives, brought her in contact with the other artists who did it so well. In the forties she had studied with folk star Josh White and had met many of his contemporaries, both the big names and the unknown older singers' singers who had brought the music along with them since childhood. She acquired a genuine sympathy for the second-class role many of these blacks had to live, even in the extremely liberal limits of the musical world. She was still angry at the slight she had received from the USO when she and White had volunteered to go overseas and had been told, "We don't book mixed company." At that point Libby had even asked Eleanor Roosevelt to intervene. But the invitation to go abroad to entertain had never come.

The blacks she met now, however, were making things happen: Ralph Abernathy, Martin Luther King and Coretta King, Sidney Poitier, Langston Hughes. . . . The Civil Rights cause attracted her, and she was ready to help it with concerts, talks, the gracious hospitality of Treetops, quiet missionary work with influential friends. There were select tours to Europe and hand-picked cities in the United States where she could be reasonably sure of her reception. She was in a unique position to help "the movement" in other ways, too. The Christopher Reynolds Foundation, which had been set up with some of the $7,000,000 from her son's estate, gave grants to Dr. King to carry his message abroad, financed a prizewinning documentary on world peace, provided seed money for a variety of causes that caught Libby's fancy.

Treetops always provided a retreat when the world got too hectic. The weekend guest list might include a composer or two; several "names" from the folk world like Alan Lomax or Paul Green; someone from Broadway, Eli Wallach or Joan Littlewood; a touch of politics, George McGovern or Martin Luther King; visitors from Hollywood, Ethel Merman, Roddy McDowell — McDowell invariably writing or arriving to cheer her up when she needed it most — or Frank Sinatra, plus the charming and unexpected newcomers whom Libby was always taking under her wing: a former lover's daughter who was in New York studying to be a dancer, a young journalist trying to break in as a writer (the invitation usually came with the proviso that the weekend must not provide material for an article), a budding artist whose work Libby admired. She had a weakness for younger men, and they for her. She was a handsome woman, always kept her figure well, and, even in her sixties, according to one admirer, she stayed slim like a dancer, no matter how much she drank. And young men — as well as mature ones — were generally most responsive. A frequent weekend visitor was Montgomery Clift, nervous, withdrawn, fighting his homosexuality and drugs, and the alcohol that finally killed him, but still exhibiting a magnetic personality when he tried. Libby was his mistress-mother, and one of his frequent complaints to her (it had begun after his role as the young Jewish soldier in *The Young Lions* who is sadistically beaten by his barrack mates) was the fact that he always got the part of the guy getting beaten up. "Why can't I do the beating up some time?" Libby was particularly sympathetic. She felt she always got beaten up, too. Her strong maternal instinct could be let out full throttle with the nearly helpless Clift, and she became too involved with him as she had been with other young men before. "It's a tragedy," she told a young writer at one point in those years, "that a woman has to undergo so much before she realizes half the affection she feels for a man is maternal." But it was a truth she could never seem to remember herself.

Yet during this time she returned, as she had before, to the one mature relationship she had maintained since she had first come to New York. In contrast to so many of the men she was attracted to who were susceptible to her dominance, perhaps even needed it, this man had always been caring — but independent; and he had loved her before success. Jennings Perry was then a top reporter, foreign correspondent, and editor of the award-winning *Nashville Tennesseean*. Perry's memories of Libby are rich — and kind. "If she had enemies, I never met them. She had a wonderful sense of humor and was invariably optimistic — sometimes childishly. And she was generally wonderful with children — especially her two adopted boys that I met in Key West on one of her vacations there. She drank pretty heavy at times. And she alarmed me driving her Mercedes that way — sometimes with a silver flask in the front seat. She had a great shape, I thought — and she always kept it, but God knows how; she was never much for exercise. I was glad, later, when she switched to sherry only."

Through some years of a marriage that very early by mutual agreement arranged itself into one of convenience, Perry had always managed to see Libby from time to time every year. Sometimes the meetings were intense and romantic. Sometimes they simply had the warmth of two old friends coming together. But in Libby's often unstable world, he was stability, dependability, real love. "Oh, my God, I've made a mess of things," she cried to him over the phone shortly after Smith died. She could let her protective wall drop with Perry. Though lots of people demanded so much of her, she knew he never did. Their times together were far removed from the New York life: country walks, deep-sea fishing trips — with Libby always dead game, bearing a gourmet picnic lunch, and invariably seasick. On several occasions they talked about Smith. "She never referred to him unkindly," Perry remembers, "but, strangely, with no particular affection either. She preferred not to talk about the whole episode. I always thought it strange, though, that she never, never referred to any of the other Reynoldses; it would have been reasonable for her to hate them. She did mention once one of Smith's nieces coming backstage at some performance to introduce herself. She appreciated the conversation — but remembered it as being very stilted. That's not surprising."

After one of these coming-togethers, Libby probably came as close as she ever did to telling someone the truth about the incident at Reynolda. Libby and Perry had been together for several days, and he was leaving soon on a writing assignment that he was not particularly looking forward to. But, he explained, the assignment carried quite a handsome fee. Then, hands in his, Libby volunteered: "Jennings, how would you like to make a million dollars? I'll tell you exactly what happened — and you can write it." Perry was, of course, interested. But it wasn't a project he could get into then. When they met again and talked about it, she put the idea off, almost as if she had never talked of it.

"Knowing her as well as I did, if she had shot Smith, I *think* I would have known it. But I'm not sure. . . . It's not the sort of thing I was going to press her on. It just didn't seem in her character to take that sort of violent action. I can imagine her committing suicide easier than I can imagine her carrying out a violent act — like shooting someone. But I don't know . . . I just don't know . . . she was very unpredictable. And she had a temper, especially when she had been drinking."

In 1960, Libby married for the third time, to Louis Schanker, an artist whose paintings, woodcuts, and sculpture are in the permanent collections of a number of museums. The marriage surprised several of her friends. One of them expressed her misgivings: "She was always the dominant, domineering one. I'm surprised she married Schanker where he dominated. His idea seemed to be to keep her 'incommunicado' on eastern Long Island, growing roses."

The show-business friends weren't so welcome anymore and Schanker carefully introduced her to the society of the Hamptons. Perhaps that was what Libby needed after all. When she had first hit on Broadway, she had told an interviewer: "I want at least one great love. A man who has achieved something in the arts. He must be more than a match for me in physical vitality and artistic achievements. . . . But one thing is sure, anyhow, I'll never be crying my heart out for a guy that loves and leaves me. . . . I never want to envy youth. I never want to be dependent. At fifty, sixty, seventy, and eighty I want to have enough charm and fascination inside myself to draw admiration and the love of men. I want to be rich inside."

In 1968, certainly rich outside and with life seeming to be kinder to her, Libby Holman came out of retirement to give a charity concert in Easthampton, Long Island. Most of the program was the "earth" music with which she had been so successful in two concerts for UNICEF given at the Dag Hammarskjöld Hall a few years before. Then toward the end of the program, she shifted into a medley of the songs that had made her famous. The sophisticated audience, reacting to the talent as well as to the nostalgia, responded with very unsophisticated and heartfelt cheers.

It was October 1930 again, when the sultry, nearsighted young college girl had to be almost led by the hand through the curtain of the Selwyn Theatre to step into the halolike spotlight:

> *My life a wreck you're making,*
> *You know I'm yours just for the taking,*
> *I'd gladly surrender*
>   *myself to you, body and soul.*

On June 17, 1971, the Selwyn Theatre on the north side of Forty-second Street a short distance west of Times Square, where Allen, Holman, and Webb had once so charmed New York audiences, was offering to a discriminating audience — which included a handful of sleepers, a number of practicing alcoholics, and assorted narcotics nodders — a double bill that consisted of something like *The Constant Fear* "(Vampires rise from the dead!") and *Ghostly Flesh* ("It will make you chill with horror!"). Slouchers occupied the doorways on either side of the Selwyn to wait out an approaching thunderstorm. Squashed pizza remains decorated the sidewalk, and a sleepy crone stared from the box-office window, as if daring you to come up and ask for a ticket. It was a long way from the opening night of *Three's a Crowd* at the Selwyn some forty-one years before.

That same June night, about thirty miles to the northeast in Stamford, Connecticut, sometime shortly after ten o'clock, the emergency room of the Stamford Hospital got a request for an ambulance to come to Treetops, in the rolling country above the town. There had been an accident.

By the time the first assistance had arrived, the garage on the estate had been aired out and the motor of the big Mercedes had been switched off. The still-graceful bikini-clad form of Elizabeth Holman Reynolds Holmes Schanker had been removed to the main house.

At sixty-five she was dead of carbon monoxide poisoning.

There are those who believe the best part of her life had really ended thirty-eight years before in Winston-Salem. In another emergency room. After another ambulance call. To another great estate.

"I wish I had been in Stamford," Jennings Perry said in a voice that tried hard to hold back the emotion. "I think I could have talked her out of it."

33

A Case — in Search of a Prosecution

IN THE CASE that has come before you, you have encountered a situation where there were no witnesses to the crime, if the two accused can be excepted. To get the first-degree murder indictments, no true expert testimony was presented by the state. Yet obviously even the simpler facts that were presented were strong enough to bring in the grand jury vote for the first-degree charge. In the manner in which they passed along the case, the earlier nonindicting grand jury showed it was similarly inclined.

Clearly grand juries can be manipulated like any other juries — mostly to do what the prosecutor wants. In a thoughtful examination of the grand jury system titled "How Well Do Grand Juries Work," *New York Times* courts reporter Dena Kleiman noted in December 1976 that "the prosecutor stands before grand jurors as a legal adviser. Theoretically, he may not attempt to influence them. But in practice, there is often little doubt how a prosecutor feels about a case. And because grand jurors often look to prosecutors for guidance, much as petit jurors look to a judge during a trial, prosecutors can influence the outcome of an inquiry." Obviously the State of North Carolina at first wanted to influence the jurors into an indictment, wanted to go to trial. But then after the state got its first want, it unexpectedly shied away from the second — the trial — as the pressure came on. In the intervening months, no contrary evidence was discovered. In theory, a resolute prosecution had spent that time solidifying the evidence in hand and adding more. There were, of course, conflicts in evidence and contradiction. But these, after all, are the sorts of questions that a trial is meant to answer. In the face of all this, a trial was resoundingly blocked.

Faced with these unresolved conflicts and contradictions, you as a reader may feel that you are more in the position of a detective than the leisurely explorer of some nostalgic, neatly concluded, all-questions-answered piece of American front-page history. You are, in fact, both detective and juror. Certainly too little first-class investigative work was done at the time. And no juror ever sat to judge Libby Holman and Albert Walker. So you may want to sit now as a juror-at-large to decide what really occurred. Then arrive at your own verdict. And in some ways you will have an advantage here over any juror in a courtroom. You will be able to consider all the evidence at your own pace — no juror can. You will be able to make any notes and diagrams that you want as the evidence is presented to you — no juror can. Write out for yourself a chain of events, a chain of logic — no juror can. You can do all this, unlectured, undirected, unharassed by defense and prosecution lawyers. None of these things could you do as a juror in court. And so you may do a much better job than any jury that might have sat.

Despite our democratic fascination with it, a trial by jury in this country is a far from ideal system. Anne Bernays, reviewing in the *New York Times Book Review* a book about the trial of Jean Harris for the shooting of Dr. Herman Tarnower, wrote that "courts are places where well-intentioned people attempt to make some sense of the irrational." The trial often does not make sense.

In a biting and thought-provoking essay published in *Newsweek* in 1978, F. Lee Bailey, certainly one of America's most publicized — if controversial — trial lawyers and presumably one of America's more practiced ones, included these comments about the drawbacks of jury trials and trial lawyers, several applying to Libby Holman's plight:

> The Chief Justice of the United States, Warren E. Burger, has lately been saying — often and pointedly — that large numbers of American

lawyers who undertake courtroom litigation are incompetent. . . . The fact is, a citizen who fails to settle his controversy, or plea-bargain it away (which is essentially the same thing), is in damned tough shape.

A trial by jury, conceived, long before there was a United States, as a great equalizer purporting to deliver to all citizens equal justice under the law, is in fact a terrifying experience, riddled with uncertainty and often happenstance. Our deification of the notion of a "fair trial" has so far submerged the value of an *accurate* trial that the latter has no real legal significance . . . someone ought to have the temerity to ask whether the *result* was correct, not simply whether the rituals were acceptable.

Laymen are invited to believe that our legal system enshrouds the trial process with an escalating system of checks and safeguards called appellate courts, which will correct affronts to justice. This is unmitigated nonsense, as all seasoned trial lawyers and jurists know — and many unwary litigants have learned painfully. . . .

We religiously refuse to make any records of a jury's deliberations (we in the profession are terrified of what such a record might reveal), and thus forfeit any ability to correct the mistakes we surely know they will make. . . . I must confess to one and all that an argument to any American appellate court that one's client ought to be granted relief because he was *innocent* — not that he didn't have a fair trial, but that despite the best efforts of a good trial judge and the earnest intentions of a jury, he was being punished for something he *damned well didn't do* — [that argument of innocence] would fall on legally deaf appellate ears. Innocence, you see, has at that level no relevance to anything.

It is apparent that any system that is willing to bet so much on the educated guesswork of a panel of laymen counts heavily on the operators of its legal machinery to squeeze maximum efficiency from the machine. Advocates entrusted with the truths and counterproofs that will lead a jury to historical truth must be skilled in all of the things Perry Mason seems to do so well. . . .

Our colleagues in medicine (who opted for licensed specialization long ago) at least use cadavers for their practice efforts, to diminish the cost of a mistake. We cut our trial teeth on real live clients. I myself had been a lawyer for all of three months when I first took over the defense of a man on trial for his life.

Our trial lawyers have no formal training. There are no schools that teach the essentials of investigation, preparation, speaking to a jury, examining witnesses, or persuading an appellate court. . . . If you say you are a trial lawyer, you are, provided you hold a license to practice law and despite the fact that your law school never really scratched the surface of any of the critically important talents mentioned above.

In view of all this — which was at least as evident in 1932 as it is today, and perhaps more so to Alfred Holman — it is no wonder that the prospect of going to trial was not an appealing one to Libby's camp.

It is apparent the state's desire to avoid a trial did not come from the fear of any member of the prosecution of suffering punishment if the trial didn't go right. And it probably did not come from a gentle concern that an innocent person might be convicted. Rather, it resulted from a slowly increasing pressure to put the lid on the whole unsavory pot.

So this will have to serve as a summary for "the prosecution that never chose to prosecute." It will be aimed toward proving a case of murder. And it points at the only two suspects. Albert Walker and Libby Holman.

The State's Case

Before backing away from the case, the State of North Carolina had apparently planned to prove (1) that it would have been physically very difficult — and totally untypical of a person intent on suicide — for Smith Reynolds to shoot himself in the manner in which he was shot; (2) that no one else could possibly have been in the room when he was shot, except for the two defendants; (3) that it was most certain those two were in the room; and therefore, (4) they must be guilty of shooting him.

If you decide those four points seem likely to be true beyond a reasonable doubt after all you read here, then you can see how severely the state judicial system was swerved from its obligations, the first of these being the obligation to provide the resolution of a trial, so that all the questions could be answered — whether or not they were embarrassing for a rich and powerful family.

We believe the facts presented in this book argue the four points above with some success. We believe also that they are points the state could have proved convincingly in a vigorous prosecution, after gathering even further evidence that would have been available at the time.

In support of this belief, perhaps the most important facts that came out in those several months between the shooting and the refusal to prosecute should be brought together into a summation.

The Condition of the Wound

Even if you are the most charitable of jurors, and even if you allowed that something unknown to any of Smith's closest family and friends had depressed him to a suicidal state, you would still have to ignore the hard physical evidence against suicide given by the condition of the wound, the position of the wound, and the path followed by the bullet as it wounded Smith and then ricochetted around the room. Study of these three points would seem to render a self-inflicted bullet wound virtually impossible.

Consider first the testimony of the doctors who tried to save Smith's life. Dr. Hanes, speaking for those at the hospital: "We found around the wound on the right temple slight evidence which we attributed to be powder burns. Not marked. Very slight. Just on the edge of the wound. A blackening of the edge of the wound which it seemed possible to us at the time were powder burns." Dr. Hanes did *not* report any powder burns inside the skull. (The prosecutor's recollections of the medical testimony for the author [page 240] are at variance with this. But here, we accept the doctor's remarks, because they were testimony a few days after the shooting, while the prosecutor was being asked to try to remember events of almost fifty years earlier.)

Consider next the statement of Dr. Hanes about examining Smith's wounds at the hospital: "On the right temple, there was a contusion . . . with a puncture wound of the skin in the middle of the swelling. . . . Just back of the left ear was another wound, just a puncture wound of the skull and scalp. . . . [This] wound at the point of exit showed nothing, merely a puncture wound of the skin."

Now consider the statement of Dr. Milton Helpern, for many years chief medical examiner for the City of New York and a forensic specialist who was called "the most celebrated coroner since the art was instituted in the twelfth century." In his book *Autopsy*, written with Dr. Bernard Knight, now Professor of Forensic Pathology at the Welsh National School of Medicine at the University of Wales, Helpern is describing a man found shot in the head; he cites certain conditions which the alert medical examiner looks for to tell him something quickly about the shooting:

> ... The medical examiner notes that the entrance wound, with some scorched skin and shrivelled hairs around it, is jagged and gaping. These facts immediately tell him that the gun was discharged at very close range, perhaps almost in contact with the head. . . .
>
> The bullet has come out through the back of the head via a great jagged wound, blowing tissue and blood with it. . . .

This carnage at the entrance and exit delivered by a gun that was "perhaps almost in contact with the head," sounds very little like Dr. Hanes's rather tidy picture of two precise "punctures." Dr. Hanes concluded his testimony by saying: "I saw no reason to suppose that the gun, held [by Smith] against the temple, could not have followed the trajectory that we found . . . it could have followed that trajectory. . . . Of course, I am just giving you an opinion, such as you would have yourself."

Dr. Hanes was not a forensic surgeon. He rarely worked with bullet wounds. *Yet he did not hesitate to make this critical judgment that so much importance was placed upon later.*

At one point in the preparation of this book, the author approached Dr. Herbert Corse, a Duke University Medical School graduate, who for twenty years headed a group of medical men who operated the emergency-room facilities of two of the larger hospitals in the Southeast. Unlike the patients of surgeon Hanes, the weekly fare of Dr. Corse was the sort of violent injury from gunshots that Hanes encountered perhaps only once, in this most publicized of cases. When asked to comment on the nature of gunshot wounds, Dr. Corse — with his twenty years in the combat zone of emergency rooms — declined: "What you need is a forensic specialist. About all we can take time to notice is that the person has been shot. I could tell that before I went to medical school. Our concern is not powder burns . . . or where the gun was . . . or if the trajectory of a bullet looks logical. Our concern is how we can help the poor guy."

But Dr. Hanes was ranging far afield. Offering the coroner's inquest profound forensic judgments. Volunteering opinions about the extreme drunkenness of Libby and Walker. Answering questions the prosecutor had never asked. It all suggested the beginning of some smart campaign to get certain statements on the record — whether they were asked for or not.

In an effort to get some useful perspective on what might have been gained if competent forensic evidence had been looked for in the case, advice was sought, when this book was being prepared, from the same Dr. Bernard Knight mentioned earlier. In addition to holding the offices already mentioned, Knight is a barrister-at-law and has testified at some of the most complex and celebrated trials in Britain, earning a worldwide reputation. Working with Dr. Hanes's testimony at the coroner's inquest and other evidence presented by the author, Dr. Knight submitted a report in December 1982. It is properly professionally cautious, but is very clearly supportive of and clear on the salient medical points brought out in the following pages of the author's summary that the reader is pursuing here. (Also see Appendix I for the complete report.)

The Position of the Wound

Pretend that your right hand is a pistol. First, make a fist, as you would if you were holding the butt of a pistol. Now extend the index finger stiffly to simulate a pistol barrel. Try now — without crooking your index finger — to place the "barrel" against your upper right temple at the hair line, aiming the pistol so the bullet will come out *behind* and *below* the left ear.* You can see that to achieve the necessary downward angle is so awkward as to be virtually impossible. Certainly it is not a natural position. Now, in response to the assertion of some that Smith was left-handed (another assertion that was never resolved), try the same thing with your left hand. An even more difficult accomplishment.

---

* The "temple" to laymen — and to some extent this applies to nonteaching doctors also — seems to designate loosely an area on the flat side of the skull, from about the height of the eyes to the point where that flat side curves up to the forehead above the eyes. A pistol pointed almost anywhere in the flat side area, or where the temple rounds into the forehead, would have resulted in a bullet trajectory that would have been unlikely to duplicate that of Smith's wound. Note that in his testimony at the inquest, Dr. Hanes locates the entry wound as "just above the right temple at the hairline."

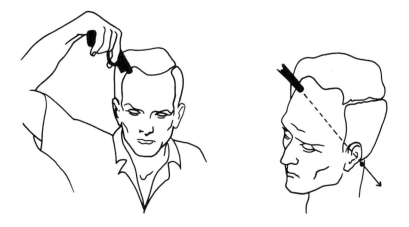

Top left and right: How Reynolds would have had to shoot himself as he was actually shot. Bottom left and right: A more natural gun angle (the one Hinckley adopted in the earlier photo, when he was threatening to commit suicide).

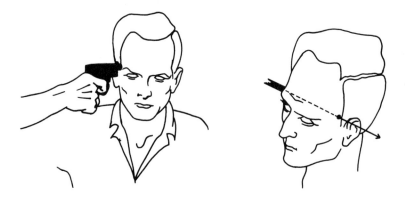

Presuming you are determined to shoot yourself in the head, where would you quickly and instinctively place the barrel? Try it with your "finger pistol." What seems natural? Most people will place the pistol just forward of their ear — or just under it, pointing rather sharply *upward*. Not putting the barrel to the upper temple. Not held some distance away from the head. There is no reason to be tentative at such a time; to the suicide, there is the last reassurance of the barrel pressed hard against the head, just before oblivion.

What has been proved here? In the first instance (where you were trying to shoot yourself in the right temple so the bullet would come out behind the left ear) not only was the angle nearly impossible — but were you to achieve it, you had to hold the pistol barrel *hard* against the head. Yet the medical evidence indicates the gun did not rest on the skin. In the second instance, where you put the gun instinctively to your head, you probably avoided by as much as four or five inches the position of the presumed entry wound high in Reynolds's forehead.

Next, consider Smith's position as reported by Libby in her single "flash" of consciousness during her long and rather medically extraordinary blackout. To quote her: "The next thing I remember — and it is just a flash — is hearing my name called and looking up and seeing Smith with the revolver at his head. And then the shot . . . and after that I don't remember anything." Note her specific mention of a revolver, which we will return to later. It is a rather surprising specific for a woman who protested she did not know much about firearms.

If he had shot himself standing above her, the path of the bullet was particularly puzzling after it emerged from Smith's head. A fragment nicked the headboard and then the doorjamb alongside it, apparently ricocheting back to exit through one of the porch screens. A fragment was found near the head of the bed and another on the floor near the headboard. But if Smith had shot himself standing and looking down at Libby in the bed, as she claimed, a bullet angling front-to-back through his head could only have spewed its fragments into the room *behind* him — away from the bed he was looking down into.

Look at the sketch of the room (p. 269) and the path followed by the bullet; then consider the way Smith had fallen, with his head near the foot of the bed and his feet draped over the side near the headboard. Try a few simple sketches of your own superimposed on what is here. There seems to be no position where Smith could have stood, looked *down* at Libby, shot *himself* through the temple, and had the bullet strike the headboard. If the wound was self-inflicted, and the bullet traveled the way it did, Smith would have had to be sitting on the upper edge of the bed in the sketch, looking out and down at the floor of the room when he pulled the trigger.

Further, as Dr. Knight points out in his summary, in the case of Reynolds's pistol, "I think that range (muzzle to skin) is more likely to be of the order of 10–20 inches; much depends on the characteristics of the weapon."

A self-inflicted wound seems out of the question.

A Questionable "Murder Weapon"

Of course, all this conjecture about the position of the gun and who held it might have vanished if a simple test for fingerprints had been possible. But this useful examination, so routine in other such cases, was never even tried — and might have revealed nothing useful if it had been. The gun that was finally found — if it was the one that killed Smith — had been handled by at least three people after it had fired the bullet! One: the person who hid it after the shooting, and who certainly would have wiped fingerprints from it before putting it back. Two: Dr. Hanes, who thoughtlessly picked it up off the sleeping porch floor at dawn. Three: estate manager Warnken, who struggled to remove the clip from it. No reliable whole prints could have remained after that. And nobody looked for partials. Yet virtually any young Winston-Salem boy who had seen a couple of good detective movies and read a few Dick Tracy comic strips would have known you didn't pick up a weapon that had been used in a shooting.

Then there was the question about where the pistol was all during the time they were looking for it. A number of alert, alarmed, and presumably observant men — all of whom were aware that a crime might have taken place — made three searches of the room, and none of them saw the gun on any of those searches. Yet at the time of the fourth search, it was lying in clear view. The only person who was moving

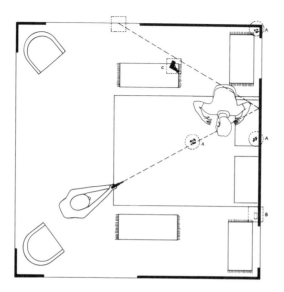

Diagrams of the sleeping porch. Found there: three bullet fragments (A), empty shell casing (B), the gun (C), only discovered after several earlier searches. A nick on the bedstand and a hole in the screen were made by the ricocheting bullet. The most logical path of the bullet — and the locations of killer and victim — must have been much as in the sketches above. Reynolds collapsed across the bed with his feet draped over the side near the pillow at upper right — and his head near the lower left corner. The empty shell casing (B) from a right-rejecting Mauser is perhaps one of the most decisive pieces of evidence for this assumption.

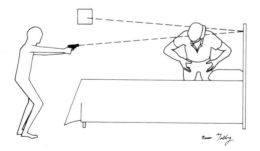

around in the upstairs of the house between the time of the third search at about 4:00 A.M. and the fourth search, about 6:00 A.M., was Albert Walker.

The fact that the weapon was missing for so long was one more thing that argued against suicide. Two innocent, anguished people rushing to the aid of their suicidal friend would have had no concern with the gun. Why hide it? Why even touch it? It did the harm! Their concern would have been all with the wounded man. Evidence in such a suicide shows that there is usually an immediate and instinctive abhorrence of the weapon that did it.

But — if you have turned a gun on someone in anger or passion, then the first instinct may be a horror at what you have done . . . followed by an awful urgency to get rid of the weapon you did it with.

A Questionable Identification

The question looms large as to whether the Mauser .32 automatic found on the sleeping porch was the gun that shot Smith. As in so many other areas of the case, the evidence was questionable and the investigation was sloppy. Walker said his own automatic was "missing" after the shooting. He spoke of owning "a Luger," which is a powerful German Army 9 mm. World War I trench pistol. A little formidable for potting rabbits and possums around Winston. Could the Mauser have been Walker's "Luger"? Was he confused . . . or devious? If the Mauser *was* his — and he wanted to pretend it was not — perhaps his first quick thought was to pretend his "missing" gun had been another automatic that *looked* similar to the Mauser. Hence the quick choice of a Luger. In both guns the bullets feed into the firing chamber from below, and from a flat magazine. They are both flat and sleek, as if cut in silhouette from a board. If a layman had seen Walker around the estate pot-shotting with the Mauser, the layman might only have been able to identify the gun as "an automatic." Then the Luger story might have held up.

Libby, on the other hand, took great pains to mention "a revolver" in her description of seeing Smith standing over her with a gun. A revolver, with its spool-like cylinder, standing out from the flat body of the gun and feeding bullets into the firing chamber, has a bulkier silhouette that even an amateur can recognize. If Libby was being careful to mention a revolver, a gun she knew Smith owned, it may have been because she was trying to support the suicide story; the most plausible thing for Smith to do would have been to commit suicide with his own revolver — brought to the sleeping porch for one more attempt to frighten Libby, or to plead with her.

What Libby didn't know when she first sent out the story to Scott about Smith standing over her with the revolver, was that the Mauser was the gun finally found on the sleeping porch when the pressure to "find a gun" got severe on Walker. She repeated her mention of a revolver in her first inquest testimony, however (page 128). But then, apparently warned about the Mauser automatic being found on the porch, she changed her story. When she talked to Moorehouse (page 202), to cover both bases, she referred both to "revolvers" and to "the little Mauser."

The Critical Timing

To summarize: 12:45 A.M., the shot. 1:00 A.M., the call for the ambulance. Fifteen minutes pass — minutes that race around the face of the clock if you are frantically casting around for what to do, what to hide when you have shot a man through the head and he is dying. An eternity to be inactive when you have seen a friend shoot himself and he needs your help.

Walker's Conflicting Story

You will remember that Walker had said it did not happen that way. Walker said that sometime after 12:30 A.M. Smith and Libby had gone upstairs, while he remained in the living room. They were upstairs "for some time" in the room Walker was using, "studying the globe," Walker said. And then Smith had come down again. At that point, according to Walker, he and Smith had some rambling exchange about Smith's wallet, which Smith then tossed to Walker, and once again Smith went upstairs.

Then Walker changed his story. Smith was actually headed upstairs,

Walker figured, "to get the German Luger" in Walker's bedside table. Walker estimated that after Smith got upstairs, another "10 minutes or so" passed before he heard what could have been a shot. The shot, Walker maintained, *and* Libby's crying *and* Blanche Yurka's arrival at the upstairs balcony came "within a few seconds of each other."

Fulcher's testimony repudiates all of this. Fulcher heard the shot at 12:45 — but not a sound after it. And he listened not far from the sleeping porch for eight or ten minutes before heading off on his rounds down to the lake.

Blanche Yurka, perhaps the only sober person inside the house at that point, heard no shot, but was wakened by the crying — quite loud and hysterical. Since Fulcher heard no crying in all the time he listened, enough time must have passed between the shot and the crying for him to get well down toward the barbecue site.

Walker claimed that his first inkling of the tragedy came when Libby came rushing down the upstairs hall right after the shot, crying that Smith had killed himself. That's when Walker testified to his own take-charge rushing about: he said Libby had collapsed in his arms at the head of the stairs. He said he tried to calm her. He said he ran to the sleeping porch and discovered Smith. He said he rushed back downstairs and telephoned for an ambulance. He said he ran back upstairs to the porch. He said he brought Smith out, unaided.

All the action he described — from hearing the shot until he came out dragging Smith — would have taken four or five minutes at least. Yet Miss Yurka, standing at the top of the stairs, contradicted almost everything Walker claimed. She testified that when she had asked Walker to investigate the crying, Libby was nowhere in sight. The next thing she saw — just seconds later — was Walker and Libby emerging from the sleeping porch together, dragging Smith.

No Libby first rushing down the hall, crying that Smith was shot.

No Walker comforting Libby.

No Walker going to the porch to investigate.

No Walker hurrying downstairs to phone.

No Walker dashing back upstairs and then dragging out Smith.

Since we do know that Walker phoned the hospital for the ambulance at some point before he met Blanche Yurka in the hall, Walker clearly knew that Smith had been shot when he was calmly pretending to Miss Yurka that he had heard nothing. Whatever his plan had been up till then, at that point, he had to change it drastically.

A Logical Reconstruction

Having been exposed to all the flaws of investigation, contradictions of testimony, trackbacks, and story changes that took place at the time, the juror-at-large is entitled to some reasonable hypothesis of what really did happen — some logical sequence of events that an aggressive prosecution might have proved, had there been a trial. That is what follows. Some of it is obviously assumption. But most of it is strongly supported by the most reliable of the testimony that was given at the coroner's inquest and developed by the questions asked in the preparation of this book.

By the night of the fatal birthday party, Smith was in a black mood. When Libby's mother and father had visited Reynolda in June, Smith — meeting them for the first time — had discovered to his strong Protestant dismay that he had married a Jew. He felt tricked. He was embarrassed in front of his friends. He was apprehensive about what his own family would say; there were all those protective provisions in his father's will, obviously aimed at him taking the wrong wife. He was fearful about the reaction of Winston-Salem society — a group he had learned, after the divorce of his first wife, to be vicious, malicious, and unforgiving.

His relationship with Libby deteriorated rapidly, and Smith began drinking more heavily. This only increased his depression and brought on more frequent periods of impotence. In other circumstances, all the impotence might have been corrected with some compassion and understanding. But he felt Libby was showing no desire to be his wife. Instead, she was mapping out her return to Broadway. If she had also told him at that point that she was pregnant, his depression might have been increased by a suspicion that the baby was not his. He feared she had already gotten all she wanted from him. His name. A claim to his money, perhaps. He didn't like or understand the Broadway crowd. And there was something very demanding and threatening about the relationship between Libby and Blanche Yurka; Libby had probably already told Smith — as she often told some of her best friends — how it alternately disturbed and intrigued her that so many attractive women were attracted to her. It all added up to the fact that Smith was losing his wife — to Broadway and to all those damn Broadway people. They were seducing her away from him.

At the birthday party, Smith was embarrassed further by Libby's drinking, by her flirting with Walker and others. And then there had been the long periods when she was off in the woods, as Smith described it "wandering around out there drunk." Smith had gotten furious when the watchman led Libby and Walker stumbling in from the darkness. A stormy scene took place between Smith and Walker, with Libby looking on unsteadily. The scene ended with Smith tossing Walker his wallet in disgust! "It's going to take more than you've got, Ab, to take care of that woman! Here's what she's after! Money!" And Smith marched out into the night. Walker knew about those dramatic walkouts. And Smith had told Walker he wouldn't be back.

Walker assumed Smith was headed for the hotel in town again. Walker started to follow Libby upstairs — but then Yurka had come down looking for her dumb after-party, and he had to send her back to bed. "Just locking up."

This time Smith had sulked around the grounds for a few minutes — then returned, intending to resume the angry alcoholic squabble with Walker and his wife. Even in its anger and its sadness, the quarreling provided a certain satisfaction.

Smith was able to trace the progress of Libby and Walker through the living room and up the stairs from the trail of sensuous clues: Libby's grass-stained slacks discarded on the living room sofa . . . her slippers under Walker's bed . . . her jersey top rolled up and dropped in Walker's bathroom. Damn! By now his wife was probably naked. With that goddamn Walker! Just like the naked parading around in her dressing room that they all had giggled about at the theater in New York!

Looking at all those clothes in Walker's room, Smith could guess what had happened. He stormed onto the sleeping porch. Anything he had seen there with Libby and Walker together would have been enough to make him livid. He would have gone after Walker first.

Choke the skinny little bastard to death! To alcohol-fogged Libby, Smith was acting like a goddamn crazy man again! Just like Hong Kong . . . and the ship . . . and Yellowstone. . . . That damn gun would come next. . . .

Walker was choking and gagging and gasping for air. Poor Ab; he had been trying to protect her. A brief drunken struggle for the gun. Hands grabbing, striking out! Figures flung up, tumbling down! Then the explosion of a cartridge . . .

. . . and Smith collapsing across the bed, blood beginning to pump from his head. The gun clattering to the floor. *My God, what had they done!*

A few frozen moments of horror. Then an awkward attempt to judge the severity of the wound. The blood was really pumping out now! It looked awful! God, was he dying?

There was a frantic effort to cover up their nakedness before anyone came on the run. But the clothes weren't there. Just a negligee. And the wet wool swimming trunks with the white Red Cross top. But no one had come. No one had heard the shot. Maybe they had some time. Maybe it just looked bad. Should they try to clean him up? Get him to bed? And get rid of that goddamn gun. Quick! The clean-up started clumsily. Bloody towels, half hidden! Bloody walls where they had stumbled around! Blood smears around the bathroom after a hurried washing-up! Oh, God! He kept bleeding! He *was* dying. Walker stumbled downstairs to call an ambulance.

As he had emerged from the little phone booth in the downstairs hall, Blanche Yurka had appeared again — waked this second time by Libby's hysterical crying. With that damn Yurka standing there asking about the crying, he knew he could not wait for the ambulance. The script had changed. He couldn't very well tell Yurka he didn't hear anything. Libby was bawling her fucking head off! When he got to the sleeping porch he shook her into a pathetic whimpering. Then he explained quickly; he hoped to God she understood. They came out together dragging Smith, along the hall, down the stairs, stuffed him into the car with Yurka's help. Then full speed to the hospital, passing the ambulance on its way in to Reynolda.

At some point in that wild evening — perhaps during the frantic clean-up period — Ab Walker had gotten rid of the gun. But when he came back to the house, all eyes turned on him to produce "the gun." After all, he had been first on the scene; if he didn't have it, who did? And he had already said the gun "was up there on the porch."

When he placed his .32 Mauser on the porch, Walker had no way of knowing that Libby would carefully specify in her testimony that Smith owned a revolver . . . had often flashed it at her . . . had been standing over her with it when she saw him in that last flash of consciousness. Walker had made a stupid mistake to hide the gun. If they had wanted to prove a suicide, leaving the gun on the scene might have done the whole thing much better.

Walker's story of his "missing Luger" was the sort of panic reaction that a thorough investigation would have turned against him with great harm. If they began to pin him down, he would just have to hope for the best.

The best was just what he got. Incredibly, his "missing gun" seemed to attract no interest at all!

At the hospital, Libby and Walker thought they were getting their last chance to get their stories straight, and Walker was desperate to see her in private — lurching through the halls, cursing at everyone, bullying the nurses, driving them out. Then hissing at Libby "Don't talk! Don't say anything!" The next morning he had blurted out to the sheriff that he would take the secret of that evening to his grave. It was one promise he made good on.

As far as getting their stories straight, Libby and Walker did have an unexpected second chance after their drunken, grappling-on-the-floor scene at the hospital. For almost forty-eight hours — from Wednesday afternoon, all Thursday, through Friday morning — they were in virtual seclusion from authorities behind the big chain at Reynolda's front gate. "Sorry, my patient is under sedation," said the Reynolds doctors. "You will get to see Mrs. Reynolds in good time," said the Reynolds lawyers. Reynolds doctors and lawyers were hard to argue with. But Walker and Yurka had free access to her the whole time!

There was always the question of how Walker's and Libby's stories would have stood up in court. But then of course they didn't have to.

The "Crazy" Know-Nothing Defense

In contrast to Walker's repeated contradictions, Libby made her only two mistakes when, the day after the shooting, she sent out the conflicting messages to Scott. She said first that she had rushed to the sleeping porch on hearing the shot and had found Smith on the bed there. Later that day Walker told her of his grilling by Scott and told her the story he had set up for himself: that the shot, the crying, and Libby's running from the sleeping porch and down the hall had come all at once, that only then had he discovered the shooting. To support his story, Walker pleaded with her to admit she had been on the porch when the shooting occurred. So she sent out the second story to Scott: she had been on the porch in bed all along.

When her lawyer father arrived, he quickly decided that her foggy memory from all the drinks might provide the excuse for all sorts of crazy changing answers. Maybe it was a defense for his daughter. But whatever her involvement, it was extreme. She would be hard to defend. She would probably crumple under a good cross-examination. On the other hand, if she didn't testify for herself, not appearing on the stand always looked incriminating to a jury.

Then Holman had the desperate idea for a forty-eight-hour blackout of his daughter's mind. No matter that it had never happened before (and would never happen again). If she stuck to that story in answering all questions, it would be impossible to trip her up: "I don't remember. . . . It is vague. . . . I can't recall. . . ." Once Libby was off the stand, it would be just a question of getting in a couple of good psychiatrist expert witnesses to defend the blackout against whatever psychiatrists the prosecution brought in to attack it. In that sort of sparring, as long as both Libby and Walker stuck to their stories, at least his daughter had a chance.*

---

* In the opinion of an experienced New York trial lawyer, Alfred Holman did indeed have a good defense with Libby's blackout, real or invented: "The questions relating to Libby's 'blackout' defense relate to an area of evidentiary law which is largely the province of experts. The proper approach to making a case which is founded on psychological premises relies on expert-opinion evidence of properly trained doctors. With this in mind, I do not think that a cross-examination of Libby would make much headway in destroying the blackout defense. She would simply answer the cross-examiner's questions by fuzzy 'I don't know' responses and thus be totally consistent with her blackout

But if Walker seemed to be getting the worst of it in pretrial or after the trial started, his lawyer would be guilty of malpractice if he didn't try to bargain Walker out of the first-degree charge. Alfred Holman's best hope for his daughter was to *prevent the case from going to trial at all.*

If prosecutor Carlisle Higgins was concerned about having "another Leo Frank case" on his hands, with another Jewish defendant getting railroaded, Alfred Holman had some real concern that both he and defense attorney Polikoff were also tempting targets for railroading as the defendant's Jewish lawyers.

Being a Jewish trial lawyer was not an attractive prospect anywhere in the United States in the 1930 — and particularly not in the South. In a widely reviewed 1976 book, *Unequal Justice*, the historian Jerold S. Auerbach wrote of the plight of the Jewish lawyer of that period among his "brothers at the bar" and before judges. A *Newsweek* article highlighted the hard truth of the book. Peter Prescott of *Newsweek* wrote:

> Barriers built of ethnic, social, religious, and educational credentials were raised [in the 1920s and 1930s] against what was perceived as "the great flood of foreign blood . . . sweeping into the bar." This foreign blood was said (by Establishment lawyers) to prevent understanding of "the Anglo-Saxon idea of self-government." Immigrant lawyers, described by the native-born as "morally unfit," a "pestiferous horde" and sometimes "Russian Jew boys," had "little inherited sense of fairness, justice and honor as we understand them."
>
> Bar associations, particularly during and after World War I, raised xenophobic patriotism to sickening heights. Attempts were made to keep Jews (never mind blacks and women) from practicing law, by movements to ban night law schools, to require a college education, to impose a "character" test on applicants from law schools. "The need for repression is great," said the journal *Bench and Bar* in 1920, "and the time for repression is now."

Welcome from your "brothers at the bar," lawyer Holman.

---

theory. On the other hand, a good prosecutor would bring in first-class psychiatrists from excellent institutions and medical colleges with pedigrees as long as one's arm. It is this kind of witness who would attempt to debunk the blackout theory. Classically then, this kind of defense becomes a fencing match between the prosecution's expert witnesses and those presented by the defense."

In spite of Holman's statements that Libby was eager for a speedy trial and "her day in court," that day loomed less and less desirable the more Alfred Holman thought of it. He had not seen one Jewish face in the Forsyth County prosecutor's office . . . or on the sheriff's staff . . . or on the high bench in Winston . . . or up at Wentworth Courthouse . . . or among the tigers of the Womble law firm . . . or in the platoons of young R. J. Reynolds executives who came and went on their mysterious business. Holman had *meant* them all to start thinking about the issue of Jewishness when he had sent the Forsyth County district attorney the telegram about the "injustices of ancient times" and the "inquisition of the Middle Ages" back in July. He hoped they were thinking.

But how could a trial be avoided? Hire the prosecutor out from under the state, to become the defense attorney? Holman had tried that. It didn't work, and could almost be taken as an attempt to bribe. Turn Libby into a fugitive from justice? That would mean the end of her career and her life really — as well as the end of any chance at support from the Reynolds fortune; her father saw her being entitled to at least *some* of all that money, after what she had put up with from Smith. Indeed, it was when Libby began telling him "what she had put up with" and about the life the two of them had, running with the smart set of Winston and in New York, that the idea for a crazy tactic came to Alfred Holman.

Some of those lively, wealthy young North Carolina people seemed to believe that one set of laws was reserved for them, another for everybody else. A court trial would soon reveal some of that. It would not be a pleasant revelation. Most of them had grown up believing their own sophisticated adventures with alcohol, sex, and finally drugs were a private part of their social charter. Alfred Holman figured that Libby's story of such adventures — *as Mrs. Smith Reynolds* — was not a tale the Reynolds family would want to take through the courts and the newspaper front pages. The papers would soon enough take an intriguing sniff at "secret hearings," "undue influence," "persecution," and "racial prejudice."

So Holman set about making sure that the prosecution knew the sort of scandalous story Libby's defense team might have to make at her trial. He knew the story would get to the Reynoldses. Then *they* might take care of the rest of his attempt to stay out of court. And they did.

APPENDIX I
The report of Professor Bernard Knight, M.D., B.Ch., F.R.C. Path., D.M.J., Barrister-at-Law, Professor of Forensic Pathology at the Welsh National School of Medicine, Home Office Pathologist

This report is an analysis based on a transcript of Dr. Hanes's testimony at the inquest in July 1932 and on other evidence supplied by the author. It argues strongly against suicide.

The forensic and medical evidence is very scanty, even allowing for the situation in 1932, so that we are in the position of having to "make bricks without much straw."

The ever-present danger is always lurking; that is, the temptation to *over-interpret* sparse and equivocal facts; this has been the curse of forensic medicine for years. But here are my findings:

PATH OF THE BULLET. One of the primary needs in this case is to definitely distinguish the entrance wound from the exit wound. There is conflicting evidence presented on this aspect.

(a) The swelling on the right temple "like a small orange" suggests that this was the site of a *contact* discharge, though other factors do not support this view. When a weapon is discharged in tight contact with the skin over a bony base such as the skull, the large volume of gas issuing from the muzzle cannot dissipate rapidly because of the unyielding base; therefore the soft tissues bulge upwards and the frequently-seen ragged, cruciate tear of a contact entrance wound is due to the gas pressure splitting this bulge from within. This does not happen in the chest or abdomen, as the gas can expand internally. However, in Reynolds' case, the actual bullet hole was said to be "a puncture wound of skin in the middle of the swelling". This does not rule out an entrance wound by any means, but one would classically expect the wound to be stellate or ragged if situated on a mound — rather than a simple puncture.

(b) Dr. Hanes seemed very vague about the "powder burns" around the wound. If one can take his opinion seriously, this would clinch the matter, but I feel his evidence is all either tentative, ambiguous or just plain wrong! He says "slight evidences which we attributed to be powder burns, not marked, very slight, just on the edge of wound, a blackening of the edge of the wound which it seemed possible to us at the time were powder burns." This is hardly convincing! However, it may be better than nothing and even in such timid terms, tends to point to an *entrance* rather than *exit* wound, especially as he is more definite about the lack of any such features in the left-sided wound at the rear of the head.

It is a pity that modern forensic tests were not carried out, such as examination of the skin for powder residues or microscopy for skin burns or hair clubbing or singeing. In modern times, a test upon the hands of the deceased and the suspects would show if they had fired a gun, especially if it was a revolver with a potentially leaky breech (automatics do not blow out propellant gases so readily). The old nitrite test for hands, prevalent in 1932, is out of favour, but perhaps could have shown something. Modern chemical tests reveal metallic elements derived from the detonator and primer.

(c) The wound on the right temple is poorly described, as far as determining entrance or exit characteristics. If it was a plain round hole, it would be most likely to be a distant *entrance* wound, since contact and very near discharges tend to split the skin, as I described earlier. Exit wounds should be stellate and *everted*, though there are many exceptions. If the gas of a contact wound raised a large swelling, then perhaps this dissipated the volume without ripping the skin, leaving only a round hole. However, there is no good description as to whether the hole was *inverted*, had a friction collar from the passage of the bullet, had a 'grease ring' or was surrounded by pink skin from the conversion of haemoglobin to carboxyhaemoglobin from the entry of carbon monoxide from the muzzle gases.

Dr. Hanes mentions 'contusion' around the temple wound and this might be used as further evidence of an entrance wound, as bruising is often marked in the vicinity. The left-sided wound behind the ear was hardly described at all, "merely a puncture wound of the skin," which tells us little. An exit is commonly stellate and more importantly, everted by the passage of the bullet, unless the tissues were supported by, say a belt, brassiere band etc. In this case this would not apply, unless Smith was already lying down on a firm surface, ... which is impossible as the bullet would then have passed into the firm surface.

If we can rely upon it, the best clue is that Dr. Hanes says that the left wound behind the ear contained shreds of brain tissue, whereas the right temple did not. This would confirm the wound behind the ear being the exit.

. . . There seems no description by Dr. Hanes of what he found inside the skull at his autopsy.

He talks utter nonsense about "damage to the brain by the bullet being largely due to the blood vessels, not so much the penetration of the bullet itself." Though vascular damage can be important, the bullet track is many times the width of the missile, due to a cavitation effect behind the bullet, when a partial vacuum oscillates with diminished amplitude, causing great damage due to lateral transfer of energy. His comments about the bullet passing "below the motor area of the brain" is also nonsense. The track would have been steeply downward, so that it would have hit the fronto-parietal cortex on the right and gone through basal ganglia to reach the left temporal lobe or temporo-occipital junction. There is no "motor area" in the brain, in the *singular* — there are two motor gyri, one on each side, extending down from the vertex to the upper temporal area.

(d) Dr. Hanes describes the external appearance of the two skull holes, but oddly, does not mention the internal aspects, which is a pity for the purpose of this analysis. Usually, when a bullet enters the skull, it punches a clean hole on the outside, as the outer table of the sandwich-like skull is supported by the central and inner layers. When it leaves the bone to pass into the cranial cavity, it usually cracks off a ring of inner table of bone, which is unsupported, so that a shelf or bevel is apparent. When it traverses the brain and hits the inside of the opposite wall, it is then the inner aspect, which is punched clean through — and the outer, i.e. final, aspect, which becomes shelved. *There is no mention of this in Dr. Hanes's report, which would be the prime object of a forensic pathologist's examination.*

However, he redeems himself a little by saying that the right temple bone defect was a small, clean-cut puncture wound. Then he says that the left-sided wound was slightly larger and the edges were roughened outwardly . . . he says "one did have a roughening of the bone as though the bone had been knocked out of the skull."

Though he is forensically a pathetic observer and witness, he gives descriptions, which, if they can be believed, give the edge to accepting that the *right* temple wound was the *entrance* and the *left* behind-ear wound the *exit.*

However, nothing is certain, both from his brief and inadequate descriptions and from the inevitable biological variations which confound attempts at dogmatic interpretation.

DISTANCE; Again, facts are scarce. Dr. Hanes talks more nonsense when he says that the fact that there was such light powder burning meant that "the muzzle must have been resting almost, if not quite on the skin or close to it." As usual, he equivocates and qualifies his opinions into a total uselessness. It is not true that slight powder burns mean close contact. The gas, carrying unburnt powder and smoke, can spurt sideways from the muzzle even in firm contact. *Slight powder burns are more likely to mean a considerable distance from the muzzle; in the case of an old revolver, maybe 20–25 inches before the powder no longer marks the skin,* though much depends on the individual weapon and ammunition.

His remark "the greater the separation from the skin, the greater the powder burn" is rubbish, unless we are considering hard contact as opposed to a fraction of an inch distance.

I think that three feet is too far to get powder burns in most cases, even with an old-fashioned revolver using black powder ammunition. An automatic produces very little powder and soot, though may still project glistening flakes of unburnt propellant. *A small round hole and very slight powder marking, with no mention of skin scorching strongly suggests a range of one to two feet.*

The swelling like an orange is harder to explain away — but I note that the autopsy revealed a large haemorrhage in the temporalis muscle; this could have occurred from rupture of a scalp artery and maybe the swelling was a haematoma, i.e. a collection of blood under the skin, rather than a gas blister.

DIRECTION. Here at least there is little doubt, except for the uncertainty whether the bullet travelled from right to left or vice versa. Assuming the entrance to be in the right temple, the trajectory would be somewhat backwards and quite steeply downwards. *If the wound were self-inflicted, then the pistol would have to be held high above the brow, certainly a difficult and atypical position.*

SUMMARY. Due to the lack of medico-legal expertise of Dr. Hanes and his scanty and tentative descriptions of the wounds, no firm conclusions can be reached. However, probabilities, as opposed to certainties can be advanced, bearing in mind the inevitable exceptions to every rule where biological factors exist.

With these important provisos, I would think that;

(a) The right temple wound is more likely to be the entrance wound.

(b) In spite of the swelling, I think that the range (muzzle to skin) is more likely to be of the order of 10–20 inches; much depends on the characteristics of the weapon. If it was indeed the Mauser automatic, this distance is still no more certain, since the Mauser was not tested for emission distance of powder burns. (It also depends on the veracity of Dr. Hanes's statement about the existence of slight powder marks.)

(c) *The position of the wound and its direction is most unlike a typical suicide shot; if the range was 20 inches or thereabouts, it could not be self-inflicted. If it was contact, which the swelling alone suggests, then Smith could just have managed to hold the weapon in the right place, though it would be an awkward and unnatural position. However, a contact discharge could hardly avoid burning the skin and leaving powder burns and soiling; even a hard contact discharge cannot form a tight enough seal against the skin to prevent this. In tight contact firings, an impression of the muzzle, forward sight or (in automatics) the ejector rod beneath the muzzle can be left on the skin around the wound.*

Unfortunately, the gaps in the data make firm conclusions (always dangerous in forensic pathology) difficult to attain.

I hope all of this is of some use; though again I must emphasize that for every forensic law, there seems to be an exception and over-interpretation is a frequent sin.

BERNARD KNIGHT

Cardiff, Wales
8 December 1982

APPENDIX II
"The Leo Frank Case"

On several occasions when Carlisle Higgins was discussing his concern about bringing Libby Holman to trial, he mentioned that he didn't want to be part of another Leo Frank case. I was vaguely aware of the outlines of the case: a young Atlanta factory superintendent was convicted of the murder of a young girl who worked at the factory. He was tried and convicted on questionable evidence. The trial and Frank's appeal were attended by great newspaper coverage and public speculation. And because Frank was a Jew, a strong anti-Jewish sentiment was inflamed by the Ku Klux Klan in Georgia. When Frank's death sentence was commuted to life imprisonment some two years after the trial, a mob formed, tried to storm the governor's mansion — then raced to a prison farm 175 miles away where Frank was being held, seized him, took him to the dead girl's grave site, and lynched him. There followed a small reign of terror against Jews in several Georgia cities — notably Atlanta — beatings in the streets, harassment in public places, and attacks on stores and businesses. Eventually nearly half the three thousand Jews in Georgia left the state. The year was 1915.

Perhaps in light of this memory, which was etched deep on the liberal South, Carlisle Higgins's concerns were well founded, even seventeen years later. Libby's press in North Carolina had not been very good. The Raleigh papers had dismissed her as "this Libby person" and an "ignorant chorus girl." That was relatively dignified. In other circles she was "the Jew girl who took over Reynolda" and the rumor giggled around was that "it looked like she had a little of the tarbrush in her, too." She was marked: a Jew fortune hunter . . . also an actress — "and you know what they say about actresses." Maybe a little black blood mixed in, too? If she were convicted of murdering "one of the most promising young men in North Carolina . . . and from such a fine family, too," Higgins was not sure what reaction might be. A lot of Reynolds factory workers had seemed to adopt the case as a family matter already. What were they capable of if angered? The rumor had already gone around, improbable as it was, that the death of Smith meant "the end of the company — because R. J., Jr., sure as hell hasn't shown any stuff for being in the tobacco business." Higgins had been a bit uneasy about bringing Libby into Wentworth after those newspaper pictures that boasted "Here Is the Cell Where the Songbird Goes." It was damn near an invitation to come get her. The Wentworth crowd had turned out all right. Good country people. A convicted Jewish murderer in the Forsyth County jail might be something else.

If all this seems far-fetched in 1980s America, the reader is invited to look at a few issues of the Atlanta, Milledgeville, and Marietta, Georgia, papers for the time in 1915 when Leo Frank was lynched and the anti-Jewish violence spilled over.

Or read the account below, from the March 8, 1982, *New York Times.* Only then — *seventy years after the trial and conviction of Leo Frank* — was the last of that tragic, violent incident put to rest, when an eighty-three-year-old Virginia man who had been an office boy for Leo Frank came forward to say that Frank had been innocent of the murder. The murderer, in fact, was the factory janitor who had been the chief witness against Frank.

AFTER 69 YEARS OF SILENCE, LYNCHING VICTIM IS CLEARED*

By Wendell Rawls Jr.
Special to the New York Times
NASHVILLE, March 7 — New but long held secret information was disclosed today in one of the most disputed trials in American history, the murder, conviction, and subsequent mob lynching of Leo Frank almost 70 years ago.

Mr. Frank, a 29-year-old Jewish factory superintendent, was convicted in Atlanta of killing one of his employees, Mary Phagan, 14, and dumping her in the basement of the pencil factory where they worked.

But in a sworn statement to the newspaper The Tennesseean, an 81-year old Virginian who, seven decades ago, was a frightened and reluctant teen-age witness in that trial, now says that he saw the real killer bear-hugging the long-haired girl at her waist and carrying her limp, unconscious body to a partly opened trap door leading to the basement on the day she was murdered.

"Leo Frank did not kill Mary Phagan," Alonzo Mann insisted in confirmation of a widely believed theory of historians.

Says Janitor Was Murderer

"She was murdered instead by Jim Conley," he asserted, referring to a factory janitor who was the chief witness against Mr. Frank.

Mr. Mann was 14 years old at the time of the murder and was working as Mr. Frank's office boy for $8 a week. He said the janitor, startled by the boy, threatened to kill him if he ever mentioned what he had seen that day.

Young Alonzo Mann was called to testify at the trial, but was asked only a few perfunctory questions. On the advice of his mother, he volunteered no information and told no one in authority what he had seen that Saturday, April 26, 1913. He said he continued to heed that advice for several years, except for an occasional confidence to relatives and a rebuffed attempt to tell an Atlanta newspaper reporter 30 years ago.

In later years, he said, he would have agreed, even been eager to talk with those who have written some 50 books about events surrounding the infamous trial. None of the authors ever approached him, he said.

But when confronted by two Tennesseean reporters, Jerry Thompson and Robert Sherborne, who were acting on a tip, he related his story and supplied them with notes, photographs, and other materials. He submitted to a lie-detector test and a psychological stress evaluation and passed both impressively, The Tennesseean said. The newspaper reported that a two-month investigation satisfied it of the historical accuracy of his information and the validity of his claims.

"Many times I wanted to get it out of my heart," the white-haired Mr. Mann said in an interview last night. "I'm glad I've told it all. I've been living with it for a long time. I feel a certain amount of freedom now. I just hope it does some good."

His lips trembled, but his clear blue eyes belied his frail physique and failing heart that pumps with the aid of a surgically implanted pacemaker. He now lives in Bristol, Va. where he said he is fond of his friends and his church.

"I know I don't have a long time to live," he said. "All I have said is the truth. When my time comes, I hope that God understands me better for telling it. That's what matters most."

But he is reluctant to tell it again. "I have laid that burden down and I don't ever want to pick it up again," he said.

According to Mr. Mann's account:

He was working with Mr. Frank in the office that Saturday morning. He had encountered Mr. Conley early that day when the burly black janitor asked to borrow a dime for beer. Mr. Mann, who is white, did not lend him the money.

He worked until about 11:30 A.M. when he left the National Pencil Company factory to meet his mother to watch the Confederate Memorial Day parade. His mother did not show up, and he returned to work.

Startled by Sight

He stepped into the first floor vestibule and walked towards the stairs to the second floor. But a movement in the shadows caught his attention. He was riveted by the scene before him: Jim Conley standing beside a trap door clutching the wilted body of a young white girl. Her head lolled on the man's right shoulder. She seemed either dead or unconscious. He saw no blood, no wounds, no rope.

The janitor looked over his left shoulder at the boy and their eyes locked. They faced each other for a few moments before the man spoke: "If you ever mention this, I'll kill you," he said.

The frightened youngster fled back to the front door and ran outside. On arriving home, he told his mother what he had seen and recalled her saying: "For God's sake, don't tell anybody else about this. You just stay out of it."

Early the next morning, a night watchman found Mary Phagan's bruised body face down in a pile of wood shavings in the basement. A ligature was around her neck, having scorched her throat. Blood had flowed from a deep cut in her scalp. There were signs of a struggle to escape. Her underclothing was ripped, but there was no evidence that she had been raped.

While Mr. Mann was out, she had come to the factory to pick up her pay, $1.20 for 10 hours work. Neither her purse nor her $1.20 was ever found.

The janitor accused Mr. Frank of the killing and said the defendant had paid him $200 to carry the body to the basement and burn it in the furnace.

Although nothing in Mr. Frank's history indicated wrongdoing, no other evidence supported the janitor, and the prosecution acknowledged that Mr. Conley had told several other versions of his story, the community and the jury were quick to convict Mr. Frank.

A wave of anti-Semitism was washing over Georgia and mobs swarmed the courthouse daily, screaming, "Kill the Jew." A local newspaper defamed Mr. Frank as "a Jew Sodomite."

Mr. Frank was sentenced to hang. He appealed his case unsuccessfully for two years before Gov. John Slaton commuted the sentence to life in prison, days before his term expired in 1915.

The commutation produced a furor of protest. Armed mobs roamed streets, forcing Jewish businessmen to board up windows and doors. A mob of several thousand people armed with guns, hatchets, and dynamite surrounded the Governor's Mansion until they were dispersed by State militiamen.

Within days of the commutation, 75 men calling themselves Knights of Mary Phagan met at the girl's grave in Marietta, Ga., north of Atlanta, and vowed to avenge her death. They armed themselves and stormed a prison farm where Mr. Frank was being held 175 miles to the southeast in Milledgeville, and where he had survived a throat slashing by an inmate a month earlier.

The mob handcuffed Mr. Frank and transported him back to Marietta and hanged him from an oak tree a stone's throw from Miss Phagan's birthplace.

In the aftermath of terror, about half the 3,000 Jews in Georgia left the state. Those who remained, hid behind locked doors, forced to survive a widespread boycott of Jewish businesses.

The Frank trial marked the rebirth of the moribund Ku Klux Klan movement that grew out of the Knights of Mary Phagan, and it also gave rise to the formation of the Anti-Defamation League of B'nai B'rith.

Recently Mr. Mann went back to Georgia and visited the grave of Mary Phagan and mused about the possibility that he could have saved her life, as well as Mr. Frank's, if he had shouted out that Saturday in 1913. But he said he often had harbored such thoughts.

"Thousands of times I've gone to bed at night with all this on my mind," he said Saturday. "I hope you folks tell the whole world what I saw and that Leo Frank was innocent."

Perhaps it's no wonder Carlisle Higgins worried about "another Leo Frank case."

Index

Inheritance and probate (*cont.*)
behalf of Reynolds's daughter,
233; Reynolds family responds to
Holman's compromise, to bank
challenge, 233–234; terms are announced by Judge Warlick, 234;
cash awards approved, 236, 244;
Reynolds Foundation established, 234–235

Inquest (events indexed in chrono-
logical order) coroner's jury
panel named, 110–111; Dr.
Hanes testifies on wound, bullet
path, conditions of participants,
111–114; Walker testifies, tells of
dispute with Reynolds, of
Yurka's arrival on the scene, of
hearing the shot, of discovering
Reynolds's body, 114–123;
Walker questioned on Libby's
Jewishness, 122–123; about his
missing gun, 122–123; Walker
taken into custody as material
witness, 124–125; Libby testifies,
127; mentions mental blackout
for the first time, 128; mentions
pregnancy possibilities, 131;
issue of the "secret" inquest,
131–132; ruling it must be public, 138–139; Fulcher testifies,
133; Walker recalled re timing of
events, 134–136; Scott testifies on
path of bullet, 136–137; Libby recalled to testify on dispute with
Reynolds the Sunday before the
shooting, 139–141; on various
threats he made against her,
59–61; 65–67; on her mental
blackout, 142; on Reynolds's impotence, 143; on his "last will"
and "suicide" notes, 144–145;
Walker recalled, 147; questioned
on conduct at hospital, 147–148;
about his return to Reynolda to
destroy evidence, 148–149; inquest jury brings in verdict, 150;
verdict questioned by *Winston-
Salem Journal*, 156

Jenney, Louisa, rumored to be hiding Libby, 169–170; 230, death in
an aviation accident, 238
Johnson, Dr. William, Reynolds
family physician, in attendance
at the hospital and caring for
Libby and Yurka after the shooting, 104, 107–108; on medical
team performing secret autopsy,
199

Kahn, Mrs. Myron, Libby's sister,
108, 152–153
Kaufman, George S., contributor to
The Little Show, 53
Keen, Charles Barton, architect of
Reynolda, 73–74
Kempner, Nick, director of *Three's
a Crowd*, 57
Kern, Jerome, composer, encour-
ages Dietz on lyrics, 50
King, Coretta (Mrs. Martin Luther
King, Jr.), civil rights leader, 254
King, Martin Luther, Jr., civil rights
leader, 254
Kleiman, Dena, New York courts
reporter, writing on pressure
placed on grand juries, 259
Knight, Dr. Bernard, forensic pathologist and author, 263, criti-
cizes faulty medical evidence, interpretation, and testimony, 265;
268
Knight vs. North Carolina, legal ruling regarding inquests with press
barred, 83
Kramer, Raymond, tutor, 86; tells
Reynolds of late prowler at the
party; 92; tells New York reporters of Reynolds's fear of kidnapping, 157

Laseter, R. E., Reynolds Company
executive and family spokesman,
called to Reynolda after the
shooting, 26; makes family statement regarding suicide, 107
Leibowitz, Sam, trial lawyer, 171